Hands-on Azure Repos

Understanding Centralized
and Distributed Version Control
in Azure DevOps Services

Chaminda Chandrasekara

Pushpa Herath

Apress®

Hands-on Azure Repos: Understanding Centralized and Distributed Version Control in Azure DevOps Services

Chaminda Chandrasekara
Colombo, Sri Lanka

Pushpa Herath
Hanguranketha, Sri Lanka

ISBN-13 (pbk): 978-1-4842-5424-0
https://doi.org/10.1007/978-1-4842-5425-7

ISBN-13 (electronic): 978-1-4842-5425-7

Managing Director, Apress Media LLC: Welmoed Spahr
Acquisitions Editor: Smriti Srivastava
Development Editor: Siddhi Chavan
Coordinating Editor: Shrikant Vishwakarma

Cover designed by eStudioCalamar

Cover image designed by Freepik (www.freepik.com)

Distributed to the book trade worldwide by Springer Science+Business Media New York, 233 Spring Street, 6th Floor, New York, NY 10013. Phone 1-800-SPRINGER, fax (201) 348-4505, e-mail orders-ny@springer-sbm.com, or visit www.springeronline.com. Apress Media, LLC is a California LLC and the sole member (owner) is Springer Science + Business Media Finance Inc (SSBM Finance Inc). SSBM Finance Inc is a **Delaware** corporation.

For information on translations, please e-mail rights@apress.com, or visit www.apress.com/rights-permissions.

Apress titles may be purchased in bulk for academic, corporate, or promotional use. eBook versions and licenses are also available for most titles. For more information, reference our Print and eBook Bulk Sales web page at www.apress.com/bulk-sales.

Any source code or other supplementary material referenced by the author in this book is available to readers on GitHub via the book's product page, located at www.apress.com/978-1-4842-5424-0. For more detailed information, please visit www.apress.com/source-code.

Printed on acid-free paper

Let this book be a daily reference guide for all the developers who use Azure Repos.

Table of Contents

About the Authors.. xi

About the Technical Reviewer xiii

Acknowledgments xv

Introduction xvii

Chapter 1: Getting Started with Azure Team Foundation Version Control 1

Lesson 1-1: Creating a Team Project with TFVC and Adding a TFVC Repo to the
Existing Team Project... 2

Lesson 1-2: Using Visual Studio Team Explorer 5

Lesson 1-3: Adding New/Existing Solutions to TFVC.. 8

Lesson 1-4: Changing Settings for TFVC in Visual Studio 16

    File Types.. 16

    Workspace Settings.. 17

    Source Control Settings... 19

    Check-Out Settings.. 19

    Check-in Policies 20

Lesson 1-5: Connecting to TFVC in VS Code 22

Summary.. 26

Chapter 2: Working with Team Foundation Version Control: Part1 27

Lesson 2-1: Exploring the Source Control Explorer.. 27

Lesson 2-2: Setting Workspace Mode to Local and Server.................................... 33

    Local Workspace Mode.. 36

    Server Workspace Mode.. 36

Lesson 2-3: Looking at Source Control Explorer Menu Items 37

Lesson 2-4: Editing and Checking In Your Changes 38

Lesson 2-5: Resolving Conflicts During Code Check-in 45

Lesson 2-6: Viewing the History and Comparing the Changes 47

Lesson 2-7: Setting Source Control Tool Options 50

Lesson 2-8: Deleting and Restoring Files 52

Summary 54

Chapter 3: Working with TFVC: Part 2 55

Lesson 3-1: Using Shelvesets 55

Lesson 3-2: Suspending and Resuming Work 64

Lesson 3-3: Doing Code Reviews with TFVC 68

Lesson 3-4: Using Lock and Unlock 76

Lesson 3-5: Applying Check-in Policies 78

Summary 83

Chapter 4: Team Foundation Version Control Branching 85

Lesson 4-1: Creating a Branch 85

Lesson 4-2: Converting a Folder to a Branch 89

Lesson 4-3: Merging and Resolving Conflicts 91

Lesson 4-4: Tracking Changesets 100

Lesson 4-5: Cherry-Picking Changesets 103

Lesson 4-6: Exploring TFVC Branching Strategies 106

    Main Only 106

    Development Isolation 106

    Feature Isolation 107

    Release Isolation 107

    Servicing and Release Isolation 108

Summary 108

Chapter 5: Team Foundation Version Control: Command Line 109

Lesson 5-1: Getting Started with the Team Foundation Command Line 109

    Developer Command Prompt for Visual Studio 109

    Team Explorer Everywhere Command-Line Client 111

Lesson 5-2: Using Workspace Commands 113

    workspaces Command 113

    workspace Command 114

Lesson 5-3: Running Various Commands 117

    get 118

    add 120

    checkin 120

    checkout (or edit) 121

    rename 122

    undo 122

Summary 122

Chapter 6: Team Foundation Version Control: Security 123

Lesson 6-1: Setting Up TFVC Security at the Team Project Level 123

Lesson 6-2: Applying Permissions at the Branch/Folder or File Level 129

Lesson 6-3: Auditing Changes and Finding Out Who Did What 134

Summary 137

Chapter 7: Getting Started with Azure Git Repos 139

Lesson 7-1: Creating an Azure Git Repo 139

    Creating a Team Project with Azure Git Repos 140

    Creating Additional Git Repos in a Team Project 142

Lesson 7-2: Cloning an Azure Git Repo 144

    VS Code 144

    Visual Studio 145

Lesson 7-3: Creating and Pushing Code to Azure Git Repos 148

Lesson 7-4: Getting Changes from Others and Sharing Code 156

Lesson 7-5: Resolving Conflicts 161

Lesson 7-6: Stashing the Changes 166

Summary 170

Chapter 8: Branching with Azure Git Repos **171**

Lesson 8-1: Creating Branches 171

Lesson 8-2: Working with Branches in Visual Studio and VS Code 174

    Visual Studio.. 175

    VS Code 183

Lesson 8-3: Merging Changes and Resolving Conflicts 185

Lesson 8-4: Using Pull Requests and Code Reviews 195

Lesson 8-5: Rebasing While Completing a Pull Request...................................... 204

Summary... 206

Chapter 9: Using the Command Line with Azure Git Repos **207**

Lesson 9-1: Getting Started with the Command Line 207

Lesson 9-2: Cloning an Azure Git Repository and Pushing Code Using the Command Line 210

Lesson 9-3: Creating a Git Repository Locally and Pushing It to Azure Git Repos 218

Lesson 9-4: Creating Azure Git Repo Branches Using the Command Line............... 222

Summary... 224

Chapter 10: Azure Git Repos: Security.. **225**

Lesson 10-1: Setting Azure Git Repos Permissions 225

Lesson 10-2: Setting Up Azure Git Repos Branch Policies 234

Summary... 240

Chapter 11: Azure Git Repos Extras... **241**

Lesson 11-1: Using Git Tags... 241

    Creating Tags with the Azure DevOps Web Portal.. 241

    Creating Tags with Visual Studio 246

    Creating Tags with the Command Line 251

Lesson 11-2: Forking a Repo 255

Lesson 11-3: Importing from an External Repository 257

Lesson 11-4: Setting Up Azure Git Repos Markdown Files as a Wiki...................... 260

Summary... 265

Chapter 12: REST APIs for Azure Git and TFVC Repos **267**

Lesson 12-1: Using Repo REST APIs from a Browser to Retrieve Data 267

Lesson 12-2: Creating a PAT to Use with REST APIs for Repos 269

Lesson 12-3: Using the Repo REST APIs from Postman 271

Lesson 12-4: Using the Repo REST APIs from PowerShell 273

Summary 276

Index **277**

About the Authors

Chaminda Chandrasekara is a Microsoft Most Valuable Professional (MVP) for Visual Studio ALM and a Scrum Alliance Certified ScrumMaster, who focuses on continuous improvement of the software development lifecycle. He works as a lead engineer in DevOps at Xameriners (Pvt) Ltd, Singapore. Chaminda is an active Microsoft Community Contributor (MCC) who is well recognized for his contributions in Microsoft forums, TechNet galleries, wikis, and Stack Overflow, and he contributes extensions to Azure DevOps Server and Services (formerly VSTS/TFS) in the Microsoft Visual Studio Marketplace. He also contributes to other open source projects in GitHub. Chaminda has published four books with Apress, and he blogs at `https://chamindac.blogspot.com/`.

Pushpa Herath is an author, blogger, and speaker at technical community events and works as a DevOps engineer at Xamariners (Pvt) Ltd.

She has years of experience in DevOps with Azure DevOps, Octopus, JIRA, and many other DevOps tools. She is an expert on functional test automation using Selenium and BDD. Pushpa blogs about technology at `https://devopsadventure.blogspot.com/`. She has published two books with Apress.

About the Technical Reviewer

Mittal Mehta has 15 years of IT experience and currently is working as a configuration manager. He also has eight years of experience working in TFS, C#, Navision, build-release, Azure DevOps, automation, and configuration in Microsoft technologies.

Acknowledgments

We are thankful for all the mentors who have encouraged and helped us during our careers and who have provided us with so many opportunities to gain the maturity and the courage we needed to write this book.

We would also like to thank our friends and colleagues who have helped and encouraged us in so many ways.

Last, but in no way least, we owe a huge debt to our families, not only because they have put up with late-night typing, research, and our permanent air of distraction, but also because they have had the grace to read what we have written. Our heartfelt gratitude is offered to them for helping us make this dream come true.

Introduction

Collaboration among developers is a vital aspect in software development. Sharing code while working in teams to achieve software delivery goals increases end-user satisfaction. Hence, source code control tools are essential for software development teams.

Azure Repos offers you both a centralized version control system and a distributed version control system.

- Team Foundation Version Control (TFVC) is the centralized version control system that comes with Azure Repos.

- Azure Git repos provide you with distributed version control and support all the popular Git repo concepts.

Hands-on Azure Repos gives you step-by-step guidance on working with TFVC and Git, while exploring best practices in each step. You will discover branching and merging techniques to resolve conflicts while sharing code with teams as well as how to track the changes you make to the code using repos. You will explore the essential command-line options, REST API usage, and security options with hands-on lessons to give you the ability to manage TFVC and Git effectively to support your teams. Additionally, code review procedures for repos and integration of a repo with other Azure DevOps features such as boards, pipelines, etc., are discussed in detail.

The hands-on steps in the book will provide you with a comprehensive understanding, from the basics to advanced topics, as you go through each chapter. Lessons comprise secrets to getting started quickly with Azure Repos in the right way and integrating it with popular development tools such as Visual Studio, VS Code, etc. The tips and tricks in the book will make you a productive developer and prevent you from taking the wrong steps while using Azure Repos.

We hope *Hands-on Azure Repos* will be your go-to resource for delivering value to your end users with software, using any platform and any language you prefer to use.

CHAPTER 1

Getting Started with Azure Team Foundation Version Control

Team Foundation Version Control (TFVC) is a centralized version control system for your source code management. Generally, a team member will have one version of each source code file on their machine while using TFVC. Branches of source code are based on paths and get created on the server. A history of version control is maintained on the source control server, not on the local developer machine. In TFVC you can apply permissions at a granular level, and restrictions can be applied at the file level, which we will discuss in Chapter 6.

In this chapter, we will explore the steps required to get started with TFVC in Azure DevOps using Visual Studio. You will be able to understand how to set up a team project to use TFVC or add a TFVC repo to an existing team project that is currently using Git repos. The steps required to set up your machine to develop with TFVC using Visual Studio will be described, and you will learn how to add new or existing solutions to TFVC in Visual Studio. Further, this chapter will discuss the different workspaces available in TFVC and the options to define and use code check-in (commit) policies. In addition, using TFVC with other developer tools such as VS Code and Eclipse will be described for you to get started even faster.

© Chaminda Chandrasekara and Pushpa Herath 2020
C. Chandrasekara and P. Herath, *Hands-on Azure Repos*, https://doi.org/10.1007/978-1-4842-5425-7_1

Lesson 1-1: Creating a Team Project with TFVC and Adding a TFVC Repo to the Existing Team Project

We discussed how to create a new team project in Chapter 1 of the first book, *Hands-on Azure Boards*, of this book series. However, let's take a quick look at creating a team project with TFVC in this lesson to keep your experience seamless.

Prerequisites: You have an Azure DevOps organization created, and you have some experience working with Azure DevOps to create team projects, or you have followed the lessons in Chapter 1 of the book *Hands-on Azure Boards*.

Navigate to your Azure DevOps organization's home page and click the "Create project" button in the top-right corner. See Figure 1-1.

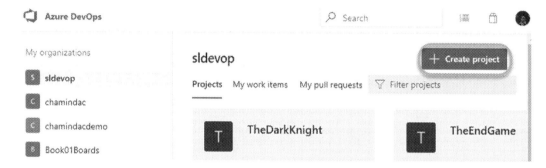

Figure 1-1. *Creating project*

In the team project creation pane, provide a name and select TFVC as the version control system. You can set "Work item process" to whatever you'd like, as discussed in detail in the *Hands-On Azure Boards* book. See Figure 1-2.

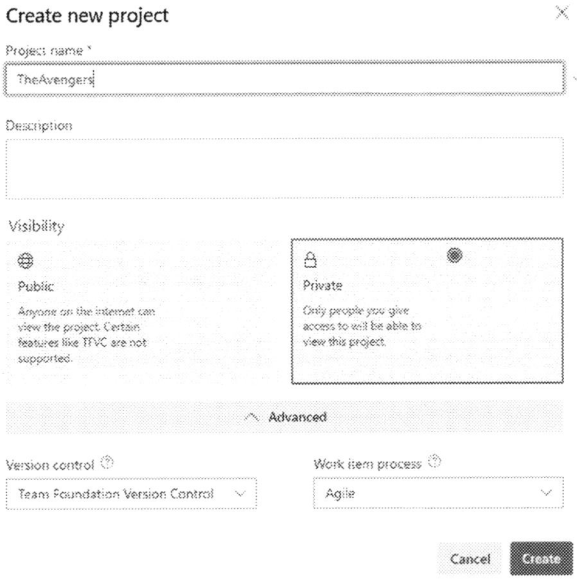

Figure 1-2. *Creating a team project with TFVC*

The created team project has TFVC set as the repo by default, and you can view it by clicking the Repos menu option in the left menu. See Figure 1-3.

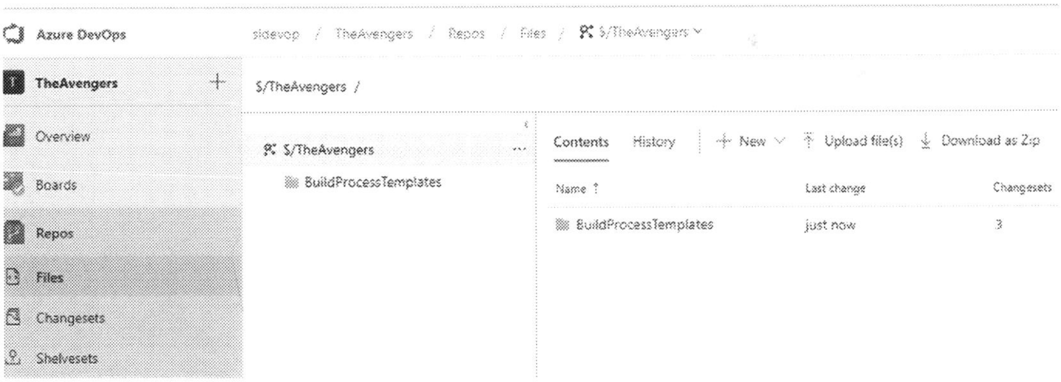

Figure 1-3. *TFVC repo*

Now, let's look at how we can add a TFVC repo to an existing team project. Unlike Git where multiple Git repos can be added to a single team project, you can have only one TFVC repo per team project in Azure DevOps. Create a new team project with Git as the version control system. Then navigate to Repos in the left menu. On the Repos tab, click the drop-down next to the Git repo name and click "New repository." See Figure 1-4.

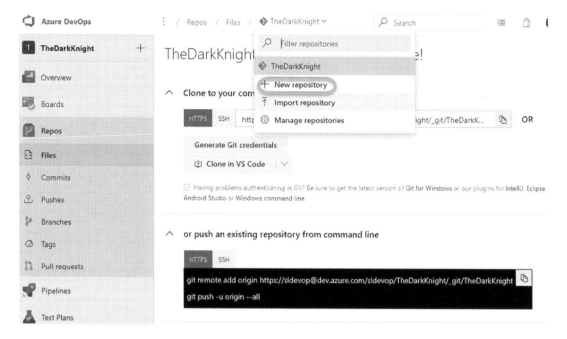

Figure 1-4. *Creating a new repo in an existing project*

In the dialog that appears, select TFVC as the repo type and click Create to create a new TFVC repo in a team project that already has Git repos. See Figure 1-5.

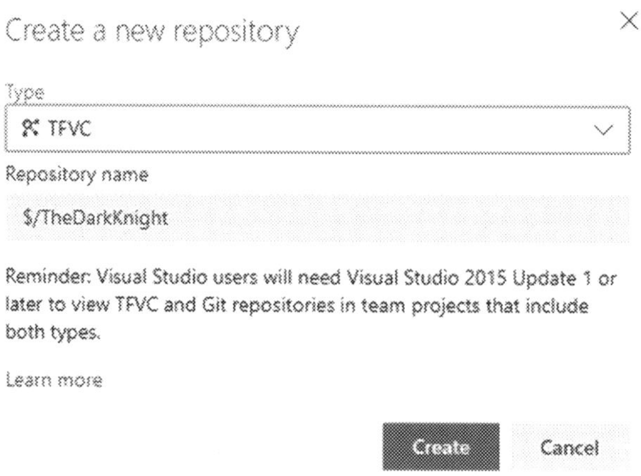

Figure 1-5. *Creating a TFVC repo*

In this lesson, we explored how to create a TFVC repo in an existing team project or create a new team project with TFVC as the source control system.

Lesson 1-2: Using Visual Studio Team Explorer

We created a new team project in the previous lesson with TFVC as the source control system. As a next step, we need to connect it to Visual Studio to get started with the source code development. In this lesson, let's discuss the steps required to get Visual Studio connected to your newly created team project in the TFVC repository, using the Team Explorer window in Visual Studio.

Prerequisites: You have Visual Studio 2019 installed on your machine and are familiar with working with Visual Studio. You have followed the steps in Lesson 1-1 of this chapter and have a team project created with TFVC as the source control system.

In Visual Studio, to open Team Explorer, you can click View ➤ Team Explorer in the menu or press Ctrl+\ and then Ctrl+M. The Team Explorer window lets you connect to Azure DevOps. You can click the Manage Connection toolbar icon to go to the Manage Connections page of the Team Explorer window. See Figure 1-6.

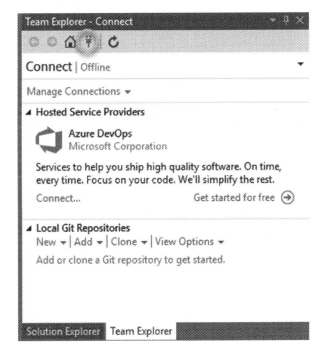

Figure 1-6. Managing connections in Team Explorer

Click the Connect link or click the drop-down next to the Manage Connections link (see Figure 1-6) and then click "Connect to a project." In Team Explorer, the Manage Connection page will open as a pop-up window. In the Connect to a Project dialog, you can see the Azure DevOps organizations you have access to if you have already logged in to Visual Studio with a Microsoft account or your organization's account. You can click "Add an account" or select a different account if you have connected more than one account. See Figure 1-7. If you click "Add an account," you will be prompted for your credentials, and you can provide them to connect your Microsoft account or your organization's account to Visual Studio.

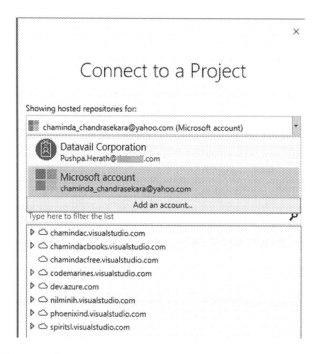

Figure 1-7. *Adding or selecting an account*

Log on from the account you used to create a team project in the previous lesson and expand the Azure DevOps services organization to view your team projects and repositories. If you are using an on-premises Azure DevOps server, you have the option to provide an Azure DevOps server URL and connect it. In the expanded view, select the TFVC repo you want to connect and click the Connect button. See Figure 1-8.

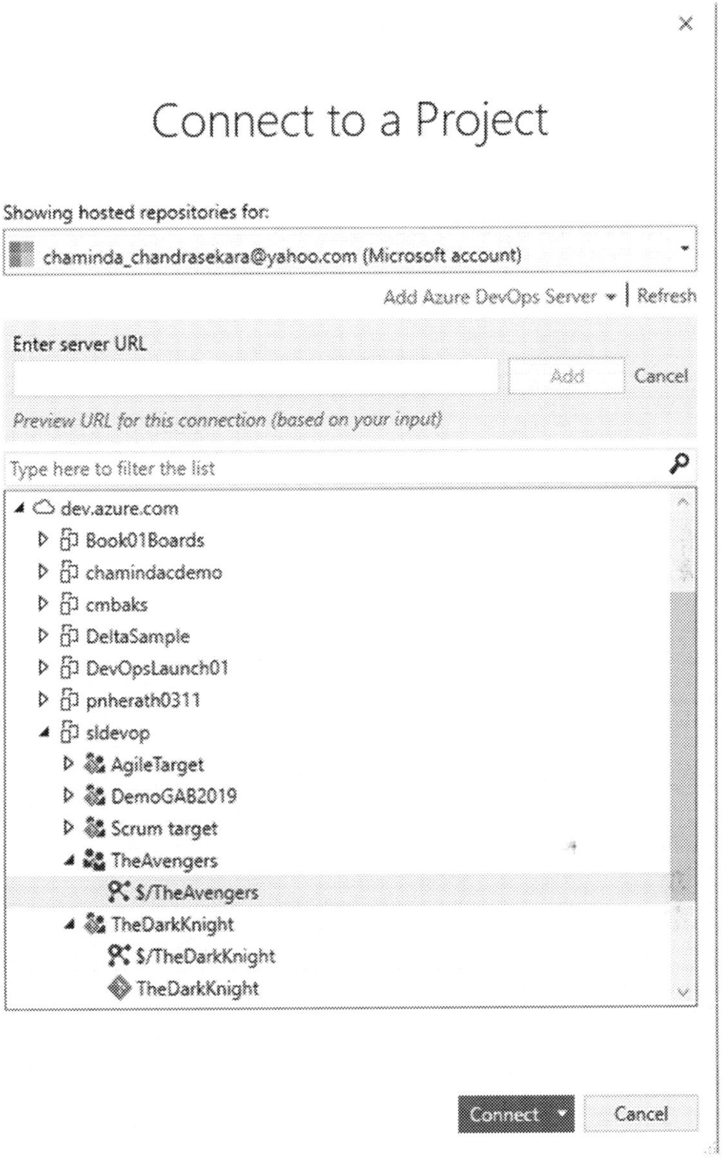

Figure 1-8. *Connecting a TFVC repo*

Once the team project TFVC repo is connected, Team Explorer will allow you to map the TFVC path of the project to a local folder and create a workspace. There are two types of workspaces, and we will discuss them in Lesson 1-4. Provide a desired local path and click the Map & Get button. See Figure 1-9.

Figure 1-9. *Map & Get button*

In this lesson, we discussed the steps required to connect and map a local path for a TFVC repository using Visual Studio.

Lesson 1-3: Adding New/Existing Solutions to TFVC

Once we map the TFVC repository in Visual Studio, we are allowed to add new solutions to version control using the Solution Explorer window of Visual Studio. Let's look at the steps to add a new solution to TFVC and how you can add an existing solution to TFVC using the Solution Explorer window of Visual Studio.

Prerequisites: You performed the steps described in the first two lessons in this chapter.

In Team Explorer, you will see the New link, which allows you to create a new solution. Click it. See Figure 1-10.

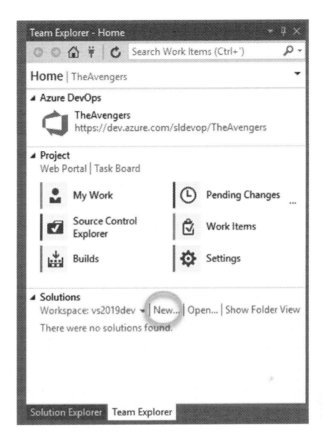

Figure 1-10. *Creating a new solution*

Then in the "Create a new project" dialog, search for *console application*, select the .NET Framework console application, and click Next. See Figure 1-11.

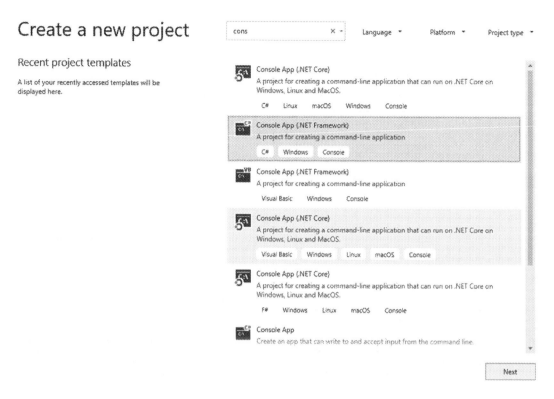

Figure 1-11. *Creating a console application*

In the next step, provide a name for the project. Do not change the Location path as the new solution is already being created in the mapped path of TFVC. Click Create to create the new application. See Figure 1-12.

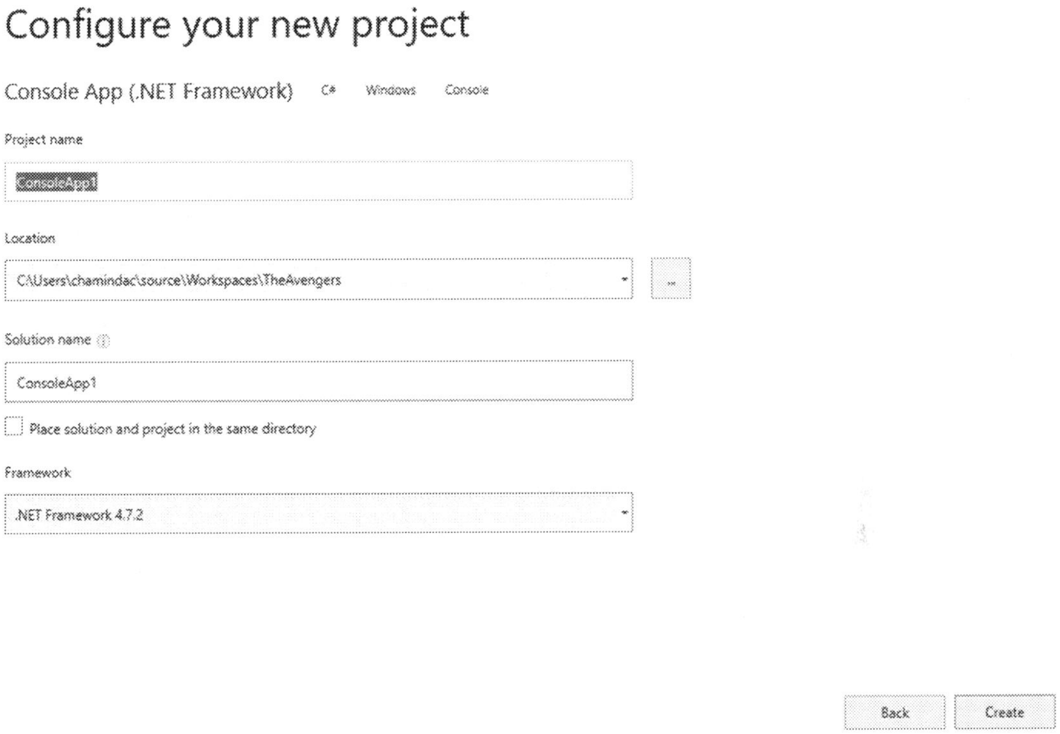

Configure your new project

Console App (.NET Framework)   C#   Windows   Console

Project name

ConsoleApp1

Location

C:\Users\chamindac\source\Workspaces\TheAvengers

Solution name ⓘ

ConsoleApp1

☐ Place solution and project in the same directory

Framework

.NET Framework 4.7.2

Back   Create

Figure 1-12. *Creating the console application in the mapped source path*

Once the new solution is created, view it in the Solution Explorer window of Visual Studio. You can open Solution Explorer by pressing Ctrl+Alt+L or by clicking View ➤ Solution Explorer in the Visual Studio menu. If you have an existing solution that you need to add to TFVC, copy all the content of the solution to the mapped local drive path of TFVC and then open that solution in Visual Studio. Once you create/open a solution in Visual Studio, go to the Solution Explorer window and right-click the solution you want to add to TFVC. Then click Add Solution to Source Control in the context menu. See Figure 1-13.

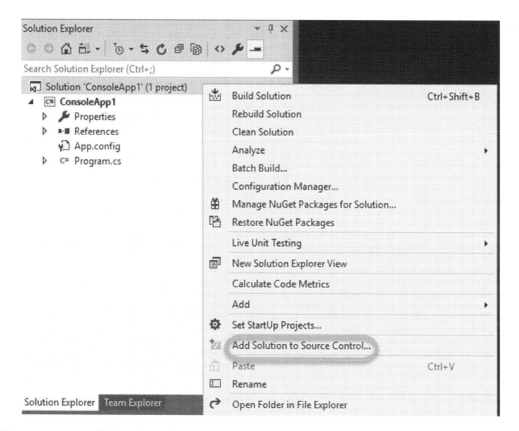

Figure 1-13. *Adding the solution to source control*

You will notice that all the files in the solution are marked with a +, indicating that they are ready to be checked in (committed) to TFVC. See Figure 1-14.

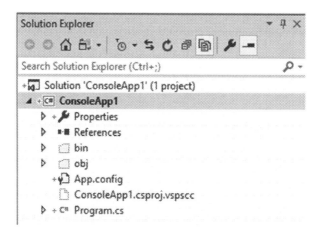

Figure 1-14. *Solution ready to be checked in*

Next open the Team Explorer window and click Pending Changes. In the Pending Changes window of Team Explorer, you will be able to see the new solution files are ready to be checked in. You can provide a comment and check in your code to TFVC. Further, you can see the Related Work Items options allowing you to add a work item, which we will discuss in Chapter 2. Note that there are some local file changes detected (this is because of the default local workspace; we will discuss the difference between the server and local workspaces that are available for TFVC in Lesson 1-4). See Figure 1-15.

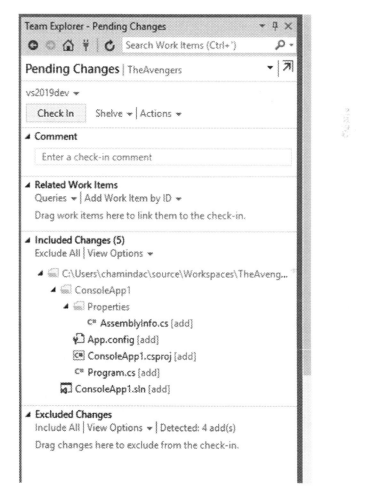

Figure 1-15. Pending changes

Click the detected changes in the Excluded Changes section. A dialog will appear, and you will be able to see the local files that should be ignored by source control. Select all the files and right-click to open a context menu. In this window, you are allowed to promote files, which will be included as changes. Or you can ignore local-only files. Since the files detected in this instance are local files, click "Ignore these local items." Note that several ignore options are available when you have selected a single file, the same file extension, etc. See Figure 1-16.

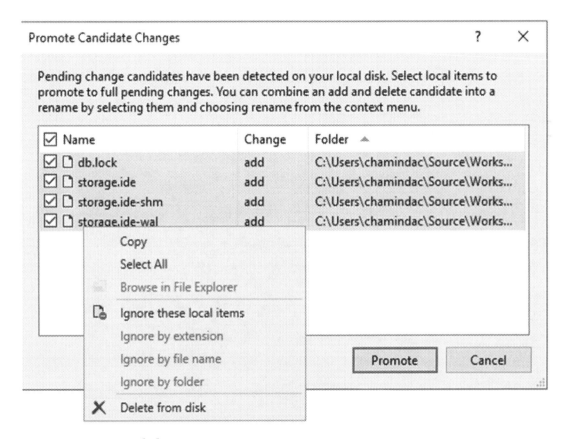

Figure 1-16. *Local changes*

You will notice a new file is added to the included changes named .tfignore in the pending changes. See Figure 1-17.

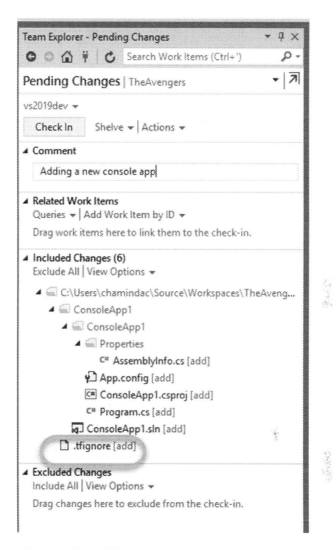

Figure 1-17. *The .tfignore file added*

Double-click the `.tfignore` file and inspect its content. The `.tfignore` file is used to specify which files/paths should be ignored from TFVC. You can define the ignore file patterns using wildcards. The `.tfignore` file contains a documentation header that itself is a good explanation of how to use the file. Provide a comment in the Pending Changes window and click the "Check in" button to commit the code to TFVC. In the Solution Explorer, the files are now marked with a lock icon indicating they are checked in to TFVC.

In this lesson, we discussed how to get a solution added to TFVC using Visual Studio's Solution Explorer. Further, we looked at how to ignore local files from getting checked in to TFVC using a .tfignore file.

Lesson 1-4: Changing Settings for TFVC in Visual Studio

There are a couple of settings you can set in Visual Studio to manage the behavior of TFVC. They are divided into two levels: project collection settings that are applicable to an Azure DevOps organization or a project collection in Azure DevOps Server and team project settings that applicable in a team project scope.

You can access the project collection TFVC settings by clicking Team ➤ Team Project Collection Settings ➤ Source Control. See Figure 1-18.

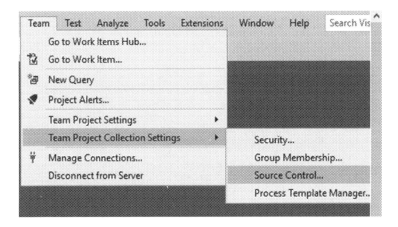

Figure 1-18. *TFVC team project collection settings*

File Types

The File Types settings let you define the enabled file types that can be added to source control and the types that are prevented from being added to source control in TFVC. See Figure 1-19.

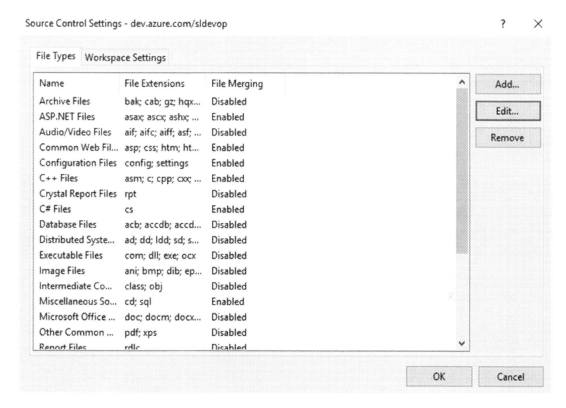

Figure 1-19. *TFVC File Types settings*

Workspace Settings

The default settings for workspaces can be set on the Workspace Settings tab of the project collection's source control settings for TFVC. See Figure 1-20.

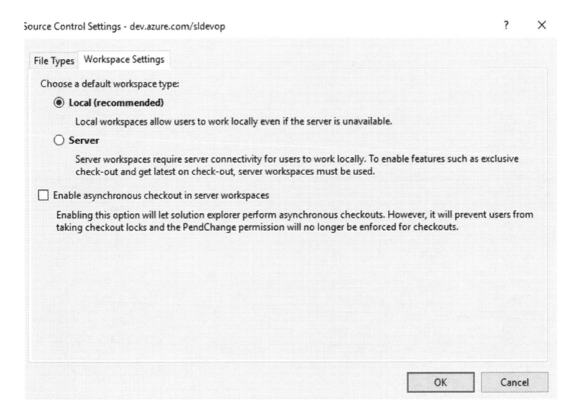

Figure 1-20. *Default workspace settings*

Team Foundation Version Control comes with two modes of workspaces, namely, local and server workspaces. By default, a local workspace is set up in Visual Studio when you connect with TFVC. Let's try to understand the difference between the local and server workspaces in this lesson.

- **Server workspace**: In a server workspace, you can handle millions of files per branch and even large binary files. The facility is there to apply locks, which we will discuss in Chapter 3. Most of the operations in the server workspace require the developer to be connected to the TFVC server. The server workspace lets you set "Enable get latest when checkout," which will download the latest version of a file when you start editing it. You should consider using the server workspace when you have more than 100,000 items in your workspace.

- **Local workspace**: A copy of the latest version of code is available on the developer's machine so the developer can work offline with the files. To check in code, the developer has to connect to the TFVC server. You should consider using the local workspace when you want to work offline often and easily restore locally deleted files. You can compare, undo, check out and edit, rename, add, and delete files easily in the local workspace mode.

We will discuss how to set the workspace mode for your development in Chapter 2.

Source Control Settings

To access the team project's source control settings, you can click Team ➤ Team Project Settings ➤ Source Control. See Figure 1-21.

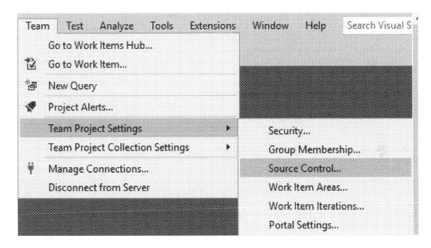

Figure 1-21. *Team project's Source Control settings*

Check-Out Settings

When you click Team ➤ Team Project Settings ➤ Source Control, the Source Control Settings dialog will open. The check-out settings let you define whether to enable multiple check-outs of files for server workspace mode as well. By default, multiple check-out is enabled for local workspace mode. Additionally, you can set the server workspace mode to get the latest version of a file for a local machine when a file is checked out. See Figure 1-22.

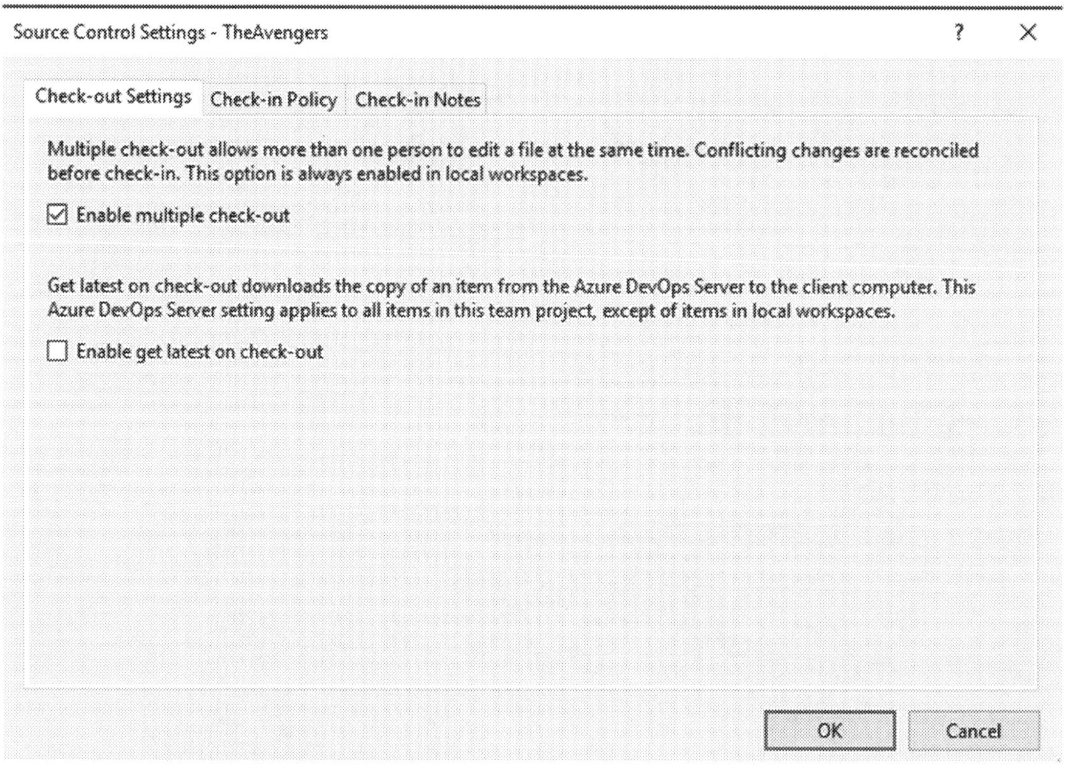

Figure 1-22. *Check-out settings*

Check-in Policies

Check-in policies help you to add conditions to check in code so that you are able to make the development team follow a given set of rules when submitting code to TFVC. There are different types of check-in policies such as making a comment mandatory, making the association of a work item to a given query mandatory, etc. We will discuss how the check-in policies work in Lesson 3-5.

Check-in Notes

Check-in notes allow you to define a note requirement for each check-in. Notes can be set as optional or required. You can specify a note title and add a note as required or not in team project's Source Control settings. See Figure 1-23.

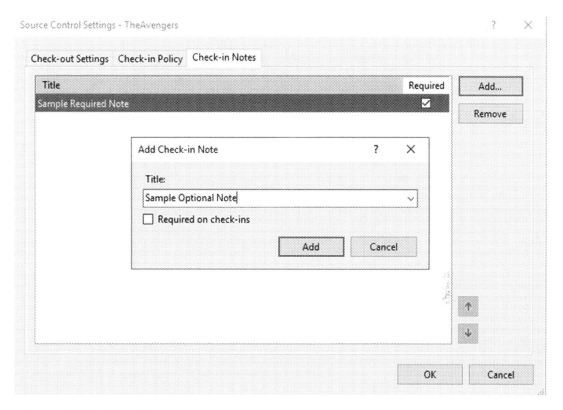

Figure 1-23. *Check-in notes*

If you try to edit a file and check in the code, you will be prompted to provide a required note. See Figure 1-24.

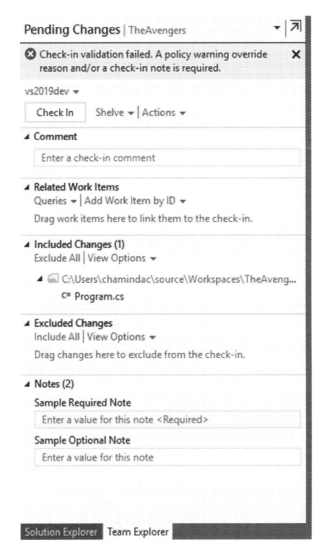

Figure 1-24. Check-in notes in Pending Changes

In this lesson, we discussed project collection and team project TFVC settings that can be used to control the behavior of how you work with TFVC.

Lesson 1-5: Connecting to TFVC in VS Code

Visual Studio Code is the lightweight cross-platform editor in the Visual Studio family. In this lesson, let's see how we can get VS Code connected to TFVC.

Prerequisites: You have installed VS Code and are familiar with working with VS Code. You must have a local workspace created for TFVC using Visual Studio or Eclipse available on your machine. If you have followed the steps in Lesson 1-2, you should have it already.

Open VS Code and press Ctrl+Shift+X, or click the cogwheel at the bottom-left corner. Then click Extensions in the context menu to open the Extensions tab in VS Code. See Figure 1-25.

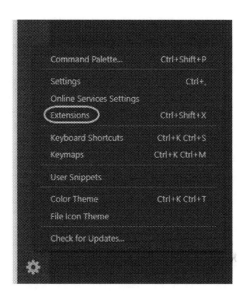

Figure 1-25. *Extensions*

Search for *Azure Repos* to get the Azure Repos extension installed. Next locate the `tf.exe` location of your machine. You can get `tf.exe` installed by installing Visual Studio or by installing Team Explorer Everywhere from `https://github.com/microsoft/team-explorer-everywhere/releases`. Team Explorer Everywhere supports macOS and Linux as well, and you can install the command-line client to get `tf.exe`. `https://github.com/microsoft/team-explorer-everywhere` contains the documentation on Team Explorer Everywhere. If you have VS 2019 installed, you typically have `tf.exe` in the path shown here:

```
C:\Program Files (x86)\Microsoft Visual Studio\2019\Enterprise\Common7\IDE\
CommonExtensions\Microsoft\TeamFoundation\Team Explorer
```

You have to go to VS Code File ➤ Preferences ➤ Setting and add a user setting as specified here with your tf.exe path:

```
{ "tfvc.location": "C:\\Program Files (x86)\\Microsoft Visual
Studio\\2019\\Enterprise\\Common7\\IDE\\CommonExtensions\\Microsoft\\
TeamFoundation\\Team Explorer\\tf.exe", "tfvc.restrictWorkspace": true }
```

Open the Settings Editor for the Azure Repos extension, as shown in Figure 1-26.

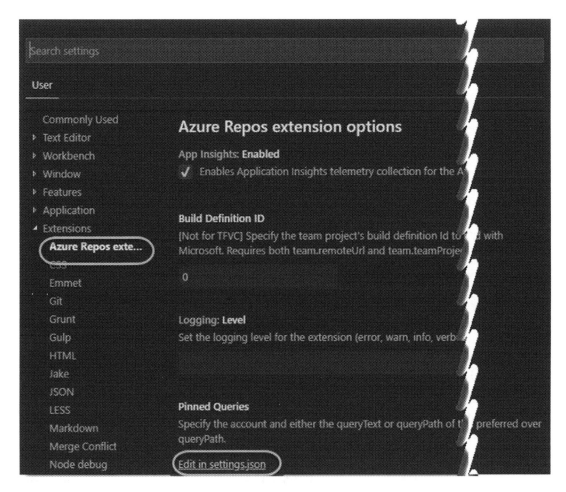

Figure 1-26. *Azure Repos extension settings*

Then update the settings file with the user settings and the tf.exe path mentioned earlier and save the settings file. Next open the local workspace folder containing the TFVC repository in VS Code. Click View ➤ Command Palette and type **team signin** in the command palette. See Figure 1-27.

Figure 1-27. *Team sign-in*

In the next two options provided, you can enter a personal access token (PAT) if you have one. How to create a PAT was explained in *Hands-On Azure Boards* book. Let's select the option to authenticate and get an access token method, as shown in Figure 1-28.

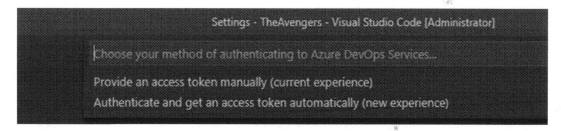

Figure 1-28. *Authenticating TFVC in VS Code*

Next copy the code provided and press Enter to authenticate. See Figure 1-29.

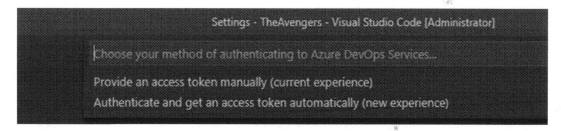

Figure 1-29. *Starting the authentication*

Provide the code and click Next in the opened browser prompt. See Figure 1-30.

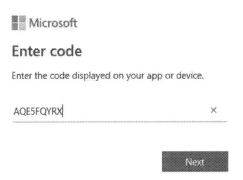

Figure 1-30. Entering code

Then provide your credentials and sign into the Azure DevOps organization when prompted and close the browser after signing in. You will be able to see the connected repo in the VS Code, and you can perform check-in and check-out operations with VS Code. See Figure 1-31.

Figure 1-31. VS Code connected to TFVC

In this lesson, we explored the steps required to connect VS Code to the TFVC repository.

Summary

This chapter took you through getting started with Team Foundation Version Control. We discussed setting up Visual Studio and VS Code to use with TFVC and explored a few useful settings. Additionally, we identified how to add a solution via the Solution Explorer window in Visual Studio to TFVC.

In the next chapter, we will discuss in detail how to use Visual Studio Source Control Explorer to work with TFVC.

CHAPTER 2

Working with Team Foundation Version Control: Part1

We discussed how to create an Azure DevOps project and access the source code using Visual Studio Team Explorer and Solution Explorer in the previous chapter. Now we have an overall idea of how to create an Azure DevOps project with TFVC as the source control system and how to connect to the project through Visual Studio Team Explorer. Hence, we can discuss more about each important section of Team Explorer to get a clearer idea of how to work with Team Explorer. One of the main windows of Visual Studio is the Source Control Explorer window, which can be launched using Team Explorer. The Source Control Explorer helps users to view and manage the source code of the project.

In this chapter, we will explore the Source Control Explorer in detail, and you will learn about many features available in the Visual Studio Source Control Explorer. Further, we will discuss how to check in your code changes, resolve code conflicts, and set different source control tool options.

Lesson 2-1: Exploring the Source Control Explorer

The Source Control Explorer is used to view and manage the source code–related files and settings of the project when you are using Team Foundation Version Control (TFVC).

Prerequisites: You followed the steps in Chapter 1. You have a solution and project available in TFVC.

Go to Team Explorer of Visual Studio and connect to the Azure DevOps project, as explained in Chapter 1. Select the Source Control Explorer. See Figure 2-1.

© Chaminda Chandrasekara and Pushpa Herath 2020
C. Chandrasekara and P. Herath, *Hands-on Azure Repos*, https://doi.org/10.1007/978-1-4842-5425-7_2

Figure 2-1. *Selecting the Source Control Explorer in Team Explorer*

We will discuss all the important sections of the source control window in this chapter. The main sections are the menu items, the folders, and the local path. See Figure 2-2.

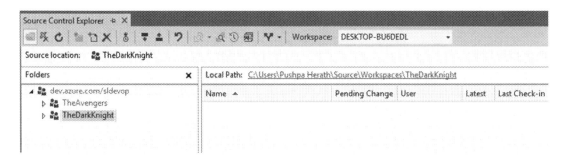

Figure 2-2. *Source Control Explorer*

Go to the Folders section of the Source Control Explorer window. You will be able to see that all the projects available in the Azure DevOps organization are listed in the Folders section. As discussed in Chapter 1, you can map the entire organization or the selected project with the local location. Right-click the mapped project. You will be able to see the context menu with the various source control options. See Figure 2-3.

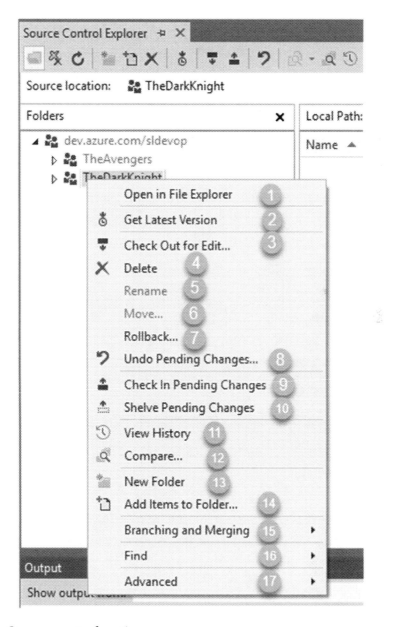

Figure 2-3. *Source control options*

Let's identify what we can do with each option in the context menu.

1. Open in File Explorer

    We can navigate to the local source control folder where we
    have mapped the source code. The workspace will open in the
    Windows File Explorer after clicking this Open in File Explorer
    menu item.

2. Get Latest Version

    While we are working in our local source control, there can be
    several changesets added to the source control in the Azure
    DevOps server. So, we need to have a way to get the latest code
    version on the server to our local source control folder.

3. Check Out for Edit

    If we need to make any changes to the existing file of the project,
    we need to check out the file first. You can open the selected file
    for editing by using this option.

4. Delete

    We can delete the selected file or the folder from the local source
    control. We have an option to undo a delete as well.

5. Rename

    We can rename the selected file or folder in the local source
    control folder.

6. Move

    We can move the selected file or folder.

7. Rollback

    We can remove the changes in the selected changesets from the
    local source control folder code and check in the pending changes
    to apply the rollback.

8. Undo Pending Changes

    We can undo the pending changes of the selected project files or
    folders from here.

9.   Check in Pending Changes

We can make several changes in the local source control folder.
If the local changes are ready to go to the server, we can check in
the pending changes. Then all the pending changes will go to the
server.

10.   Shelve Pending Changes

There may be situations where we are in the middle of an
implementation that is not completed. Hence, we can't check
in those changes to the server. But we all know that if something
happens to our development machine, we will lose all the
pending work we have done. As a solution to this, we can keep our
incomplete code on the server using shelve sets. We will discuss
more about shelve sets in Chapter 3.

11.   View History

We can open the history window where we can find all the
changeset details of the project.

12.   Compare

We can compare the local work source control folder version
to the server version using this option. This allows you to select
which local version you want to compare to the server version.

13.   New Folder

We can add a new folder to the selected project.

14.   Add Items to Folder

We can add files to the selected folder using this option. After
selecting this option, a window will open where you can browse
and select the files to add to the project.

15.   Branching and Merging

Development teams follow different branching strategies to
make their development work more organized. So, they are using
separate branches for feature development, as well as some
branches for testing purposes. At one point in development,

teams merge these branches. Hence, we can create new branches and merge the branches using this option when we use TFVC as the source control system. Also, we can convert folders to the branches with this option. We will discuss more about branching with TFVC in Chapter 4.

16. Find

This is a search option available in source control. We can search for labels, changesets, and shelvesets with this tool.

17. Advanced shows more advanced options. See Figure 2-4.

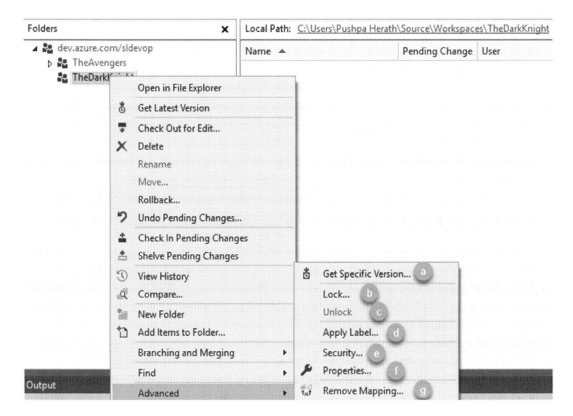

Figure 2-4. *Source control advanced options*

a. We can select the specific version and overwrite the local files.

b. We can lock the selected file and restrict the file editing by another user.

   c. We can unlock the selected file and allow editing by other users.

   d. We can apply labels for the code versions.

   e. We can navigate to the Azure DevOps project security section using this option.

   f. We can navigate to the Project Properties window from this option.

   g. We can remove the source code from the local workspace using this option.

In this lesson, we discussed some of the features available in the Source Control Explorer. We were able to get a basic idea of Source Control Explorer concepts such as check-in, rollback, shelve set, branches, and check-out.

Lesson 2-2: Setting Workspace Mode to Local and Server

Team Foundation Version Control is a centralized version control system, which allows users to have one version of the source code in the local working machine. This local workspace can have two modes that we will learn about in this lesson.

There can be two modes of the workspace: local mode and server mode. We will discuss the similarities and differences of these two modes in this lesson.

Go to the Source Control Explorer window and you will be able to find the Workspace option at the top of the window. See Figure 2-5.

Figure 2-5. *Workspace option*

You can see the currently selected workspace. Expand the drop-down and select Workspaces to add or edit workspaces. After clicking Workspaces, the Manage Workspaces window will open, which allows us to see all the workspaces we have access to. Also, there are buttons to add, edit, or remove workspaces. Here we have another interesting option to access the remote workspaces of the current user. If the same user has created workspaces on different machines for this project, the user can list all those workspaces here by checking the "Show remote workspace" box. See Figure 2-6.

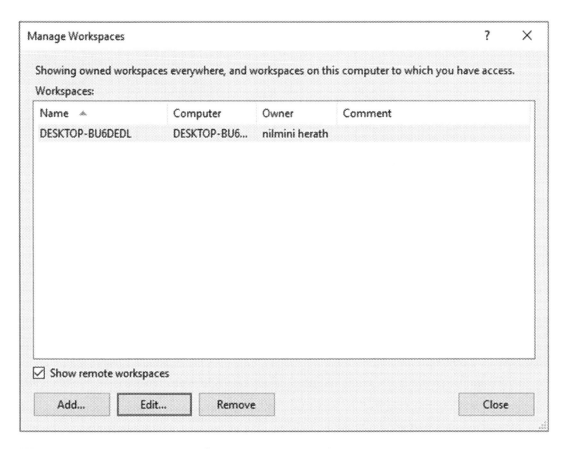

Figure 2-6. Managing a workspace

Select the workspace in the list and click the Edit button. This will open a window where you can see the server path and local path of the workspace. You will be able to find the Advanced button at the bottom of the window. Click that button to learn more about the workspace. See Figure 2-7.

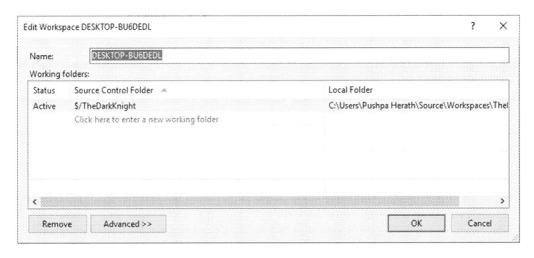

Figure 2-7. Editing the workspace

After clicking the Advanced button, another window will open with more details of the workspace. See Figure 2-8.

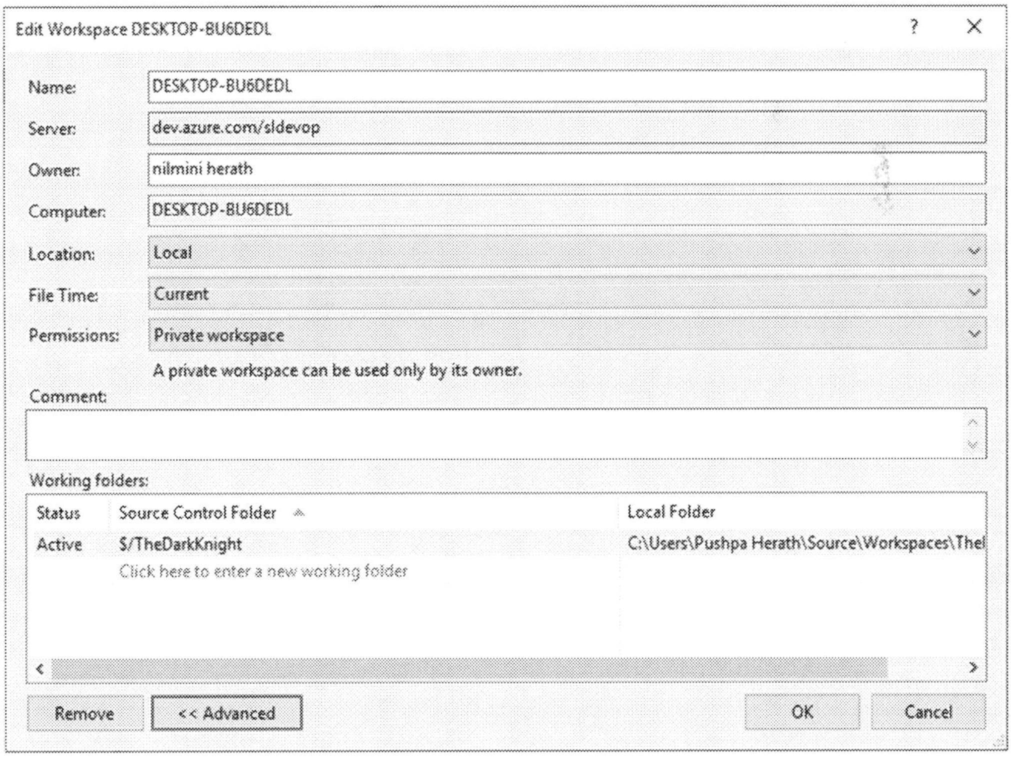

Figure 2-8. Editing the workspace window with more details

We can find the name of the workspace listed here. Also, we can edit the name of the workspace from this window. Next in the list, we can find the server, owner, and computer name of the selected workspace.

We can select the location of the workspace from this window. We can specify the location as local or server. The next item in the list is File Time. We can give two values as the file time: current and check-in. We can control the permission of this workspace using the Permissions section. Here we have three permission types available. They are private, where only the workspace owner can access the workspace; public (limited), which allows valid users to access the workspace, but they don't have any administration permission for the workspace; and, which means any valid user has admin and contribution permission for the workspace.

So far, we have discussed the options available in workspaces. Now we will discuss the local and server workspace modes.

Local Workspace Mode

If we work in the local workspace mode, we can perform most of the source control operations without connecting to the Azure DevOps server.

The following are the source control operations you can perform in local mode:

- Checking out a file for edit

- Pending add, delete, rename, or edit new files and folders

- Undoing pending changes

If we need to perform a check-in, shelve, view history of items, merge, or branch, we need to go online. These actions don't work in offline mode.

Server Workspace Mode

For almost all the actions, the server workspace needs to be connected with the server. Otherwise, you have to take the codebase offline and later edit the existing files without having the capability to undo or add new files, projects, etc. When the connectivity is available, you can get the solution back to online mode.

In this lesson, we learned how to create multiple workspaces with different modes. Also, we discussed workspace permission control capabilities. Further, we discussed the capabilities and limitations of the server workspace mode and local workspace mode.

Lesson 2-3: Looking at Source Control Explorer Menu Items

So far, we were able to identify Source Control Explorer operations and local and server workspaces. In this lesson, we will discuss more about Source Control Explorer operations. We can find the menu items at the top of the Source Control Explorer window. We will discuss those menu items in this lesson. See Figure 2-9.

Figure 2-9. *Source control menu items*

1. We can hide or show the folder section by clicking this folder icon.

2. We can show or hide deleted items in the source.

3. We can refresh the source by clicking this menu icon.

4. Select a folder in the Folders section and click this folder icon in the menu. The new folder will be added to the selected folder.

5. Add existing items in the selected local folder to version control.

6. Delete the selected file or folder.

7. Get the latest version of the source in the server.

8. Check out the selected file for edit.

9. Check in any pending changes to the server.

10. Undo any pending changes.

11. Compare the source with the local version.

12. Compare the folder content with the server version.

13. See the history of the selected files.

14.   Search for the changesets.

15.   Create branches.

In this lesson, we were able to identify the source control menu items. All these menu items act as quick access to the Source Control Explorer operations.

Lesson 2-4: Editing and Checking In Your Changes

So far, we discussed different operations available in the Source Control Explorer. So, let's try to learn how to use those operations while working with the code.

Prerequisites: You followed the steps in Chapter 1. You have a solution and project available in TFVC.

Go to the Source Control Explorer and open the solution file. See Figure 2-10.

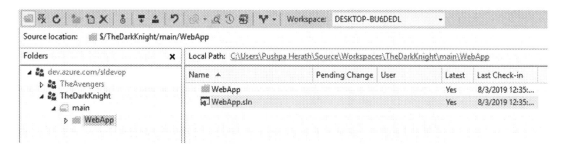

Figure 2-10.   *Moving to a solution using the Source Control Explorer*

Go to the Solution Explorer. We can see the source code open in the Solution Explorer. Let's select a file and make a small change to it. If any change has been made to a file, it will be indicated with the red check mark. Right-click the changed file to identify the different actions we can do with this file. See Figure 2-11.

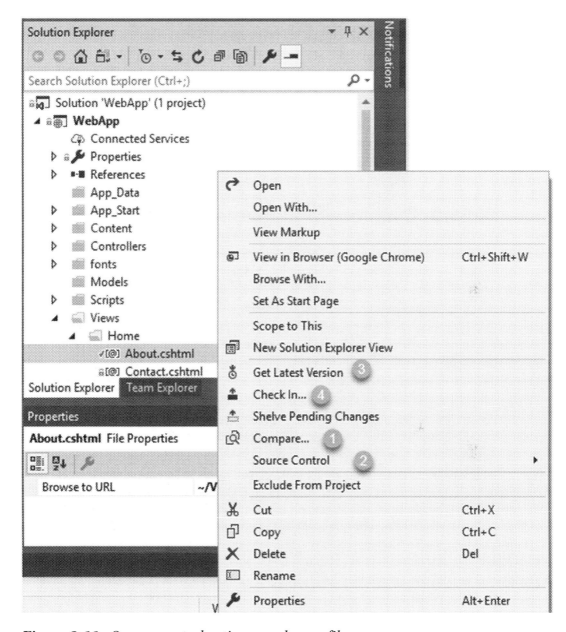

Figure 2-11. *Source control actions on change file*

1. **Compare**

    We can compare the file versions using the compare option in this
    pane. After selecting the Compare option, the Compare window
    will open. See Figure 2-12.

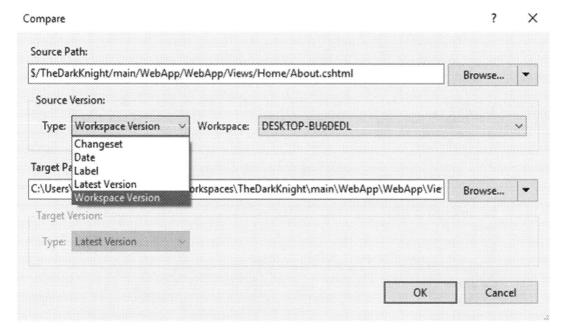

Figure 2-12. *Comparing the source and local versions*

In the Compare window, we can select the type of source version.
Here we can compare the different source versions with the latest
version of the local changes we have done to the project source.

- **Workspace Version**: We can compare the pending changes to the
  source version in the selected workspace.

- **Latest Version**: We can compare the pending changes to the
  latest source version.

- **Label**: We can give an existing label for the source and compare
  that labeled version to the pending changes.

- **Date**: We can compare the source changes done on a specific day
  to the pending changes.

- **Changeset**: We can select the changeset and compare the
  pending changes to the selected changeset version.

After we select any of these comparison option, we will be able
to see the comparison between the pending changes and the
selected source version. See Figure 2-13.

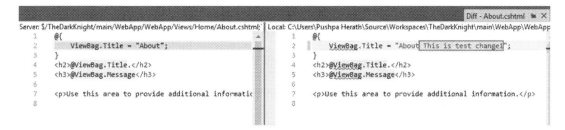

Figure 2-13. *Code comparison*

2. **Source Control**

   Move the mouse on to the source control; a pane will open with
   the four source control options. See Figure 2-14.

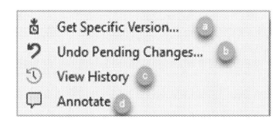

Figure 2-14. *Source control pane options*

a. The Get window will open after selecting the Get Specific Version item from
   the pane. You will find some change overwrite options in the Get window,
   which allows us to overwrite the selected file content with the selected
   source version. See Figure 2-15.

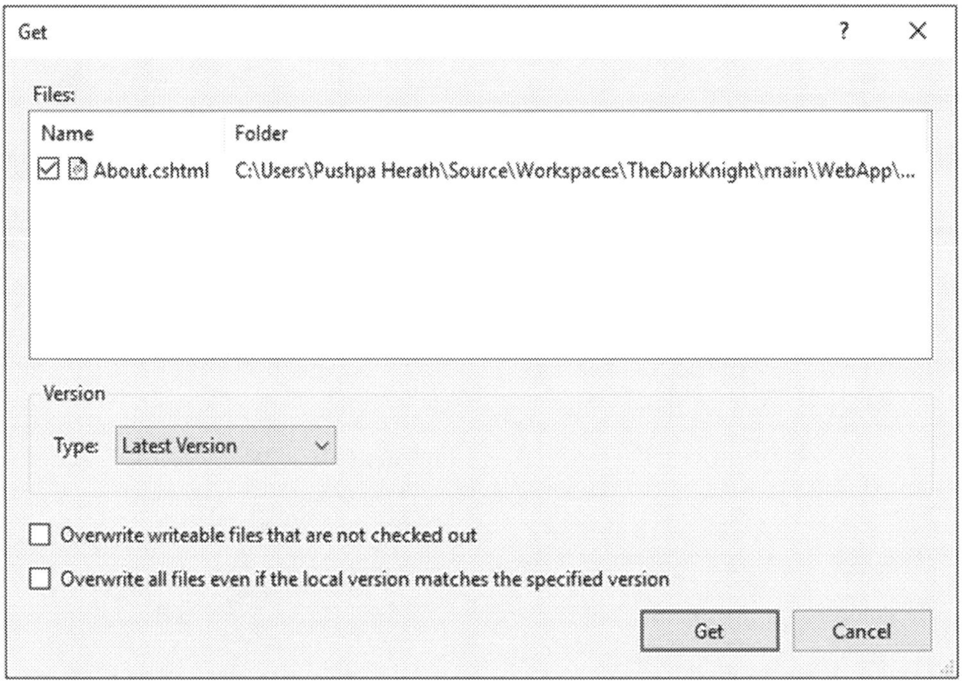

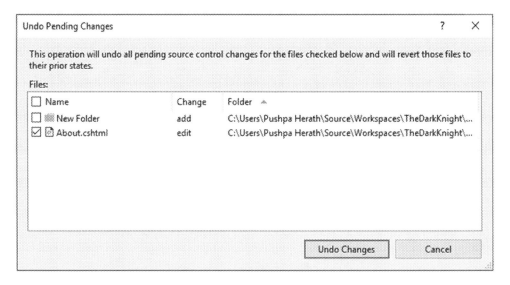

Figure 2-15. *Get version window*

  b. You can select Undo Pending Changes to remove the pending changes. After we select the Undo Pending Changes option, the window will open where we can select the file and undo the change. See Figure 2-16.

Figure 2-16. *Undoing the pending changes*

    c. The View History option allows you to access the changeset details.

    d. We can use Annotate to identify who has done the changes in the selected file. See Figure 2-17.

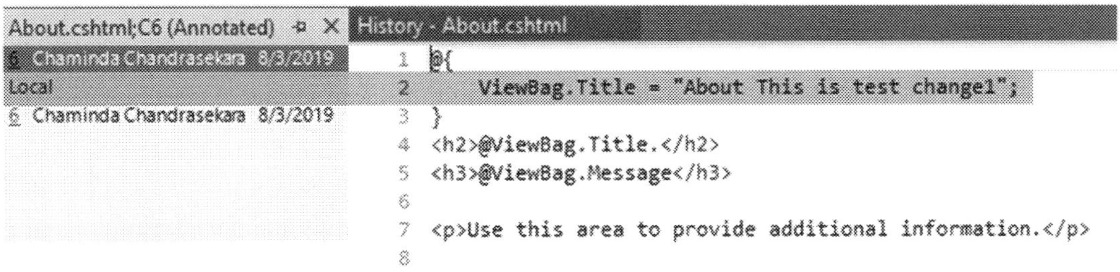

Figure 2-17. Annotate

3. **Get Latest Version**

We can get the latest version of the selected file from the server. If there are any changes that have been done to the same file by another team member, we will get change conflicts. You can resolve the conflicts using the Resolve Conflicts window, which we will discuss more specifically in the next chapter.

4. **Check in**

We can check in the pending changes using this menu option. But there is a check-in best practice we have to follow.

Before checking in the code, get the latest version from the server and resolve any conflicts. Then build the solution to verify that no build issues occurred while resolving the conflicts and test the application. Again, get the latest version from the server to verify there are no new changes; after that, check in the code. After clicking the check-in icon in the menu, the Pending Changes window will open. See Figure 2-18.

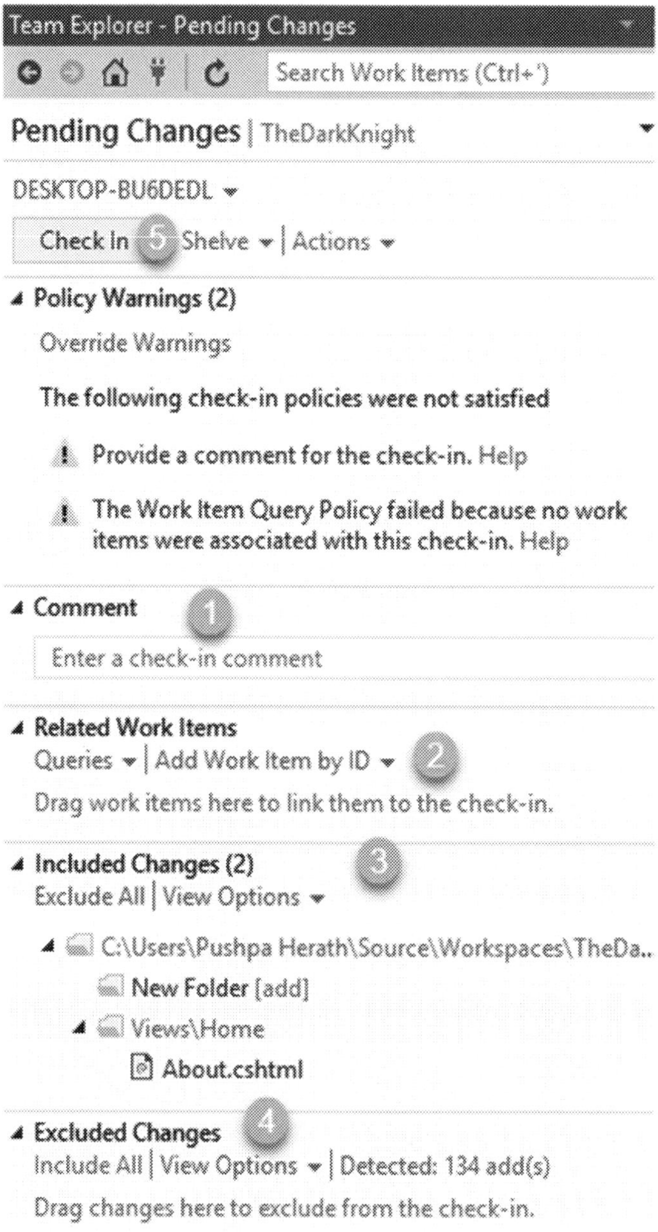

Figure 2-18. *Pending Changes window*

1. Add the comment to the changeset to identify what the change is about.

2. Add the work item for the changeset to track the user story completion.

3. All the changes will be listed in the include section. We can exclude the files from this section if we don't want to send the changes to the server.

4. All the excluded files will be listed here.

5. After adding the work item and the comment, we can check in the code. The override warning policy will bypass all policies and allow the user to check in the code.

In this lesson, we made a simple change to a file in the project to identify the version comparison capabilities in the Source Control Explorer. Further, we discussed different source version filtering options. Finally, we saw how to check in the changes to the server.

Lesson 2-5: Resolving Conflicts During Code Check-in

We know as a best practice we need to get the latest code from the server before we check in any pending changes to the server. But if the same file has changes on the server, we may get change conflicts.

Prerequisites: You followed the steps in Chapter 1. You have a solution and project available in TFVC.

Let's try to identify the options available in the Source Control Explorer to resolve these conflicts. See Figure 2-19.

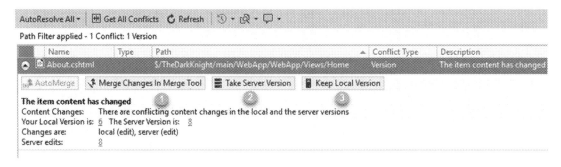

Figure 2-19. *Conflicts window*

Let's identify main three options available in the change conflict window.

1. **Merge changes in Merge tool**

   We can open the Merge tool to do the code merge. See Figure 2-20.

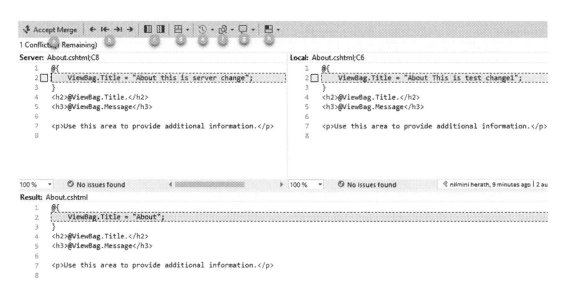

Figure 2-20. *Merge tool*

   a. We can select the changes from both the server version and the local version and see the final version using the result section. To keep the selected changes, we can click the "Accept merge" button.

   b. We can use this to move to previous differences and conflicts. Also, we can use this to move to next differences and conflicts.

   c. We can pick the change to the left (server) or right (local) as the change to be used in merged.

   d. We can change the view of the Merge Tool window. We have vertical view, horizontal view, and mixed view.

   e. The changeset list will open.

   f. We can see the comparison of the server version and the local version.

   g. We can use an annotation to see the owner of each change.

   h. We can change the focus between the server version window, local version window, and result window.

2. **Take Server Version**

   We can directly specify to get the version on the server. Then we can select the local folder file content to replace with the server content.

3. **Keep Local Version**

   We can keep the local version instead of the server version.

In this lesson, we explained the change conflict resolve options available with the Source Control Explorer. We discussed the three options available to resolve conflicts.

Lesson 2-6: Viewing the History and Comparing the Changes

While we work with TFVC, we can check in the code changes to the server. Each and every check-in is saved as a changeset. We can track all the changes made to the source code by every member of the team using changesets. So far, we have discussed several ways of accessing the changeset details in the source control system.

Prerequisites: You followed the steps in Chapter 1. You have a solution and project available in TFVC.

We can find all the changes made by team members using this list. See Figure 2-21.

Source location: C:\Users\Pushpa Herath\Source\Workspaces\TheDarkKnight\main\WebApp\WebApp\Views\Home\About.cshtml

Changeset	Change	User	Date	Path	Comment
9	edit	nilmini herath	8/3/2019 8:48:45 PM	S/TheDark...	Updated About.cshtml
8	edit	nilmini herath	8/3/2019 7:45:18 PM	S/TheDark...	Updated About.cshtml
6	add	Chaminda Chandrasekara	8/3/2019 12:35:18 PM	S/TheDark...	Add solution

Figure 2-21. *Changeset details*

1. **Change Set Details**

   Select the changeset from the list and click the Changeset Details
   icon. This will open the Changeset Details page in Team Explorer
   where we can find all the details of the changeset. See Figure 2-22.

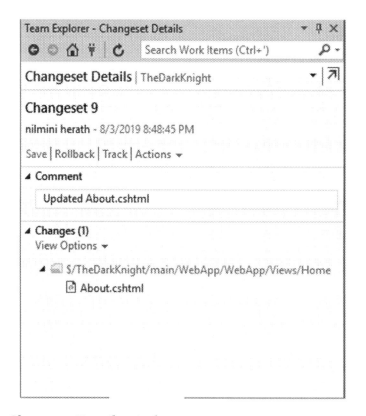

Figure 2-22. *Changeset Details window*

2. **Compare**

   We can select the two changesets from the list and compare the two selected changesets using this option.

3. **Track changeset**

   We can track the changeset.

4. **Get version**

   We can get the selected changeset version.

In the Changeset Details window, we can see two tabs available. One is for changesets, and the other is for the labels. Similar to the changesets, we can use labels to compare and get the labeled version code to the local workspace.

In addition to this window, we can do the same changeset comparison in the Azure DevOps server web portal.

Go to Azure DevOps and move to the Changesets section under Repos. See Figure 2-23.

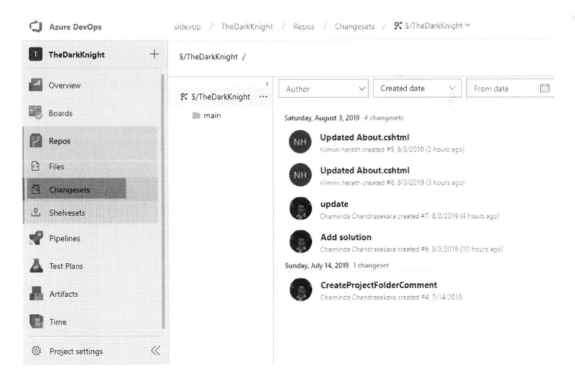

Figure 2-23. *Changesets section*

In the Changesets section, you will be able to see the list of changesets. We can filter the changesets list using the filters available. We can filter by author, created date, and date duration. Select one of the changesets from the list to open it. You will be able to see the comparison between the changeset version with the latest source version. See Figure 2-24.

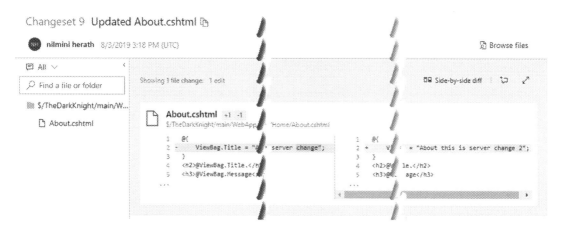

Figure 2-24. *Changeset comparison*

In this lesson, we discussed changesets. We identified the basic menu items in the changeset window and the use of it. Also, we discussed how to access the changeset details on the Azure DevOps server. Further, we learned how to search and compare changeset versions with the latest source code in the Azure DevOps server web portal.

Lesson 2-7: Setting Source Control Tool Options

In the Visual Studio Options window, you can set certain options for TFVC source control. Let's look at the options available.

Click Tools ➤ Options in the Visual Studio menu. See Figure 2-25.

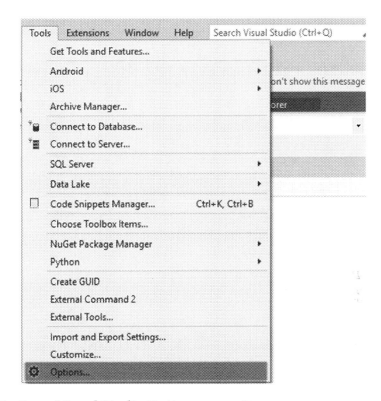

Figure 2-25. *Open Visual Studio Options menu item*

The Options window will open where we can find the source control tools. Go to Source Control and select Visual Studio Team Foundation Server. See Figure 2-26.

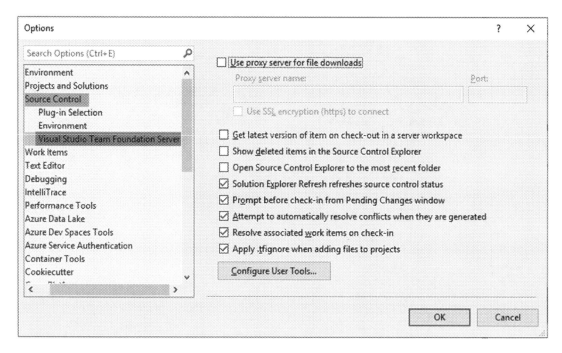

Figure 2-26. *TFVC options*

You can define your preferred options to work with TFVC in this Options window. For example, you can set the option to show deleted files in the Source Control Explorer window. Try setting your preferences and enhance your experience as per your needs.

In this lesson, we discussed how to change preferences for TFVC behavior in your Visual Studio instance.

Lesson 2-8: Deleting and Restoring Files

TFVC allows you to delete files, folders, or branches and restore them. Let's look at how you can perform a restore of a deleted file or folder.

Prerequisites: You followed the steps in Chapter 1. You have a solution and project available in TFVC.

In the Source Control Explorer, delete a file by selecting it and clicking the Delete toolbar button. Then check in your pending changes, confirming the delete.

The deleted file is not by default visible in the Source Control Explorer. You can use the Visual Studio options for Team Foundation Version Control as explained in the previous lesson and enable "Show deleted items" in the Source Control Explorer. Or you can just click the show/hide deleted items toolbar option in the Source Control Explorer to achieve this. Then right-click the deleted item and click Undelete. See Figure 2-27.

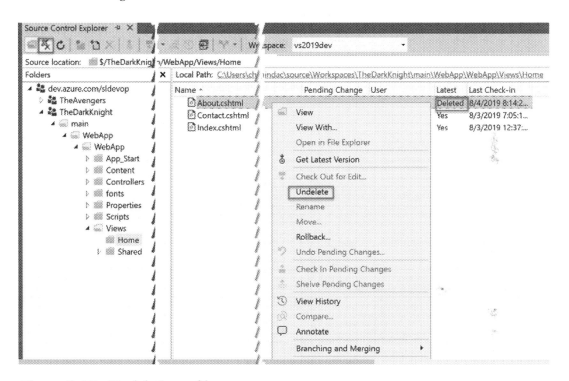

Figure 2-27. *Undeleting a file*

The file, folder, or branch will be restored with the contents it had when it was deleted and become a pending change. You can check in the pending changes to fully restore the file, folder, or branch.

In this lesson, we explored the capability to restore a file, folder, or branch in TFVC using the Source Control Explorer.

Summary

In this chapter, we discussed actions you can perform while using Team Foundation Version Control and the Source Control Explorer. Further, we explored how to check in files, resolve merge conflicts, and view the history of changes made to the source code. Additionally, we discussed the options you can set in Visual Studio to control the behavior of TFVC and how to restore deleted files, folders, or branches.

In the next chapter, we will explore how to use shelvesets, suspend and resume work, apply locks, use check-in policies, and do code reviews with TFVC.

CHAPTER 3

Working with TFVC: Part 2

Team Foundation Version Control (TFVC) is highly integrated with Visual Studio. In this chapter, we'll cover how to use Visual Studio Team Explorer and Source Explorer, or Team Explorer and Solution Explorer, to do TFVC operations such as adding projects and solutions, checking in and out, deleting files, restoring files, undoing changes, and more.

Specifically, we will explore how to use shelvesets. You'll also learn how to suspend and resume work with Visual Studio using Team Explorer, how to do code reviews with TFVC, how to set up version control locks, and how to create check-in policies.

Lesson 3-1: Using Shelvesets

Shelvesets are somewhat similar to changesets, which we discussed in the previous chapter. However, a shelveset is not merged or committed to your code branch, and when the other team members get the latest version of code, they will not get any shelvesets, like they would changesets. Shelvesets are added to the TFVC server and kept safe but not merged with your codebase. You can think of them as changesets that are on an isolated shelf outside of your codebase. Shelvesets are useful to make sure your in-progress work is saved in TFVC centrally without adding it to the codebase because it is halfway-done work that should not disturb other team members' work. For example, at the end of a day's work, if your work is only partially completed, you should not check it in as a changeset. Instead, you can save it as a shelveset so that it is securely stored in TFVC centrally and will be available to you in case something happens to your development machine. Let's look at how to create and use shelvesets.

Prerequisites: You followed Chapters 1 and 2. You have a solution and project available in TFVC.

© Chaminda Chandrasekara and Pushpa Herath 2020
C. Chandrasekara and P. Herath, *Hands-on Azure Repos*, https://doi.org/10.1007/978-1-4842-5425-7_3

Shelvesets will not get lost if something happens to the development machine as they are available in TFVC, and you can obtain them by finding them in Visual Studio Team Explorer.

Open a solution that is checked in to TFVC. Start making some modifications to the code such as declaring a new variable, as shown in Figure 3-1.

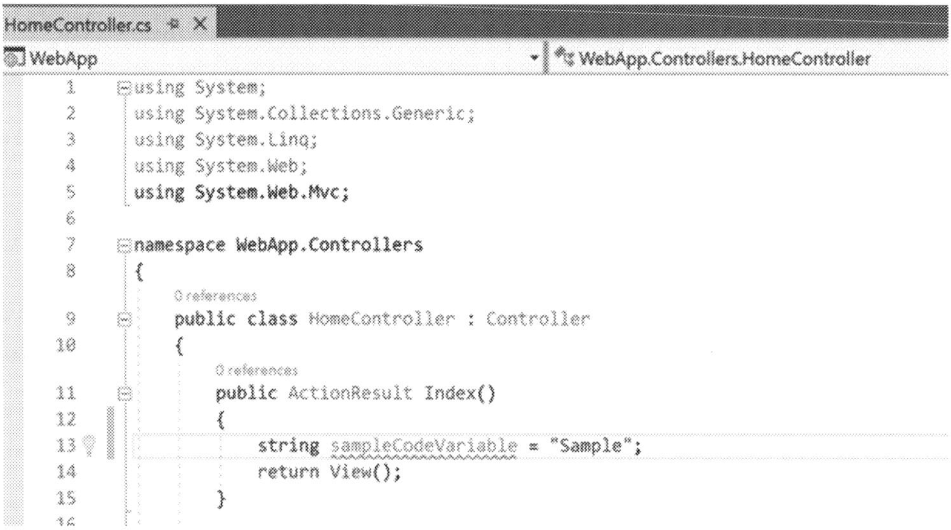

Figure 3-1. *Sample code modification*

Open the Team Explorer window in Visual Studio and go to Pending Changes. In the Pending Changes window, you will be able to provide a comment and check in the source code. However, instead of checking in, click the Shelve link to get started creating a shelveset with your pending changes. See Figure 3-2.

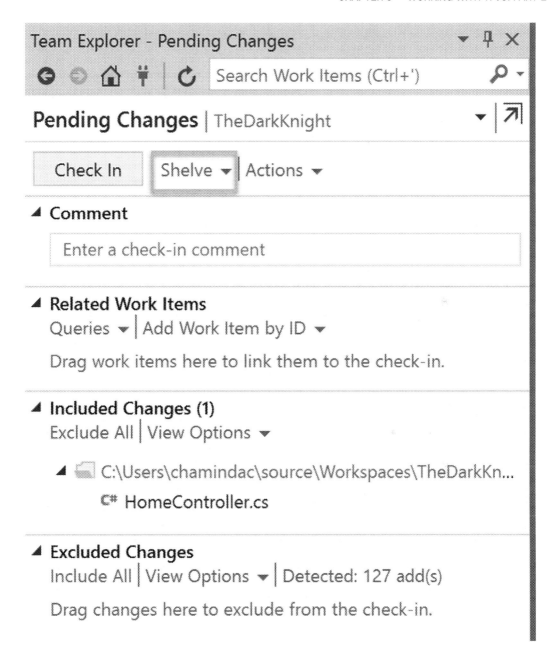

Figure 3-2. *Pending Changes window*

Once you click Shelve, a pane will appear, and you will be able to provide a name for the shelveset. The "Preserve pending changes locally" check box is by default selected, and as the label states, when this option is selected, the pending changes will be available for you to work on further after you create the shelveset. Let's uncheck the

"Preserve pending changes locally" option to see what happens to the pending changes. The other option, "Evaluates policies and notes before saving," will demand for check-in policies and note policies to be applied for the shelveset as well. We will discuss the check-in policies later in this chapter; we discussed notes in Chapter 1. You can click the Cancel button to cancel the shelve operation. Click the Shelve button to create the shelveset. See Figure 3-3.

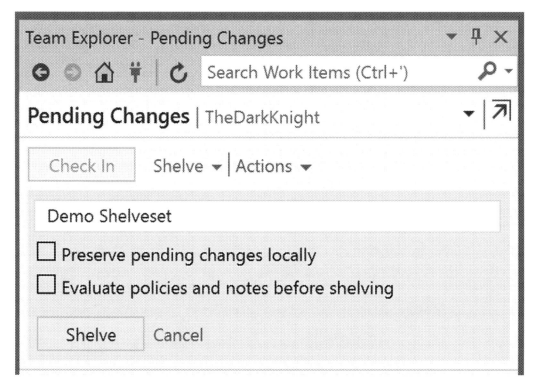

Figure 3-3. *Creating a shelveset*

Once the shelveset is created, you can see that the pending changes are also undone. This is because we have unchecked the "Preserve pending changes locally" option. If you kept it checked, your pending changes may still be visible to you after creating the shelveset. In that case, make sure to undo pending changes before continuing with this lesson.

Once you shelve your changes, they are securely stored in TFVC as a shelveset. In a situation where you want to stop your current work and make a quick fix to the existing codebase, you can use a shelveset without preserving the pending changes. Then you can perform any quick fix on your codebase and check it in. Next, you can unshelve the shelveset and get your pending changes into your local codebase to continue working. This is actually manually suspending and resuming work with the help of shelvesets. We will discuss the options for suspending and resuming work in Visual Studio with TFVC later in this chapter.

To confirm that a shelveset is available in TFVC centrally, you can go to the web portal of Azure DevOps Services/Server and open the Shelvesets tab. On this tab you will be able to search the shelvesets by name of the shelveset or by name of the creator of the shelveset. See Figure 3-4.

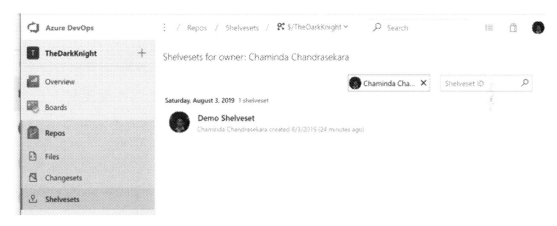

Figure 3-4. *Shelvesets in the Azure DevOps web portal*

Clicking the shelveset name will take you to the details of the shelveset, and you can inspect each code file change in the browser. See Figure 3-5.

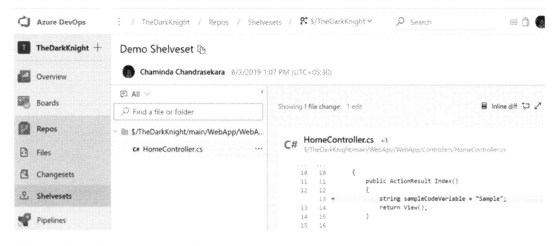

Figure 3-5. *Shelveset details*

Now that we do not have the code changes we have done locally, let's check how we can find the shelveset and get the changes back into pending changes mode so that we can continue the work on our codebase. This operation is called *unshelving*.

In the Pending Changes window, you can click the Actions down arrow to open the Actions context menu. In the context menu, click Find Shelvesets. See Figure 3-6.

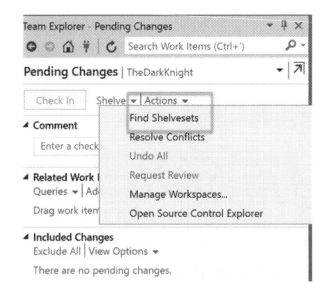

Figure 3-6. *Find Shelvesets option in Pending Changes*

In the Find Shelvesets window, you can provide the name of the shelveset or the name of the creator of the shelveset to search for a shelveset. In the found shelveset, you can right-click and open the context menu. In the context menu, you have options to view the details of the shelveset, unshelve the shelveset, delete the shelveset, and request a code review on a shelveset. See Figure 3-7. We will discuss code reviews with TFVC later in this chapter. Click View Shelveset Details.

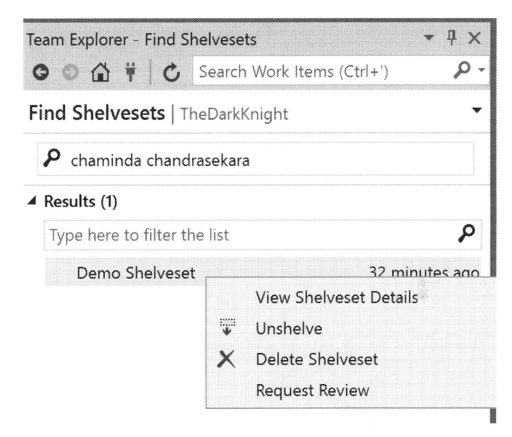

Figure 3-7. *Viewing a shelveset*

In the shelveset details, you have the option to unshelve changes in a shelveset partially by excluding files from unshelving. You can request a code review or open the shelveset in the browser. The Delete Shelveset option is also available in the shelveset details. See Figure 3-8. Click Unshelve Changes.

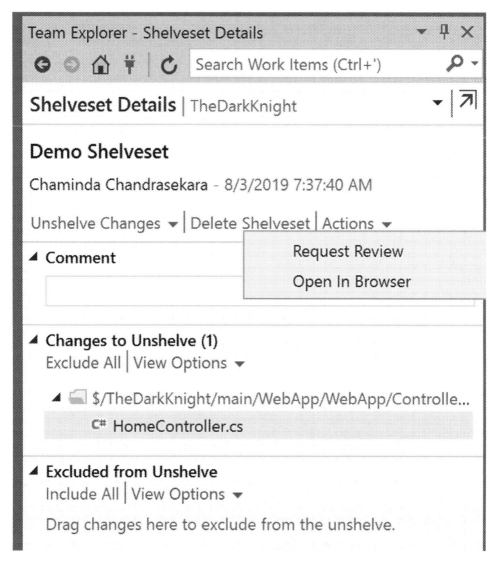

Figure 3-8. *Shelveset details*

Once you click Unshelve Changes, you will be able to see two options. One is to preserve the shelveset on the TFVC server after the unshelving is done. The other option lets you restore the check-in notes and the work items associated with the pending changes. Click the Unshelve button. See Figure 3-9.

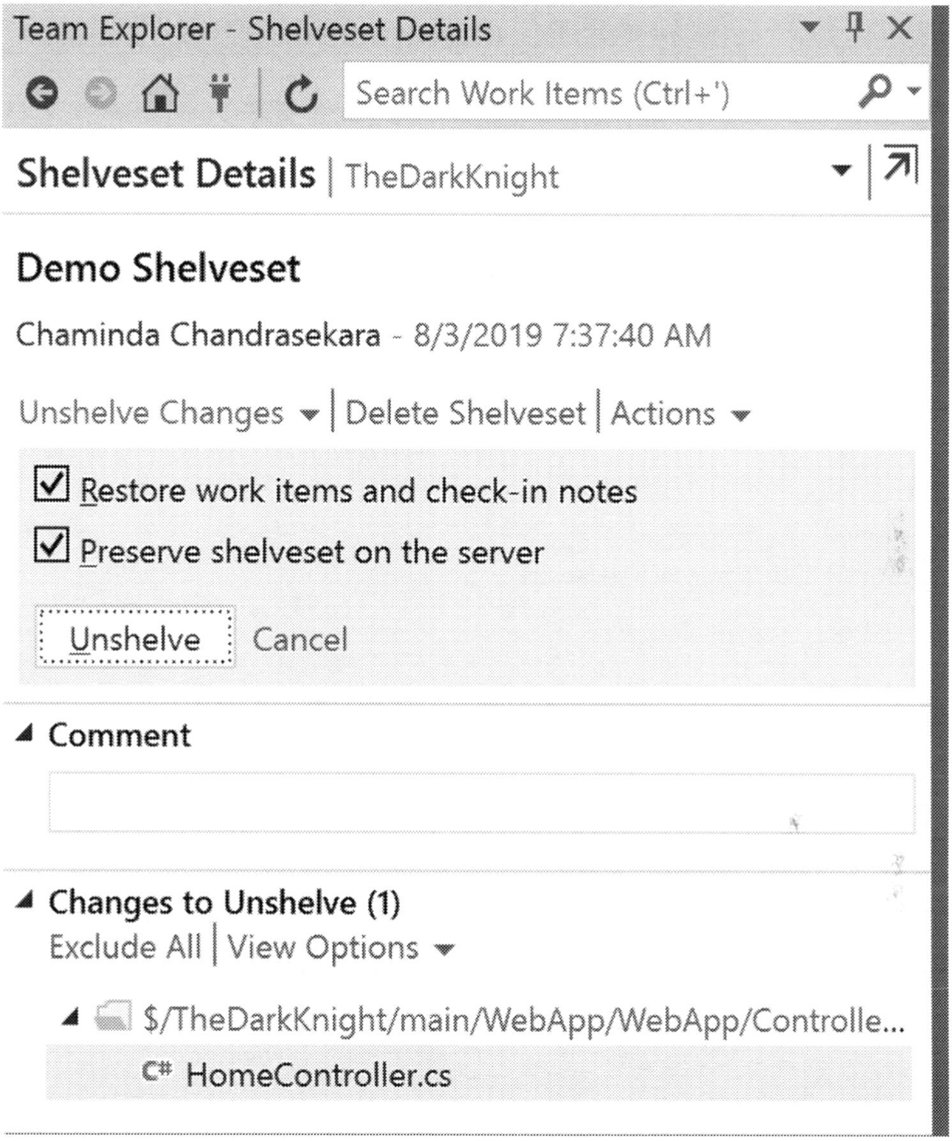

Figure 3-9. Unshelving

Once the shelveset is unshelved, you will be able to see that the previous pending changes reappear in your code files. There could be merge conflicts while unshelving, but they can be resolved the same way as described in Chapter 2.

In this lesson, we discussed the steps of shelving and unshelving and the usage and benefits of shelvesets.

Lesson 3-2: Suspending and Resuming Work

The suspend and resume work is an option available in Visual Studio while using TFVC as the version control system. You can stop your current work while preserving all your changes in suspend mode and automatically undo all your pending work with suspend. It even captures bookmarks or any breakpoints made in Visual Studio and keeps track of the opened code windows and other windows in Visual Studio.

Suspending work is useful when you need to stop your current code changes to switch to other higher-priority work. Once you perform the high-priority work and check the changes in, then you can resume your work using the resume work feature in Visual Studio. Let's look at the steps to suspend and resume work.

Prerequisites: You followed Chapters 1 and 2. You have a solution and project available in TFVC.

Make some code changes and save. Then in Team Explorer, click My Work. See Figure 3-10.

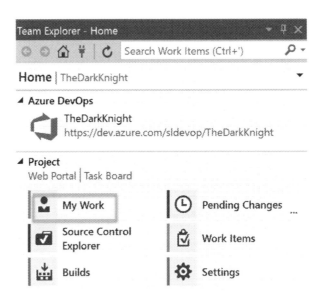

Figure 3-10. *My Work window*

In the My Work window, you will be able to see the in-progress work as edits. If you click View Changes, you will be taken to the Pending Changes window. You can click the Actions menu and add a work item by ID to the in-progress work or drag and drop a work item from the available work items. With or without adding a work item, click the

Suspend button. See Figure 3-11. The added work item can be removed from in-progress work by right-clicking the added work item and clicking Remove from In Progress in the context menu.

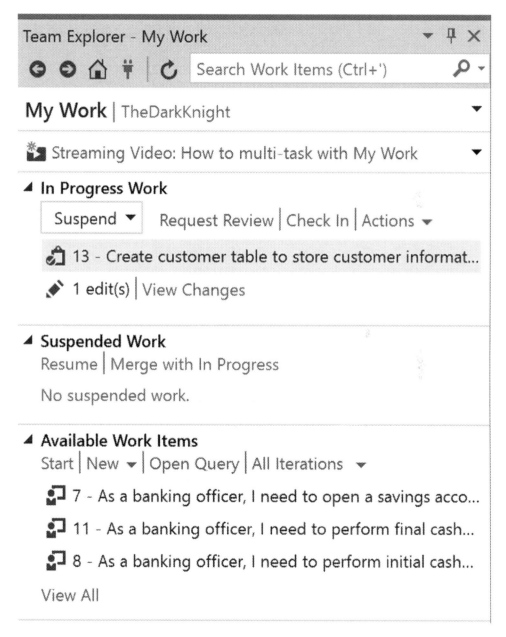

Figure 3-11. Suspending work

The suspend work description will be autofilled with the work item title, if you have added a work item. You can add your own description by updating the autofilled description. Then click the Suspend button. See Figure 3-12.

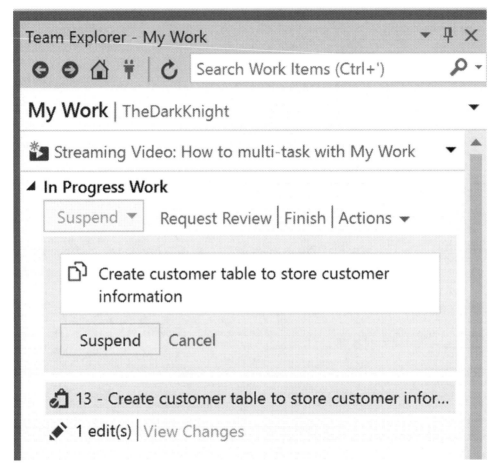

Figure 3-12. *Suspending the work*

Once you suspend the work, if you inspect the shelvesets, you will be able to see that a new shelveset has been created. The suspend-resume actually works with the help of shelvesets behind the scenes. See Figure 3-13.

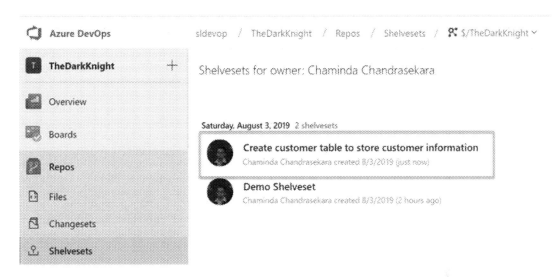

Figure 3-13. *Shelveset created by suspending work*

In Visual Studio you will be able to see that the pending changes are undone once you suspend the work. Now you can do any other code changes on your original codebase before you started the suspended changes. You can check in those changes and later resume the work that you were doing.

To resume work, you can go to My Work in the Team Explorer window of Visual Studio. You can click Resume, and the previously suspended work will be available in your solution as pending changes. You can even resume suspended work while you are already have pending changes by clicking Merge within Progress Changes. See Figure 3-14. If there are any conflicts while you are resuming work due to pending changes or changesets you created after suspending work, you can resolve the merge conflicts in the same way as explained in Chapter 2.

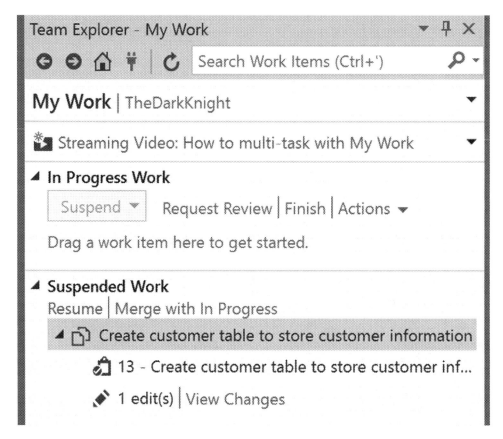

Figure 3-14. *Resuming work*

Once the work is resumed, the shelveset created behind the scenes is also deleted automatically.

In this lesson, we explored how we can suspend and resume work, which works with the shelvesets concept of TFVC.

Lesson 3-3: Doing Code Reviews with TFVC

Code reviews are important to maintain good-quality code in your projects. TFVC offers a code review integrated with Visual Studio Team Explorer. Let's look at the steps to do a code review.

Prerequisites: You followed Chapters 1 and 2. You have a solution and project available in TFVC.

Make some code changes in your project by opening it in Visual Studio. Then go to My Work in the Team Explorer of Visual Studio. You can drag and drop a work item or add a work item by ID to the in-progress work using the Actions menu. You can do this before requesting a code review to notify the reviewer of the work item that you are working on. However, work items are not mandatory for you to request a code review. Click the Request Review button to start a code review request. See Figure 3-15.

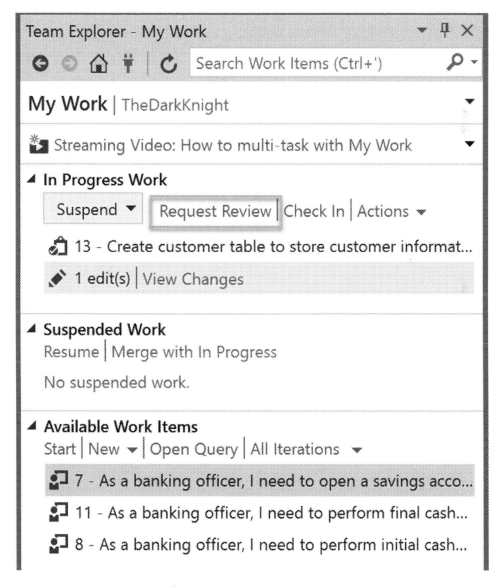

Figure 3-15. *Initiating a code review request*

A new code review request subject will be automatically filled in with a selected work item title if you have added a work item to the in-progress work. You can edit the subject and provide a description as well with the request. The team project name will be tagged, and you can select one or more reviewers for the core review request by clicking Add Reviewer. After selecting the reviewer, click Submit Request. See Figure 3-16.

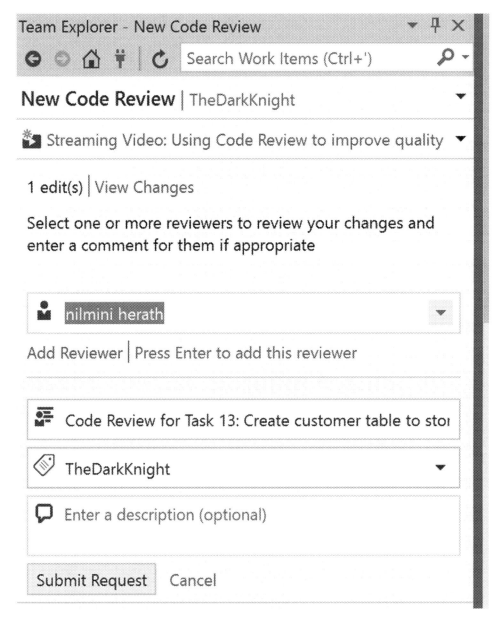

Figure 3-16. *Submitting a code review request*

After submitting code review request, it will appear under My Code Reviews & Requests in your My Work. See Figure 3-17. You can suspend the work as we discussed in the previous lesson and work on something else until you receive feedback from the reviewer.

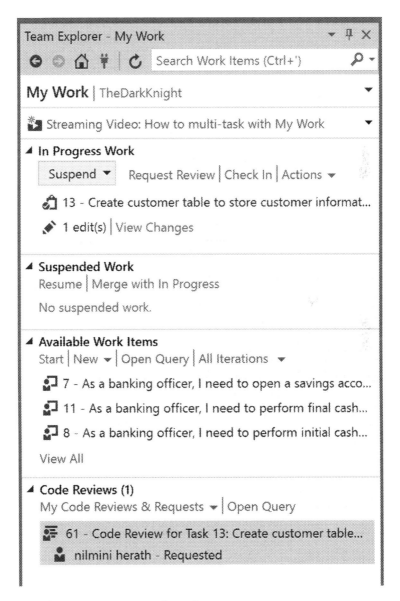

Figure 3-17. *Code review requests listed*

In the My Code Reviews & Requests drop-down, you can filter the requests for recently closed, recently finished, incoming requests, and your code review requests. See Figure 3-18.

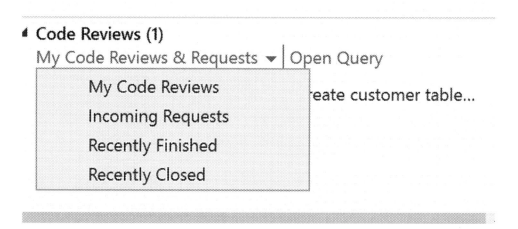

Figure 3-18. *Filtering code reviews*

If you inspect the shelvesets, you will find a shelveset for code review is created automatically. See Figure 3-19.

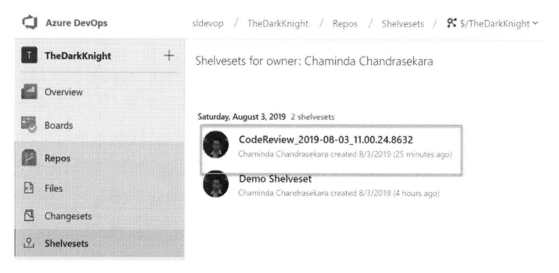

Figure 3-19. *Shelveset created for code review*

The reviewer receives the code review request in their My Work in Team Explorer. The user can accept to do a code review or decline it. See Figure 3-20.

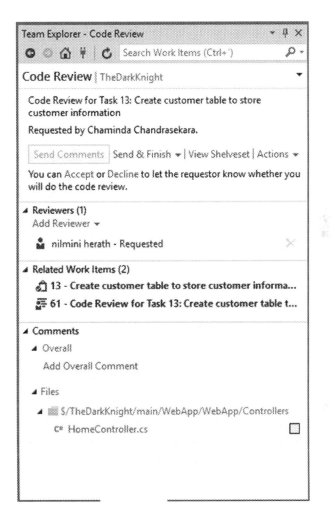

Figure 3-20. *Accepting or declining*

The reviewer can click files to view the code changes and add file comments for the review. See Figure 3-21.

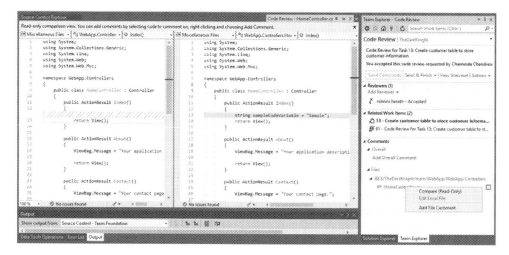

Figure 3-21.   *Reviewing the files*

The Action menu lets the reviewer open the related work item. The reviewer can add an overall comment and send and finish the code review with Looks Good for approval or ask to do more changes. See Figure 3-22.

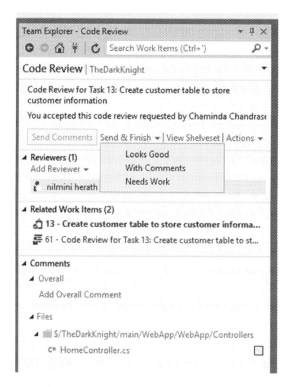

Figure 3-22.   *Approving the code review*

Once the code review is approved, the initiator of the code review can see it in their My Work. See Figure 3-23.

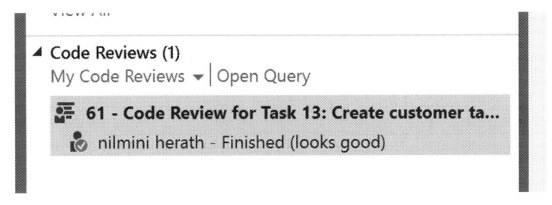

Figure 3-23. *Code review approved*

In addition to requesting a code review on pending changes, you can request code reviews on changesets or shelvesets. See Figure 3-7 for how to request a code review for a shelveset using Find Shelvesets in Team Explorer. You can request a code review for a changeset in the Source Control history view by right-clicking the relevant changeset. See Figure 3-24.

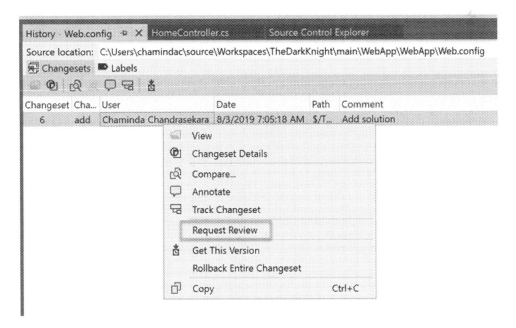

Figure 3-24. *Code review for a changeset*

In this lesson, we discussed the code review procedure with TFVC, which is an essential activity for any development team to ensure high-quality and maintainable code.

Lesson 3-4: Using Lock and Unlock

Locking/unlocking files is a useful feature in TFVC because it allows you to temporarily apply a lock on a file or folder in the TFVC server. The locked file will be prevented from check-out by other users, and you can prevent merge conflicts by applying a lock. This should be used with caution, though, as you should not block other team members from doing their work on the code. You might want to apply a lock on a code file or a folder in a situation where you will be doing a major and impactful change, which absolutely requires avoiding merge conflicts, so that the critical change in the code can be checked in to TFVC after you have completed it without any conflicts. Let's look at how you can lock and unlock a file or folder in Visual Studio Source Control Explorer.

Prerequisites: You followed Chapters 1 and 2. You have a solution and project available in TFVC.

Open the solution in Visual Studio and open the Source Control Explorer. Then you right-click the required file or folder and click Advanced ➤ Lock in the context menu to lock the file or folder. See Figure 3-25.

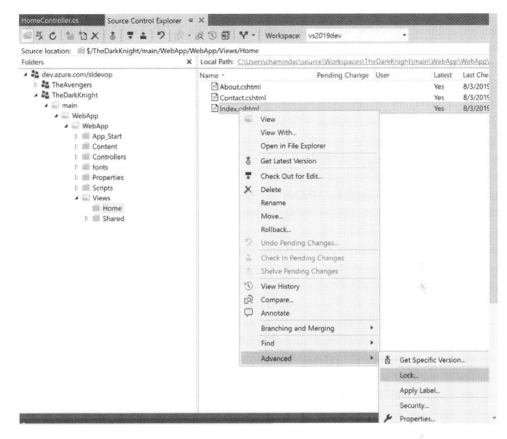

Figure 3-25. *Locking a file*

A dialog will pop up, and you can click Lock to lock the file for you exclusively. See Figure 3-26.

Lock

Files:

Name	Folder
☑ 📄 Ind...	$/TheDarkKnight/main/WebApp/WebApp/Views/Home

Lock   Cancel

Figure 3-26. *Lock file dialog*

The file will be checked out and will be locked for others so that only you will be able to edit the file. See Figure 3-27. Until you remove the lock, no one will be able to check in any changes to the file/folder.

Local Path: C:\Users\chamindac\source\Workspaces\TheDarkKnight\main\WebApp\WebApp\

Name ^	Pending Change	User	Latest	Last Che
About.cshtml			Yes	8/3/2019
Contact.cshtml			Yes	8/3/2019
✓ Index.cshtml	lock, edit	Chaminda Chan...	Yes	8/3/2019

Figure 3-27. *Locked file*

You can right-click the file/folder in the Source Control Explorer and click Advanced ➤ Unlock to unlock the file. Or once you check in the file, the lock will be removed.

In this lesson, we explored the file/folder lock/unlock option in TFVC to identify the capability to edit a file/folder in isolation, while preventing others from making changes to it.

Lesson 3-5: Applying Check-in Policies

Check-in policies are useful for setting up control over how the changes are checked in to the source control system. You can ensure the team is adhering to the procedures so that the quality of changesets will be higher and more meaningful. Let's look at creating check-in policies in Visual Studio and how they get applied to the check-in attempts.

Prerequisites: You followed Chapters 1 and 2. You have a solution and project available in TFVC. You have a few user stories, and you have a shared query with the active user stories. We covered how to create work items and write queries for work items in the *Hands-on Azure Boards* book of the series.

Open the solution in Visual Studio and make some code changes. In the Visual Studio menu, click Team ➤ Team Project Settings and go to the Source Control tab to open the Source Control options for the team project. Then in the dialog, go to the Check-In Policy tab and click the Add button. There are several check-in policy options available. See Figure 3-28.

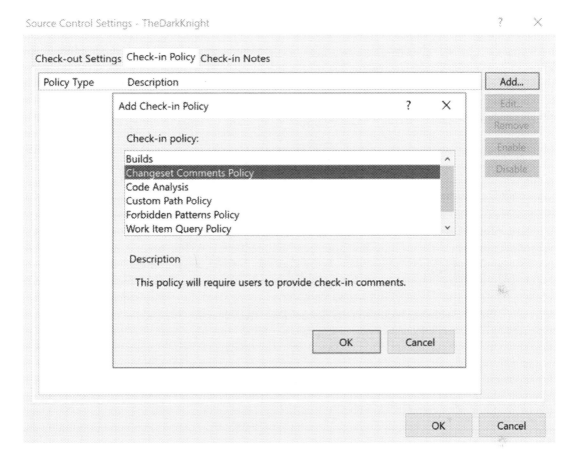

Figure 3-28. *Adding a check-in policy*

Build policies will be discussed in the *Hands-On Azure Pipelines* book. Let's select the changeset comment policy and add it. This will make a comment for a check-in mandatory when trying to check in pending changes. See Figure 3-29.

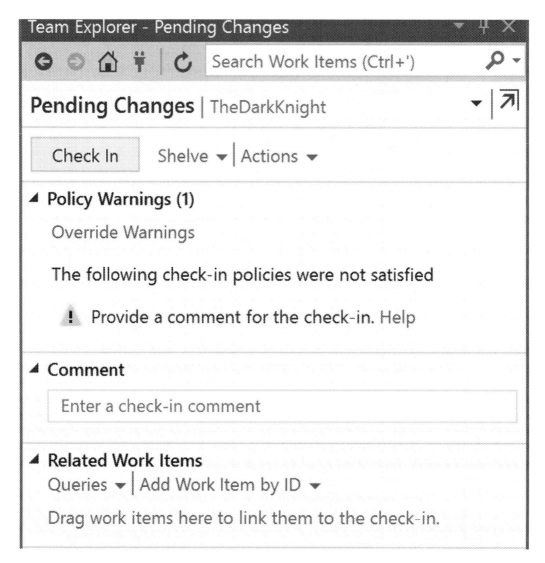

Figure 3-29. *Comment policy applied*

We can try adding a work item query policy as well. Select a work item query in the dialog box that appears when you select the Work Item Query Policy. See Figure 3-30.

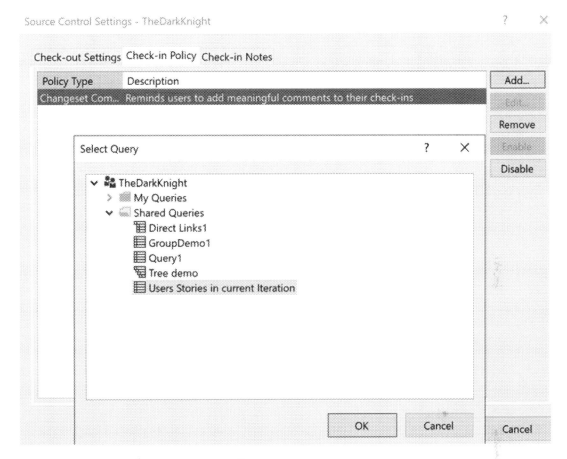

Figure 3-30. *Work item query policy*

This will make associating a work item from the given query mandatory when checking in a pending change. See Figure 3-31.

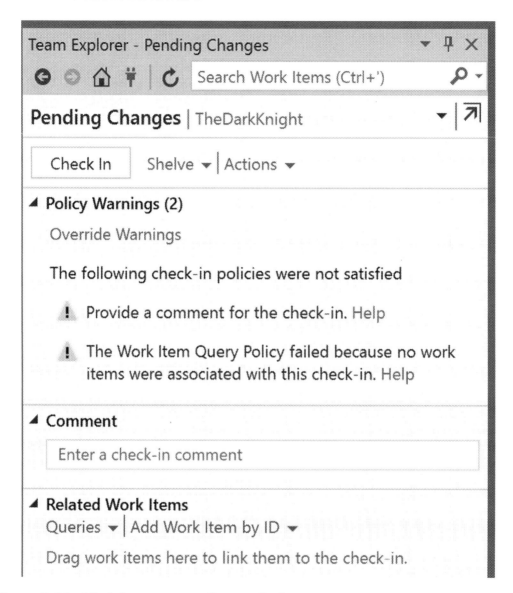

Figure 3-31. *Work item query policy applied*

You can try other policies and apply them and see how they affect your team's check-in experience.

In this lesson, we explored check-in policies, which are useful to maintain standards and proper collaboration and communication when working with codebases.

Summary

In this chapter, we discussed how to use shelvesets and how the shelvesets help to do code reviews as well as suspend and resume work in this chapter. How to use locks and the checking policies were also described. With this chapter and the previous chapter, you have gained a comprehensive idea of how to work with Team Foundation Version Control.

In the next chapter, we will discuss the branching feature of TFVC, which will give you an in-depth idea of how to create and work with branches as well as some useful branching strategies with TFVC.

CHAPTER 4

Team Foundation Version Control Branching

After going through the previous chapters of this book, you now have a good understanding of the source control capabilities of Team Foundation Version Control (TFVC). Branching is the most important capability of any source control system because it helps the development team to manage their source code in isolation while creating new features and hotfixes. You will learn about the branching capabilities of Team Foundation Version Control throughout this chapter.

Lesson 4-1: Creating a Branch

In development, you might want isolation when trying to add new features to the project or doing a hotfix. In some scenarios, the entire team can work in one branch, but sometimes it is better to have separate branches for each feature development or hotfix. This lesson will explain how to create a branch in TFVC using the Visual Studio Source Control Explorer.

Prerequisites:

- Azure DevOps project with TFVC as the source control system
- Mapped local workspace of the project on the working machine

Go to the Source Control Explorer. Select the folder or branch you want to create a branch with. You can move the mouse over the folder or branch and right-click and select Branch, or you can use source control menu items to create a branch. See Figure 4-1.

© Chaminda Chandrasekara and Pushpa Herath 2020
C. Chandrasekara and P. Herath, *Hands-on Azure Repos*, https://doi.org/10.1007/978-1-4842-5425-7_4

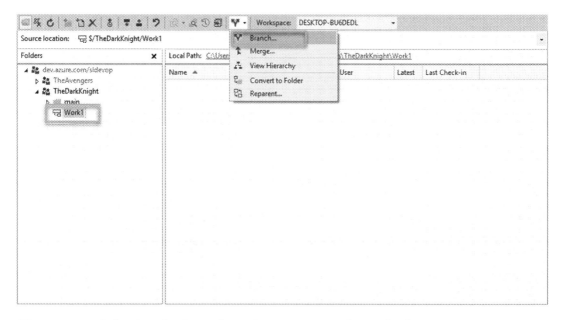

Figure 4-1. *Selecting the Branch option to create a branch of main*

Alternatively, you can create a branch by right-clicking a selected branch and then selecting the Branching and Merging ➤ Branch option, as shown in Figure 4-2.

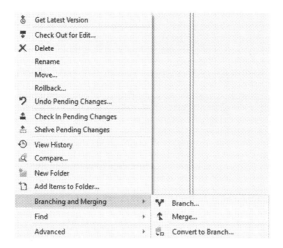

Figure 4-2. *Creating a branch*

The Branch window will open. You will be able to define the new branch name and decide on a source version to create a new branch. See Figure 4-3.

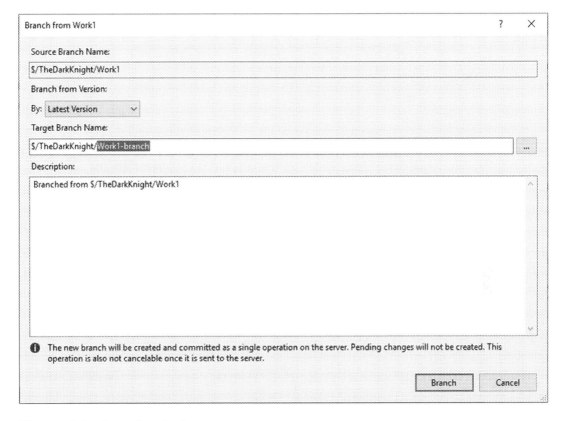

Figure 4-3. *Branch window*

For the source version, you have following options in the Branch from Version drop-down:

- **Latest Version**: Latest version in the source

- **Changeset**: Select a version using changesets

- **Date**: Select a version with a specific date

- **Label**: Select a labeled version

- **Workspace**: Select a version of the selected workspace

After selecting the source version, click the OK button to create a new branch. You might get a pop-up that allows you to accept or deny the branch creation. See Figure 4-4.

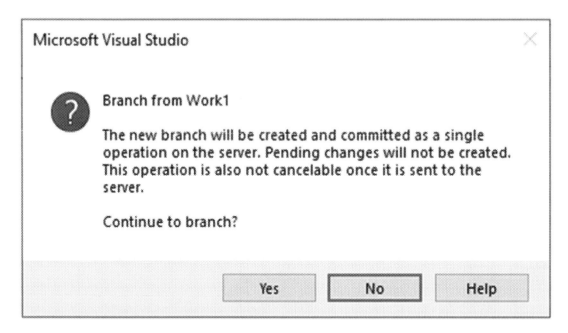

Figure 4-4. *Branch creation verify pop-up*

Now the new branch creation is completed. Go to the Source Control Explorer. You will be able to see the new branch. See Figure 4-5.

Figure 4-5. *Newly added branch in the Source Control Explorer*

In this lesson, you learned how to create a new branch using the Source Control Explorer. Also, we discussed the ability to create a branch with different source versions.

Lesson 4-2: Converting a Folder to a Branch

In TFVC we can have both folders and branches in the source control system. Sometimes we need to work on code that is not related to any of the branches. For that type of situation, we can create a folder inside the source control system and maintain the source code inside the folder. While you maintain your code inside a folder, you might later need to add the source code inside the folder to a branch. In TFVC we have an easy option to do this: converting a folder into a branch. This lesson will explain how to convert a folder into a branch.

Prerequisites:

- Azure DevOps project with TFVC as the source control system

- Mapped local workspace of the project on the working machine

- Mapped project with a folder in the source control system

Go to the Source Control Explorer. Select the folder that you need to convert to a branch. Select the branch drop-down among the source control menu items and select the Convert to Branch option. See Figure 4-6.

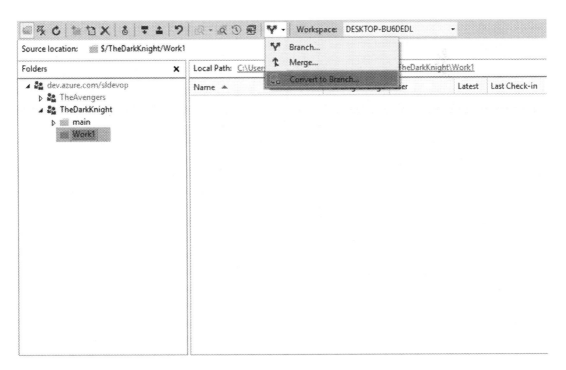

Figure 4-6. *Selecting Convert to Branch from the source control menu*

After selecting Convert to Branch, you will be able to see the window where you can find basic details about the new branch being created using the folder. See Figure 4-7.

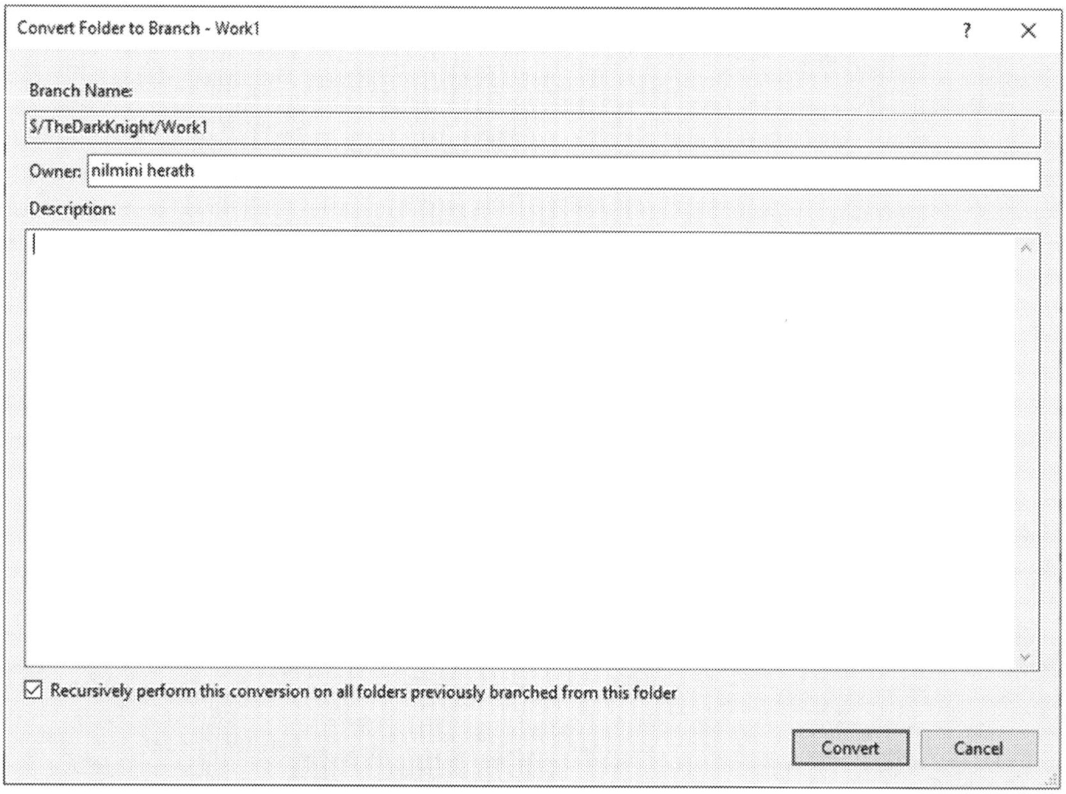

Figure 4-7. *Converting the folder to a branch*

You can give the branch a name or keep the default branch name. Also, you will be able to see the owner of the branch. You can also give a description to the branch. When you are ready to convert the folder to a branch, click the Convert button.

You will be able to see that the folder has been converted to a branch. See Figure 4-8.

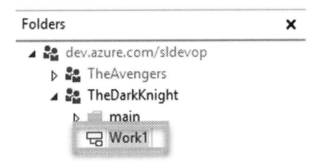

Figure 4-8. *Branch created using a folder*

In this lesson, we discussed how to convert folders to branches easily with the Source Control Explorer.

Lesson 4-3: Merging and Resolving Conflicts

Development teams can decide to use certain branch structures according to their project requirements. Each team needs to decide the best branching structure suitable for their project requirements or they will face more complex problems when trying to merge the branches. No matter how many branches a team has, the team needs to be able to merge these branches correctly. This lesson will explain how to merge branches and resolve any conflicts that occur while merging.

Prerequisites:

- Azure DevOps project with TFVC as the source control system

- Mapped local workspace of the project on the working machine

- Multiple branches with the same source version

We have the master branch, the Develop branch, and two Feature branches in the source control with the same source version. See Figure 4-9.

Figure 4-9. *Branches with the same version of source code*

We have a master branch where we maintain the code ready to deploy to production. We have a development branch where we merge all the feature changes to. We are developing two features. So, we have two Feature branches in the source control system. This is the sample branch structure we are going to use with this lesson. Figure 4-10 shows the branching hierarchy of our sample branching structure.

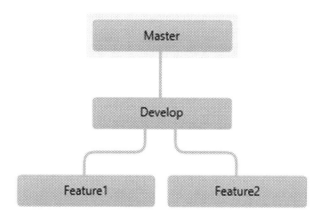

Figure 4-10. *Branch structure*

Multiple team members are developing Feature1. So, they create a local workspace for the Feature1 branch. After their implementation is completed, they check in the code changes to the server. After the Feature1 implementation is completed, the Feature1 branch is merged with the developer branch.

Go to the Source Control Explorer. Select the Feature1 branch and then click the branch icon in the source control menu. Then in the menu Click on Merge. See Figure 4-11.

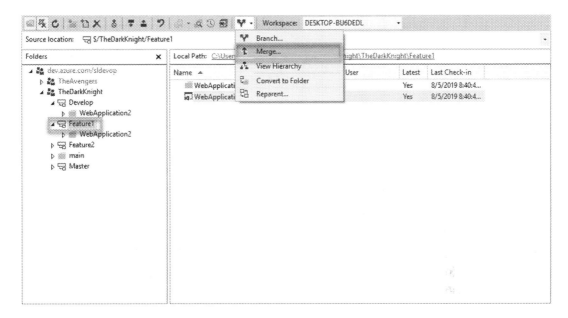

Figure 4-11. *Merging the changes*

The Source Control Merge Wizard will open. We are going to merge the Feature1 changes with the Develop branch. So, our source branch is Feature1, and the target branch is the Develop branch. You have two merge options available in the wizard. You can merge all the changes up to a specific version, or you can merge changes in specific changesets. See Figure 4-12.

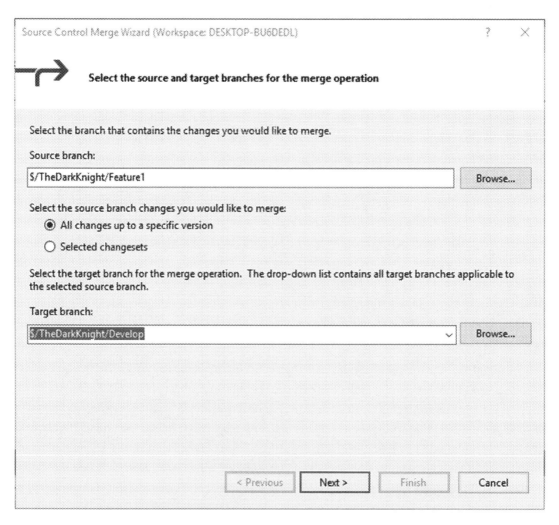

Figure 4-12. *Source Control Merge Wizard, step 1*

After deciding which changesets to merge, you can click Next to move to the next step of the wizard. This sample merge takes place with all the changes up to a specific version.

In step 2 of the wizard, select the source branch version. See Figure 4-13.

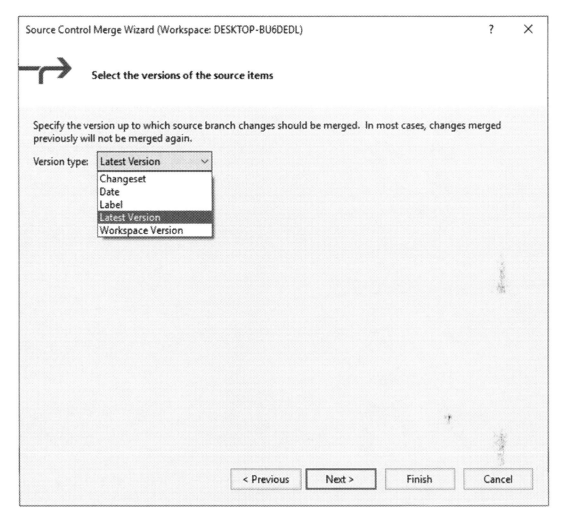

Figure 4-13. *Selecting a source version*

After selecting the source version, click the Next button to move to the next step of the wizard. You will be able to see the final step of the wizard. Click the Finish button to finish the wizard. See Figure 4-14.

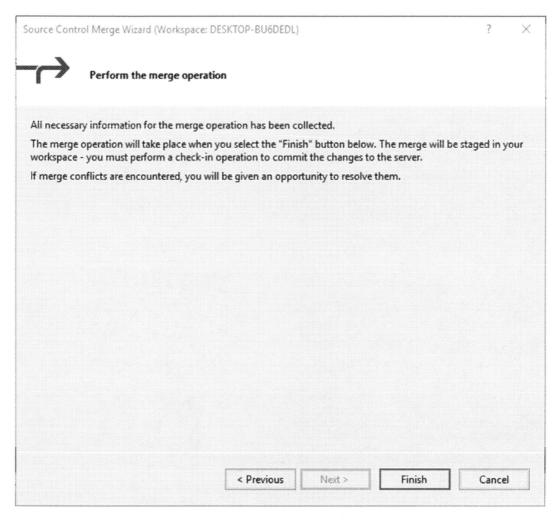

Figure 4-14. *Source Control Merge Wizard, final step*

After clicking the Finish button, you will be able to see that the merge process starts. If you don't have any merge conflicts, you will be able to complete the process without any warnings. If the merge succeeds, the Feature1 branch on the server and the local development branch should have similar content. If you compare these two branches, there should not be any differences in the files.

Go to the Source Control Explorer. Select the Feature1 branch. Click the Compare icon in the source control menu. See Figure 4-15.

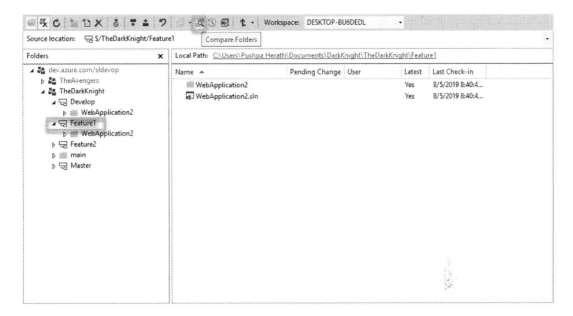

Figure 4-15. *Open compare for Feature1 branch*

After clicking the Compare icon, a window will open. You can select the source branch and target branch to compare. Also, you can select the view option to display the comparison result. After selecting the branches and view options, click OK to start the comparison. See Figure 4-16.

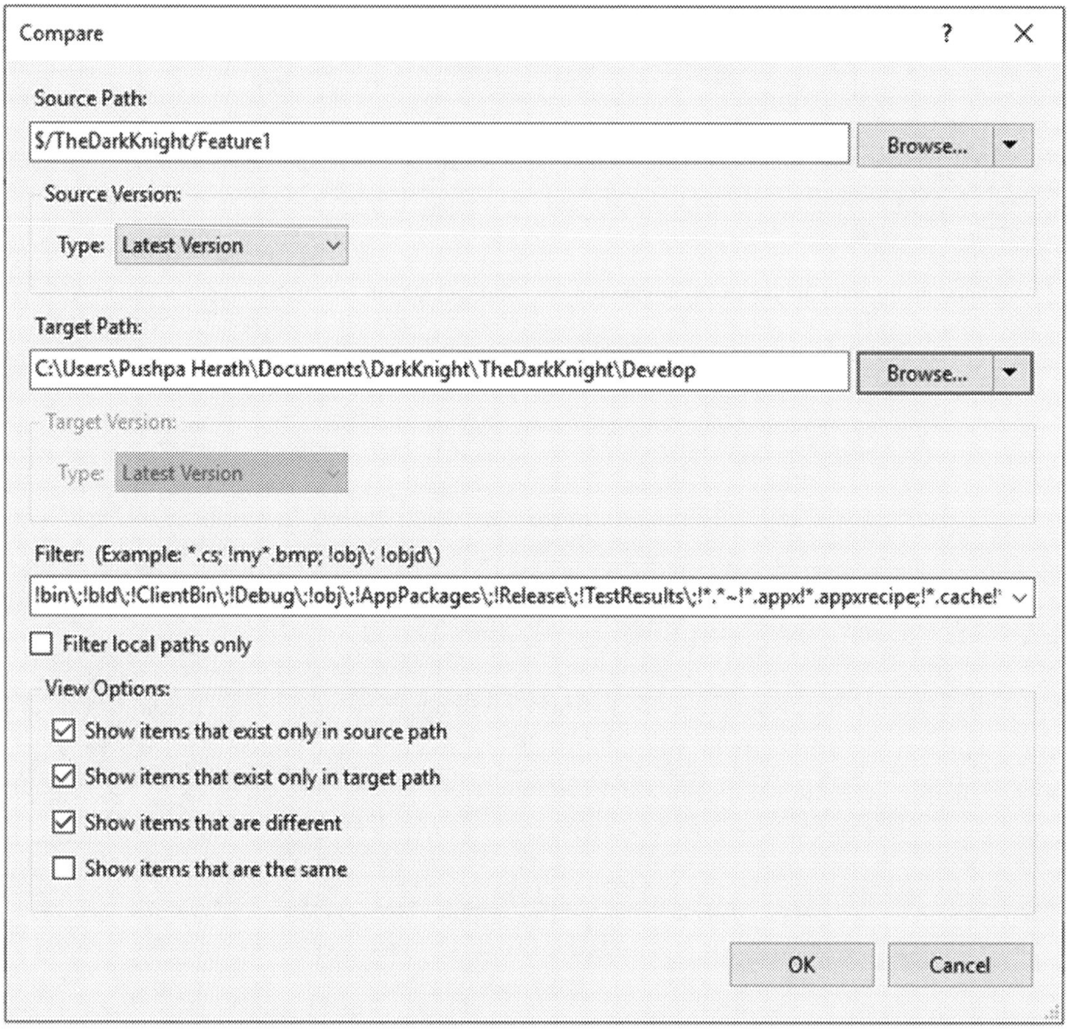

Figure 4-16. *Comparing Feature1 and Develop branches*

If the branch merging succeeded for this merge, you will get the comparison result with zero differences. This might change according to the situation. See Figure 4-17.

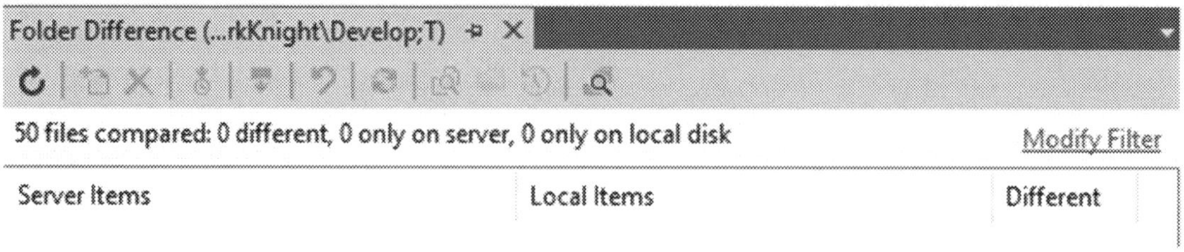

Figure 4-17. *Merge branch comparison*

Since there are no issues, you can check in the local Develop branch changes to the server.

So far, we have discussed the basic merge concepts. Now we will discuss how to solve merge conflicts.

Let's consider following scenario. We have the Develop branch. Also, there are Feature1 and Feature2 branches. Parallelly, two different teams develop Feature1 and Feature2. At the beginning, both branches have a similar version to the Develop branch. Then the Feature1 changes are merged with the Develop branch. Now the Feature 2 changes are going to be merged with the Develop branch. But on the server, the Develop branch has a new version of the `About.cshtml` file. Also, we have changed that same file in the Feature2 branch.

So, select the Feature2 branch as the source and the Develop branch as the target. Merge the changes using the merge wizard. At the end of the merge, you will be navigated to a conflict page. See Figure 4-18.

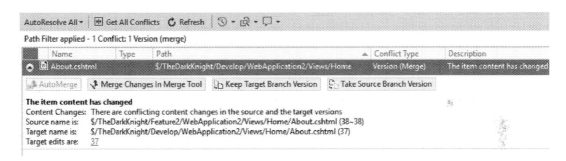

Figure 4-18. *Merging the conflicts*

Select Merge Changes in the merge tool and select the changes you want to keep. Finally, click the Accept Merge button to merge the changes. See Figure 4-19.

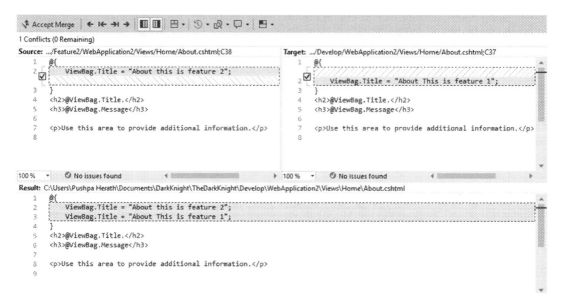

Figure 4-19. Comparing the changes

After resolving all the conflicts, the branch merge can be completed. You can compare the branches. Then you will be able to see all the files with the differences listed in the comparison area. You can verify that you have merged the branches correctly by comparing these files. After the merge is completed, you can check in the Develop branch changes to the server.

This lesson explained how to merge branches. Also, you learned that you have two options to select the merge. One is to merge all the changes up to the current one; the other option is to merge only the selected changesets. Further, we discussed how to resolve merge conflicts.

Lesson 4-4: Tracking Changesets

Now we are familiar with main source control operations such as creating branches, converting folders to branches, merging branches, and resolving merge conflicts. After every merge, it is better if we have a way to track the changes done to each branch. This lesson explains how we can track the changes done to each branch.

Prerequisites:

- Azure DevOps project with TFVC as the source control system

- Mapped local workspace of the project on the working machine

- Multiple branches with the same source version

- Multiple check-in and branch merges

Go to the Source Control Explorer. Select the project. Then click the History icon on the Source Control Explorer menu. See Figure 4-20.

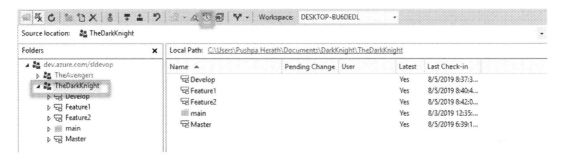

Figure 4-20. *Clicking the History icon*

The changeset list will open. You can see all the changes made to the project using this list. If you want to see the changes made to a specific branch only, select the branch in the Source Control Explorer.

Now we have the changeset list of the entire project. See Figure 4-21.

We can track the changes from this page. Select one changeset and click the Track Changeset icon in the menu. See Figure 4-21.

Changeset	User	Date	Comment
39	nilmini herath	8/6/2019 9:22:18 PM	Merge feature2 with develop
38	nilmini herath	8/5/2019 9:44:42 PM	Create API - Feature 2 complete
37	nilmini herath	8/5/2019 9:41:54 PM	Merge feature 1 to develop
36	nilmini herath	8/5/2019 8:52:17 PM	As a banking officer, I need to open a savings account for a customer- Feature complete
35	nilmini herath	8/5/2019 8:42:00 PM	Branched from $/TheDarkKnight/Develop
34	nilmini herath	8/5/2019 8:40:47 PM	Branched from $/TheDarkKnight/Develop
33	nilmini herath	8/5/2019 8:37:37 PM	Branched from $/TheDarkKnight/Master
32	nilmini herath	8/5/2019 8:32:10 PM	add master slotution
20	nilmini herath	8/5/2019 6:39:12 PM	Add solution to main
11	Chaminda Chandrasekara	8/4/2019 1:51:28 PM	resore
10	Chaminda Chandrasekara	8/4/2019 1:44:23 PM	delete file
9	nilmini herath	8/3/2019 8:48:45 PM	Updated About.cshtml
8	nilmini herath	8/3/2019 7:45:18 PM	Updated About.cshtml
7	Chaminda Chandrasekara	8/3/2019 6:07:13 PM	update
6	Chaminda Chandrasekara	8/3/2019 12:35:18 PM	Add solution
4	Chaminda Chandrasekara	7/14/2019 11:33:34 AM	CreateProjectFolderComment

Figure 4-21. *Clicking the Track Changeset icon*

The Tracking Changeset window will open. You will be able to select the branches in the Branches section. After selecting the branches, click Visualize to track the changes. See Figure 4-22.

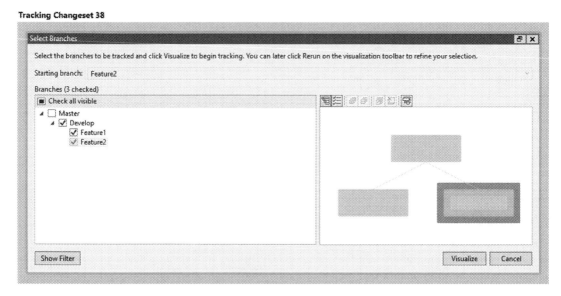

Figure 4-22. *Tracking the changeset*

The Tracking Changeset hierarchy view will open. See Figure 4-23.

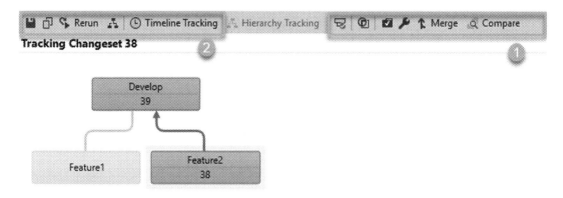

Figure 4-23. *Tracking Changeset hierarchy*

Let's try to identify the menu items in the Tracking Changeset window. You can see we have highlighted two areas in Figure 4-23. In the toolbar on the right are these icons (from right to left): Compare icon, Merge icon, Settings icon to move to the settings window, Source Control icon to move to the Source Control Explorer, Changeset icon to navigate to the Changeset Details page, and Tracked Changes icon to display only the branches with the changes in the selected changeset.

In the toolbar on the left of Figure 4-23 (from left to right), we can save the visualization, copy the visualization, rerun the tracking, go to the visualization hierarchy view, and do timeline tracking.

Timeline tracking is an interesting feature where we can track the changes by changed dates. See Figure 4-24. If you hover the mouse over the feature changeset number, you can see all the relevant details of the changeset.

Figure 4-24. *Timeline tracking*

We can use these features to identify our application development process behavior.

In this lesson, you learned how to do changeset tracking. Further, we discussed how to use the hierarchical view of the changeset time tracking to clearly display the behavior of our application development progress.

Lesson 4-5: Cherry-Picking Changesets

We discussed how to create branches and how to merge them in the previous lesson. We know how to merge all the changesets in a branch with another branch. Also, we saw that there is an option in the Source Control Merge Wizard where we can select only one changeset or multiple changesets to merge. This option is called *cherry-pick*ing. You will learn more about cherry-picking in this lesson.

   Prerequisites:

- Azure DevOps project with TFVC as the source control system

- Mapped local workspace of the project on the working machine

- Multiple branches

- Multiple check-ins and branch merges

Go to the Source Control Explorer. Select a branch with changesets. We selected the Feature1 branch. Then click Merge to start the merge wizard.

Select "Selected changesets" in the Source Control Merge Wizard. See Figure 4-25.

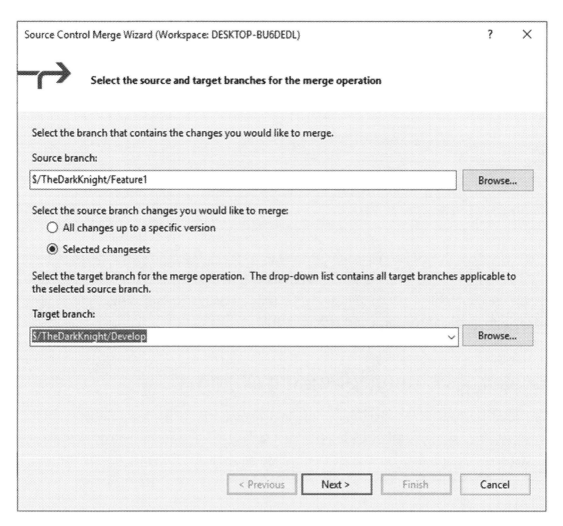

Figure 4-25. *Selecting a changeset option*

Click the Next button to move to the next step of the wizard. You will be able to see the changesets here. You can select the changesets you need to merge from the list and click Next to move to the next step of the wizard. See Figure 4-26.

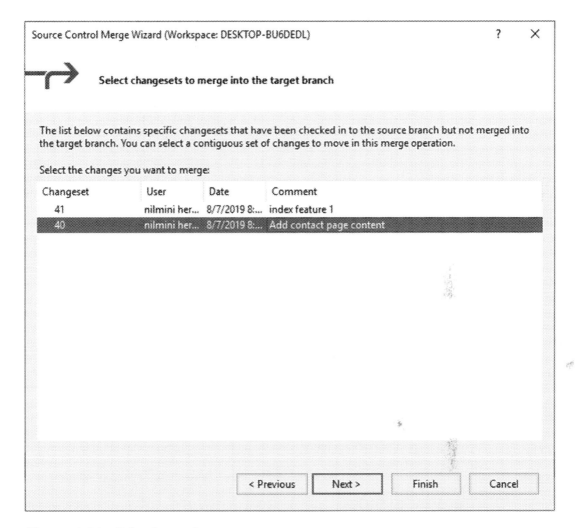

Figure 4-26. *Selecting a changeset*

After clicking the Next button, you will navigate to the final step of the wizard. Click Finish to end the wizard. This merges the Feature1 changes with the Develop branch.

Now go to the Source Control Explorer and check in the changes to the server. You will be able to see the merged changes in the Develop branch.

Lesson 4-6: Exploring TFVC Branching Strategies

Selecting a suitable branching strategy for a team is an important part of the automation process. Branching strategies can vary depending on the needs of a team, and teams are free to create their own branching strategies according to their requirements. Let's identify some commonly used TFVC branching strategies in this lesson.

Main Only

This is a basic branching strategy with one branch. If we are using this branching strategy, we need a way to identify development changesets and the changesets go to production in a given release. A main-only branching strategy is controlled using labels to identify releases or any other important milestones. Once a release is made, the branch is labeled on the changeset that the release is taken. See Figure 4-27. However, this strategy may create clutter in the source control system as changesets from multiple features may get added randomly to the main branch, which makes it really difficult to isolate a feature change if a need arises.

Figure 4-27. *Main only*

Development Isolation

The main purpose of this branching strategy is always maintaining a stable main branch. So, create dev branches from the main branch and do the development in the dev branch. When merging the dev branch with the main branch, first merge the main branch to the dev branch with forward integration (FI) to make sure any changes in the main branch are applied to dev and resolve conflicts if any. Then integrate changes from the dev branch to the main branch using reverse integration (RI). See Figure 4-28.

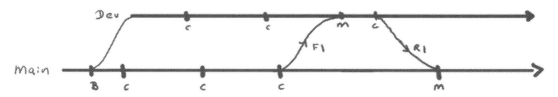

Figure 4-28. *Development isolation*

Feature Isolation

The concept of this branching strategy is to create separate branches from the main branch or from the dev branch for each feature. Frequently merge the parent branch to the feature branch. But the feature branch merge to the stable parent branch time is decided by the team upon completion of the feature. Some teams decide to merge the feature branch to the dev or main branch when the definition of done is met. This gives feature isolation in the stable branches, which might be useful in managing the codebase. See Figure 4-29.

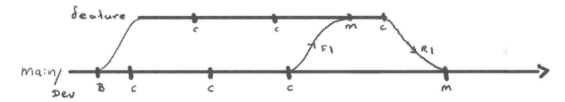

Figure 4-29. *Feature isolation*

Release Isolation

Create release branches from main. Always merge the changes from the release branch to main when a hot fix is made. But never merge the main branch changes back to the release branch because it is maintained as the production-deployed code. You can use different permission restrictions to prevent unwanted branch merges, which we will discuss in Chapter 6. See Figure 4-30.

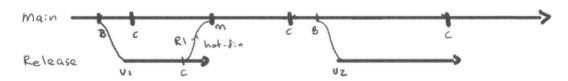

Figure 4-30. *Release isolation*

Servicing and Release Isolation

The servicing branch model is useful when you need to release service packs to your customers until the next major release is made. There should never be forward integrations happening from main to service or from service to release branches in this strategy. For subsequent releases, you can create new servicing branches and release branches. See Figure 4-31.

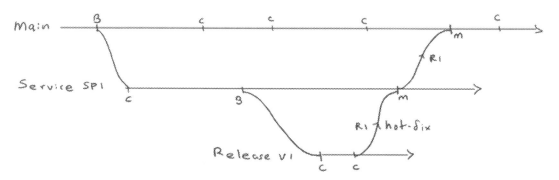

Figure 4-31. *Service and release isolation*

You can further introduce hotfix branches to the service and release isolation strategy, but it is not a recommended approach.

In this lesson, we discussed a few common branching patterns used with TFVC. You may use these patterns in combination to achieve a branching strategy suited to your project's needs.

Summary

In this chapter, we explored the branching and merging abilities of TFVC. We discussed how to resolve merge conflicts and the available options for branching and merging. Further, we explored the commonly used branching patterns to understand the possible strategies for implementing a branching structure for a given project's needs.

In the next chapter, we will discuss the command-line options available for TFVC. These command-line options will be especially useful in performing administrative tasks with TFVC.

CHAPTER 5

Team Foundation Version Control: Command Line

The command line in Team Foundation Version Control (TFVC) allows you to perform almost any action that you can do with Visual Studio; in fact, there are additional actions that can be performed in TFVC using only the command line. In this chapter, let's explore the command-line capabilities of TFVC so you can perform additional administrative and general actions, including and beyond the actions you can perform with Visual Studio. The purpose of this chapter is to get you started with TFVC commands so that you are familiar with how to use them. Once you know how to use the commands described in this chapter, you will be able to use many other TFVC commands in the same way.

Lesson 5-1: Getting Started with the Team Foundation Command Line

The Team Foundation Version Control command line comes as `tf.exe`. This command-line tool enables you to perform several command-line actions in TFVC. Let's look at how we can enable the usage of the `tf` command line on a computer.

Developer Command Prompt for Visual Studio

If you have Visual Studio installed on your computer, you have the developer command prompt for Visual Studio. When you open the developer command prompt, you can type `tf vc help` to list the TFVC commands available. See Figure 5-1.

© Chaminda Chandrasekara and Pushpa Herath 2020
C. Chandrasekara and P. Herath, *Hands-on Azure Repos*, https://doi.org/10.1007/978-1-4842-5425-7_5

Figure 5-1. Developer command prompt

To get detailed help for the commands, you can type tf msdn commandname. For example, if you type tf msdn add, a browser window will open with Microsoft documentation for the add command. See Figure 5-2.

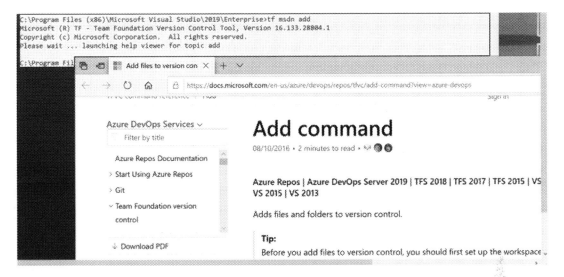

Figure 5-2. Running the tf msdn add command

Team Explorer Everywhere Command-Line Client

The tf command-line client can be downloaded from https://github.com/Microsoft/
team-explorer-everywhere/releases. You should download the TEE-CLC ZIP file
and extract it to use the tf command line. As a prerequisite, you need to have the Java
runtime installed and JAVA_HOME set in your environment path variables for Windows
systems. See Figure 5-3.

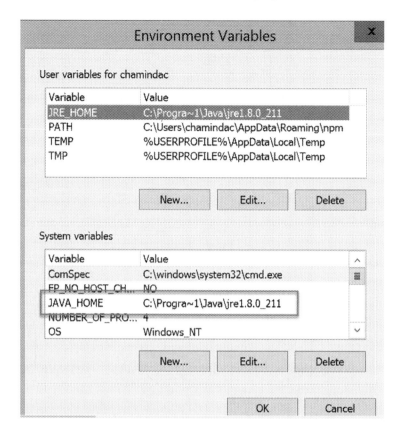

Figure 5-3. *Setting JAVA_HOME*

Then you can open a command prompt, navigate to the folder where you have extracted the tf command-line client, and execute the tf eula command to accept the end-user license agreement (EULA). You have to press the Enter key a couple of times to get to the end of the agreement, where you will be prompted to accept the license agreement. See Figure 5-4.

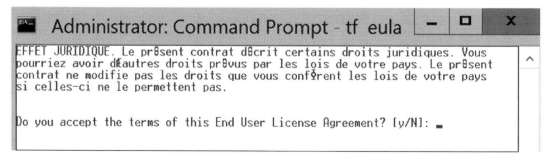

Figure 5-4. *EULA for TF CLC*

Note that there are slight differences when using the developer command prompt for Visual Studio versus when using the command-line client. For example, `tf vc help` and `tf msdn commandname` are not valid commands in the command-line client. However, most of the Team Foundation Version Control commands work with both options.

In this lesson, we discussed how to get started with the command line for Team Foundation Version Control.

Lesson 5-2: Using Workspace Commands

There are two commands related to TFVC workspaces. In this lesson, we'll look at them to understand the usage.

workspaces Command

The `workspaces` command allows you to view information about the workspaces on the system. For example, you can execute the `workspaces` command with the following syntax to obtain any workspace on any computer you have for your username (see Figure 5-5):

```
tf workspaces /collection:https://dev.azure.com/chamindac /computer:*
Collection: https://dev.azure.com/chamindac
```

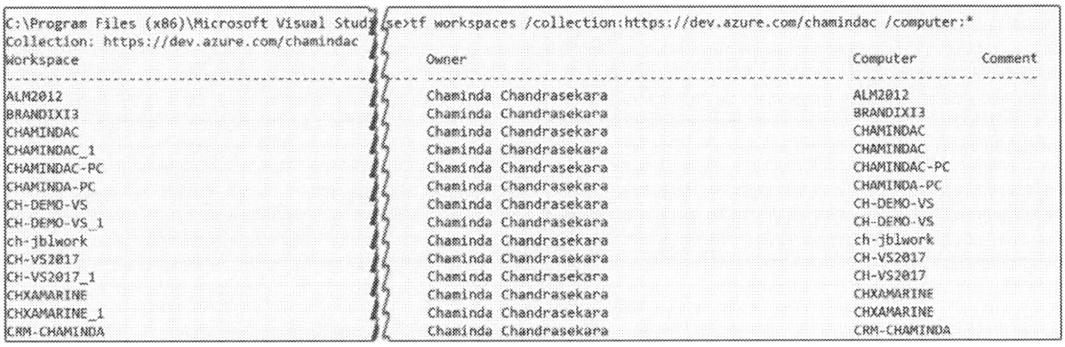

Figure 5-5. *Getting all the workspaces for the current user*

You can pass /owner:* in addition to the previous command to get all the workspaces of all the users, or you can specify a username to retrieve workspace information for a given user on all computers for the team project collection (Azure DevOps organization). The /remove: workspace names command allows you to remove one or more workspaces. If you're listing more than one workspace, then separate the names with a comma. There are a few other arguments and options you can pass to the workspaces command to perform different actions. Type tf msdn workspaces at the developer command prompt to see the full list of arguments and options in the Microsoft documentation.

workspace Command

Using the workspace command, you can view, modify, create, or delete a workspace. Let's try a few commands.

Create a folder named beta1 and open the developer command prompt for Visual Studio. Change the directory to the beta1 folder. Then execute tf workspace / new beta1 /collection:azuredevopsaccounturl. This will open a dialog asking for confirmation to map the beta1 folder to the new workspace. Click OK to create the workspace. See Figure 5-6. You may be prompted to get the latest version of code, but you can skip that by clicking No.

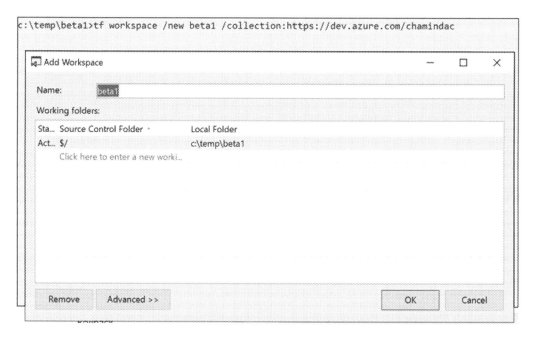

Figure 5-6. *Creating a new workspace*

The workspace is created for the current user. Now, if you run the command `tf workspaces`, you will see the new workspace called `beta1`. See Figure 5-7.

```
c:\temp\beta1>tf workspaces
Collection: https://dev.azure.com/chamindac
Workspace Owner                          Computer      Comment
--------- -------------------------- ----------- ----------
beta1        Chaminda Chandrasekara VSCookBook

c:\temp\beta1>_
```

Figure 5-7. *New workspace beta1*

Create another folder named `beta2` and execute `tf workspace /new beta2;usernameofanotheruser /collection:azuredevopsaccounturl` to create a workspace for a given user. Then click OK at the prompt. See Figure 5-8.

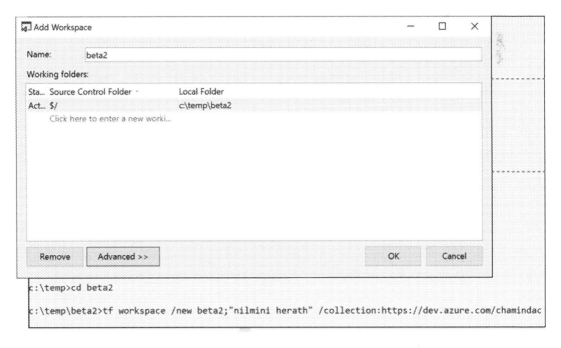

Figure 5-8. *New workspace for another user*

Execute the `tf workspaces` command to see the two new workspaces available on the machine with two owners. See Figure 5-9.

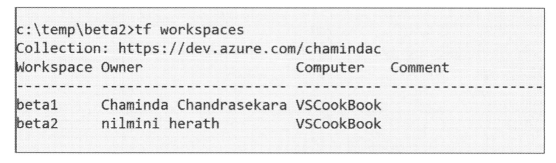

```
c:\temp\beta2>tf workspaces
Collection: https://dev.azure.com/chamindac
Workspace Owner                    Computer   Comment
--------- ---------------------- ---------- ----------------
beta1     Chaminda Chandrasekara VSCookBook
beta2     nilmini herath         VSCookBook
```

Figure 5-9.   *Workspaces*

From the mapped local folder, you can just execute `tf workspace` to open the workspace property editor. In the pop-up window, you can click the Advanced button to view and edit the workspace properties. See Figure 5-10.

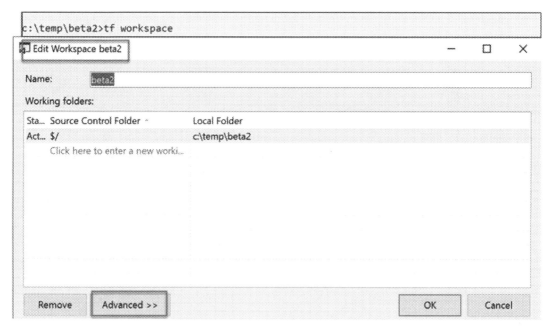

Figure 5-10.   *Editing a workspace*

You can delete a workspace using `tf workspace /delete workspacename; ownername`, as shown in Figure 5-11.

```
c:\temp\beta2>tf workspace /delete beta2;"nilmini herath"
A deleted workspace cannot be recovered.
Workspace 'beta2;nilmini herath' on server 'https://dev.azure.com/chamindac' has 0 pending change(s).
Are you sure you want to delete the workspace? (Yes/No) Yes


c:\temp\beta2>tf workspaces
Collection: https://dev.azure.com/chamindac
Workspace Owner                     Computer    Comment
--------- ------------------------- ----------- ---------------------------------------------
beta1     Chaminda Chandrasekara VSCookBook

c:\temp\beta2>
```

Figure 5-11. *Deleting a workspace*

You can execute `tf msdn workspace` at the developer command prompt for Visual Studio to open the documentation for the command.

In this lesson, we looked at a few actions we can perform with the `workspace` and `workspaces` commands. You will find these commands useful for doing administrative tasks in TFVC.

Lesson 5-3: Running Various Commands

You learned how to add files, check in files, check out files, rename files, etc., using Visual Studio with TFVC. You can perform these actions using the command line as well. Let's try them in this lesson using the workspace we created in the previous lesson.

Prerequisites: You followed the previous lesson and created a workspace.

Open the `beta1` workspace folder created in the previous lesson or create a new workspace that is mapped to the Azure DevOps organization. Then create a new team project named LearnTFVC with Team Foundation Version Control. Creating a team project was explained in the *Hands-On Azure Boards* book of this book series. See Figure 5-12.

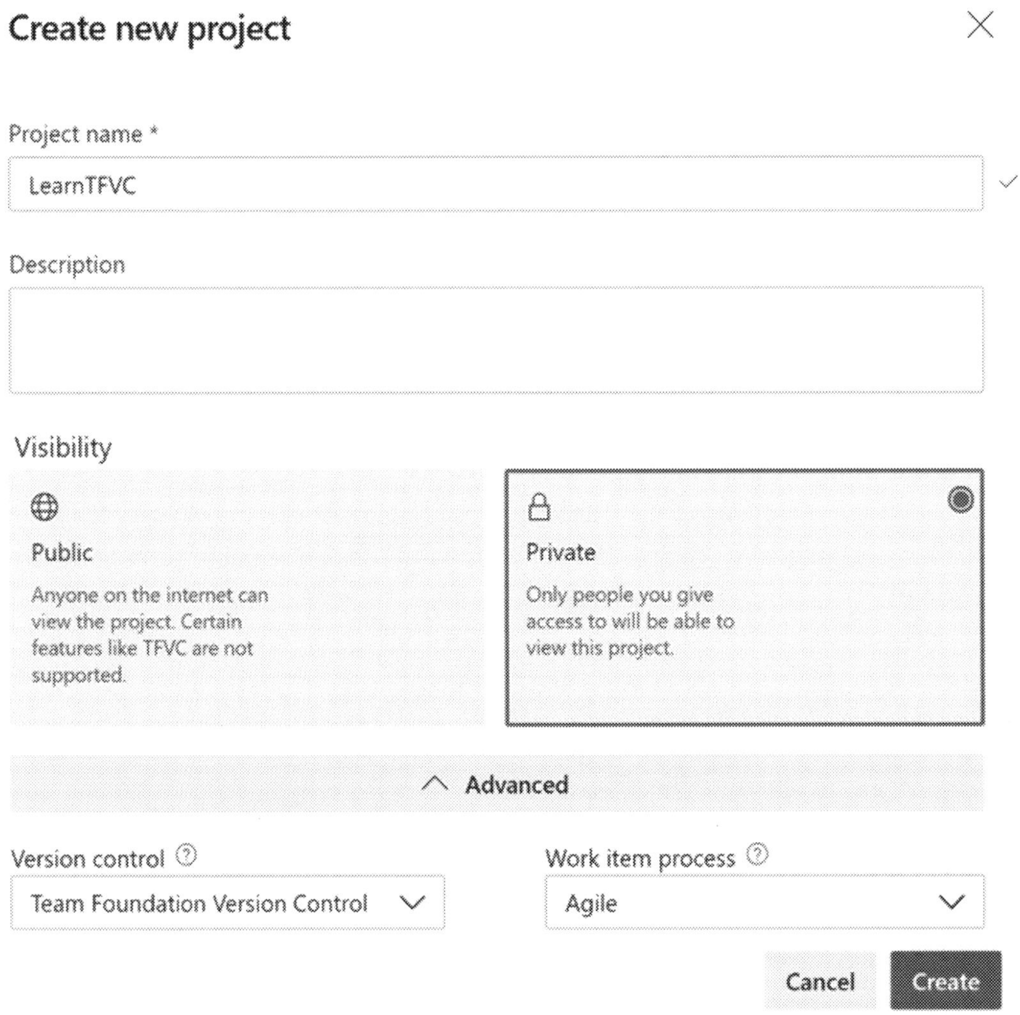

Create new project   ✕

Project name *

```
LearnTFVC
```
                                                                    ✓

Description

Visibility

⊕

Public

Anyone on the internet can
view the project. Certain
features like TFVC are not
supported.

🔒

Private   ◉

Only people you give
access to will be able to
view this project.

∧ **Advanced**

Version control ⓘ

```
Team Foundation Version Control    ∨
```

Work item process ⓘ

```
Agile                              ∨
```

Cancel   **Create**

Figure 5-12. *Creating a team project*

get

Open the developer command prompt for Visual Studio and change the directory to the
workspace folder of the Azure DevOps organization. We can use the get command to
get the latest version of $/LearnTFVC. Execute tf get $/LearnTFVC from the workspace
folder. See Figure 5-13.

```
c:\temp\beta1>tf get $/LearnTFVC
c:\temp\beta1:
Getting LearnTFVC

c:\temp\beta1>
```

Figure 5-13. *Getting the latest version*

You can use the -version parameter to specify a version to get. To access the documentation to learn more about the tf get command, execute tf msdn get from the Visual Studio command prompt. Since we have gotten the latest version for the path $/LearnTFVC, you will find that a LearnTFVC folder is created within your workspace folder. See Figure 5-14.

```
c:\temp\beta1>dir
 Volume in drive C is Windows
 Volume Serial Number is C247-3C56

 Directory of c:\temp\beta1

08/20/2019  11:29 PM    <DIR>          .
08/20/2019  11:29 PM    <DIR>          ..
08/20/2019  11:29 PM    <DIR>          LearnTFVC
               0 File(s)              0 bytes
               3 Dir(s)  76,096,212,992 bytes free
```

Figure 5-14. *LearnTFVC folder in workspace*

add

Create a folder named main inside the LearnTFVC folder. Then, using Visual Studio or Visual Studio Code, create a simple Console Application project in the main folder. Now from the LearnTFVC folder, you can execute tf add *.* /recursive to add all the files in the project to source control to make the files pending changes. The bin and obj folders will be ignored by default. See Figure 5-15.

```
c:\temp\beta1>cd learntfvc

c:\temp\beta1\LearnTFVC>tf add *.* /recursive
main

main:
ConsoleApp1

main\ConsoleApp1:
ConsoleApp1
ConsoleApp1.sln

main\ConsoleApp1\ConsoleApp1:
ConsoleApp1.csproj
Program.cs
Items matching the following exclusions were ignored: bin;obj

c:\temp\beta1\LearnTFVC>
```

Figure 5-15. *Running the tf add command*

You can use tf msdn add to open the documentation at the developer command prompt for Visual Studio to learn more.

checkin

From the LearnTFVC folder, execute tf checkin /comment:"Add New Console App" /recursive to check in all the files added. You will get a pop-up window that lets you associate work items, select files, deselect files to check in, and so on. Click the Check In button. See Figure 5-16.

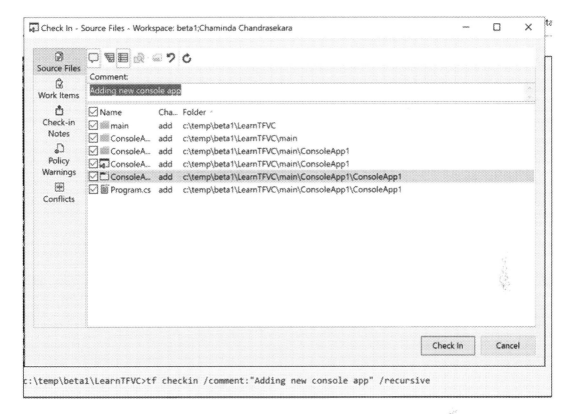

Figure 5-16. *Running the tf checkin command*

Once you click the Check In button, the files will be checked in. To learn more about the checkin command, execute tf msdn checkin at the developer command prompt of Visual Studio.

checkout (or edit)

To check out a file, you can execute tf checkout filename or tf edit filename. Then you can make changes to the file and check in the file. It is possible to recursively check out files in the folder of a given path or check out all the files recursively from the workspace using /recursive. For more information about the checkout command, execute tf msdn checkout or tf msdn edit from the developer command prompt for Visual Studio.

rename

To rename files, you can use `tf rename oldite newitem`. For example, `tf rename classx.cs classy.cs` will rename `classx.cs` to `classy.cs`. You can use `/lock` to lock a file exclusively to prevent other users from checking it in or out. To open the documentation for more information about `rename command`, execute `tf msdn rename` at the developer command prompt for Visual Studio.

undo

The `undo` command is a really useful command allowing users to discard pending changes. You can use `tf undo filename` to undo a pending change in a given file. The `/workspace:workspacename` command can be used with `tf undo` to discard changes in a remote workspace. If the workspace not specified, the workspace of the current folder is considered for the command. `/workspace:workspacename;workspaceowner` can be used with `tf undo` to discard changes of other users' workspaces. However, when you undo changes in a remote workspace, before working in that remote workspace, a `get all` command should be performed in the remote workspace. `tf undo` will discard any locks applied on files in that workspace.

In this lesson, we explored the command-line options to add files to TFVC, check files in and out, and rename files. `tf undo` is a really useful tool we learned about in this lesson; it can undo changes in missing workspaces (due to the unavailability of the remote machine) or workspaces owned by users who are no longer available, discarding the pending changes and removing the locks on files in remote workspaces and workspaces owned by other users.

Summary

In this chapter, we explored several commands available in TFVC. Now you have a good understanding of how to use TFVC commands. There are many other commands available in TFVC such as `tf lock`, `tf branch`, `tf merge`, etc. You can execute `tf vc help` to get a list of the `tfvc` commands available. Then you can execute the `tf msdn` command at the developer command prompt for Visual Studio to open the documentation for a given command.

In the next chapter, we will explore the security and permissions management features of Team Foundation Version Control.

CHAPTER 6

Team Foundation Version Control: Security

Security is a crucial part of any source control server. The Team Foundation Version Control (TFVC) server offers various security methods to improve the safety of the team's source code content. In this chapter, let's look at how to control the access of TFVC and maintain a secure codebase.

Lesson 6-1: Setting Up TFVC Security at the Team Project Level

We can control access to the project source code in several ways. One mechanism is to control access is from the team project level. This lesson will give you an idea about the available security options in an Azure DevOps team project for TFVC.

Prerequisites:

- Azure DevOps project with TFVC as the source control system

- The ability to log in to Azure DevOps as the administrator

Go to the project settings of the Azure DevOps project. Select Repositories in the Repo section. You will see the repository security control options available in Azure DevOps. See Figure 6-1.

© Chaminda Chandrasekara and Pushpa Herath 2020
C. Chandrasekara and P. Herath, *Hands-on Azure Repos*, https://doi.org/10.1007/978-1-4842-5425-7_6

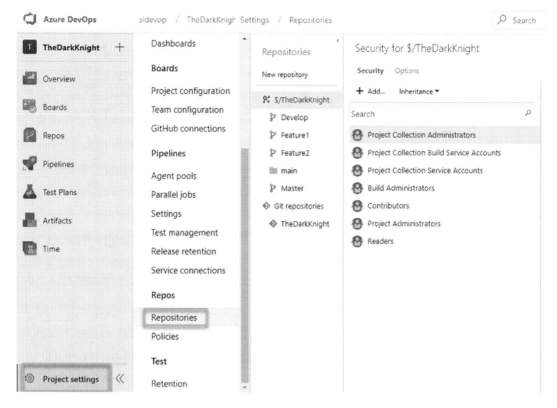

Figure 6-1. *Moving to the repository's security controls*

Also, you can move to the security control page through the repository page. Go to the Azure DevOps repository. Select the Files section. At the top of the repository, you will see a drop-down icon in front of the repository name. Click the drop-down and select "Manage repositories" to move to the security controls of the repository. See Figure 6-2.

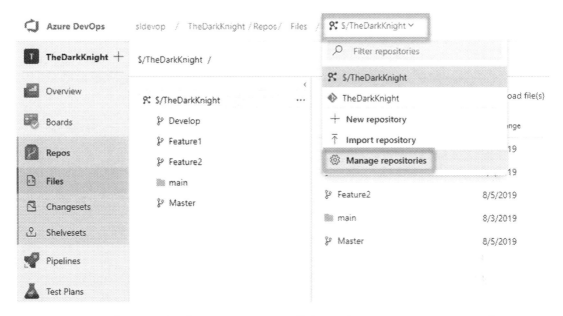

Figure 6-2. *Selecting the "Manage security" drop-down item to move to the security controls*

Now we are on the repository security control page. You can see the Azure DevOps groups listed on the permission control page. Each group has been set up with different permissions for the repo. In addition to these default security groups, you can add individual users or groups and control the access to the repository. See Figure 6-3.

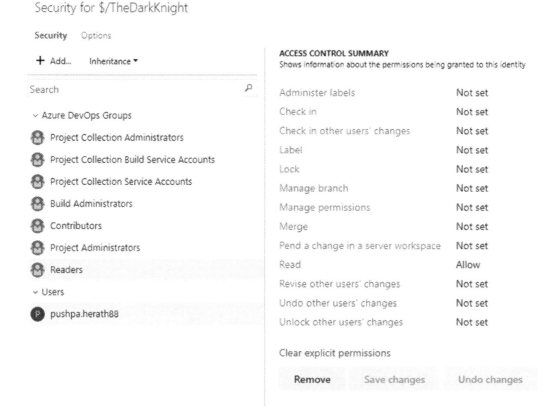

Figure 6-3. *Azure DevOps groups and individual users*

Azure DevOps allows you to control the repository access using the following options:

- **Administer Labels**

  The user with this permission can edit or delete the labels added by other users.

- **Check in**

  The user with this permission can check in the changes. Also, the user with this permission can revise any committed changes.

- **Check in other users' changes**

  When multiple users work in the same workspace, the users with this permission can check in the changes made by other users.

- **Label**

  A user with this permission can label the changesets.

- **Lock**

  Users with this permission can lock the folders and files, preventing other users from checking out the file or the folder.

- **Manage branch**

  Users with this permission can convert folders to branches, edit properties, reparent branches, and convert branches back to folders.

- **Manage permissions**

  Users with this permission can control other users' permissions for folders and files.

- **Merge**

  Users with this permission can merge changes into the given path/branch.

- **Pend and change in a server workspace**

  Users with this permission can add a pending changeset to the server workspace by doing actions such as checking out, adding/editing files, etc.

- **Read**

  Users with this permission can read the content of files and folders.

- **Revise other users' change**

  Users with this permission can change the comments of checked-in files not only made by themselves but also by others.

- **Undo other users' change**

  Users with this permission can undo the changes made by another user.

- **Unlock the other users' changes**

  Users with this permission can unlock files and folders locked by
  another user.

In front of each of these permissions, you will see the value as Not Set, Allow, or
Deny. Project administrators can change these permissions by clicking these values.

So far, we have discussed all the crucial parts of the security controls. Further, you
will see an Options link next to the Security link. Click the Options link. You will see a
toggle that allows you to enable or disable web editing of the repository. See Figure 6-4.

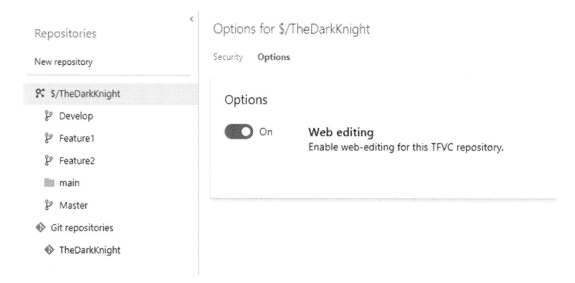

Figure 6-4. *Enabling or disabling web editing*

Let's see how this option works by disabling web editing. After disabling web editing,
go to the repository and select a file. Click the Edit button. You will see a message that
explains that web editing has been disabled. See Figure 6-5.

Figure 6-5. *Web editing disable message*

This lesson explained the Azure DevOps security permissions of the repositories. We were able to learn about different TFVC repository permissions available in Azure DevOps.

Lesson 6-2: Applying Permissions at the Branch/Folder or File Level

We discussed how to do access control for an Azure DevOps TFVC repository in the previous lesson. Now you have the idea about the access control options available in Azure DevOps. Let's discuss further the repository access control within this lesson. We will discuss how to control the permission of a branch, folder, or file.

Prerequisites:

- Azure DevOps project with TFVC as the source control system

Open Visual Studio and connect to the Azure DevOps project using Team Explorer. Move to the Source Control Explorer of the project. Here you can see the branches, folders, and files of the selected project.

Let's discuss how we can control the access of a branch of the project.

Right-click a branch and select the Advanced option from the pane. Then you will see another pane with a few options. Select Security from the pane. See Figure 6-6.

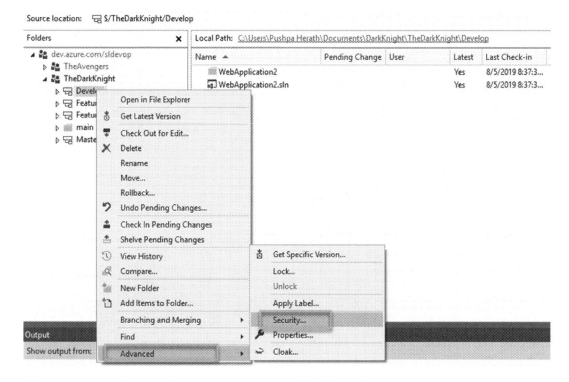

Figure 6-6. *Selecting the Security option of the branch*

You might be asked to enter the Azure DevOps credentials before navigating to the Azure DevOps security section where you can control the access permission to the specific branch. In this example, we can control the access permission of the Develop branch. These changes will not affect the other branch permissions. See Figure 6-7.

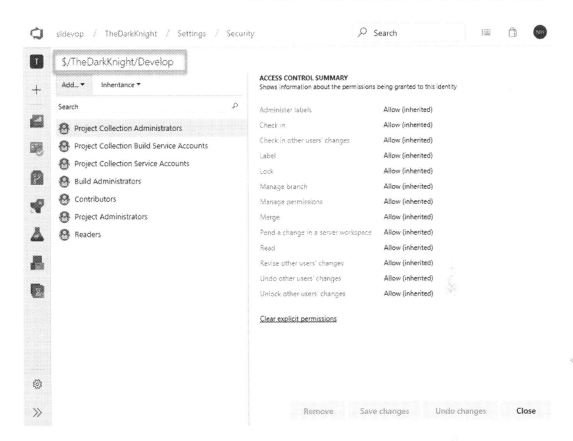

Figure 6-7. *Permission of the branch*

You have seen how to control the permission of the branch. Let's see how to control the permission of a folder.

Go to the Source Control Explorer. Select a folder and right-click it. A pane will open. Select the Advanced option and then Security. See Figure 6-8.

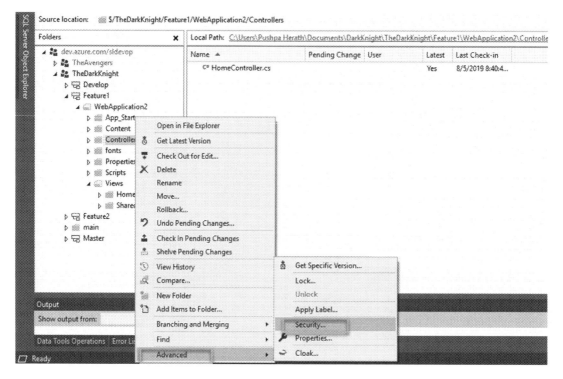

Figure 6-8. *Security option for a folder*

After selecting Security, you will navigate to the folder security page where you can control the security of the selected folder. See Figure 6-9.

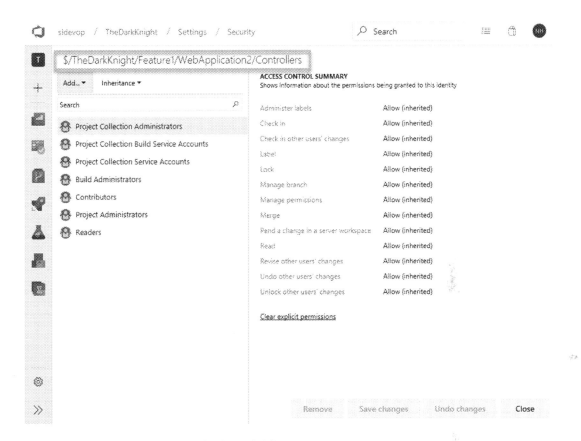

Figure 6-9. *Security control of the folder*

Let's see how we can control the security of the file. Go to the Source Control Explorer and select the file for which you want to change the permission. Right-click the file, select the Advanced option, and then select Security, as explained earlier. You will be navigated to the Azure DevOps security control page where you can control the permission of the selected file only. See Figure 6-10.

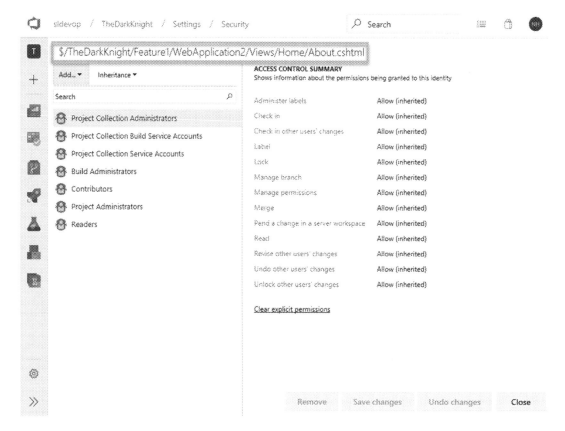

Figure 6-10. *Security control of the file*

This lesson explained security control at the branch level, folder level, and file level. You can set different access permissions for each file in the repository. By using these options, you can maintain a stable codebase securely in a TFVC repository.

Lesson 6-3: Auditing Changes and Finding Out Who Did What

While working as a team with a common codebase, sometimes we need to track who has made changes in each part of the code. So, let's discuss how we can track the changes easily with Visual Studio.

Prerequisites:

- Azure DevOps project with Team Foundation Version Control as the source control system

Go to Visual Studio's Source Control Explorer. Select the file with the change. Right-click the file and select the Compare option in the menu. See Figure 6-11.

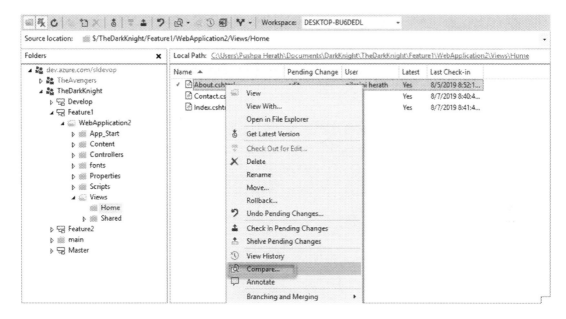

Figure 6-11. *Selecting Compare*

The Compare window will open. You can select the source file and target file from this window. Also, you can select the file source version to compare and the workspace. In this example, we are comparing the workspace version of the file with the source version. You can see the comparison between the two versions of the file in Figure 6-12.

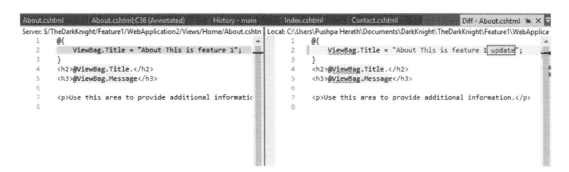

Figure 6-12. *File version comparison*

With this comparison option, we can compare the changes made in each file.

Visual Studio Team Explorer has another option where we can track the person who made each change in a file.

Go to the Source Control Explorer. Select the file and right-click it. A pane will open. Select Annotate from the pane. See Figure 6-13.

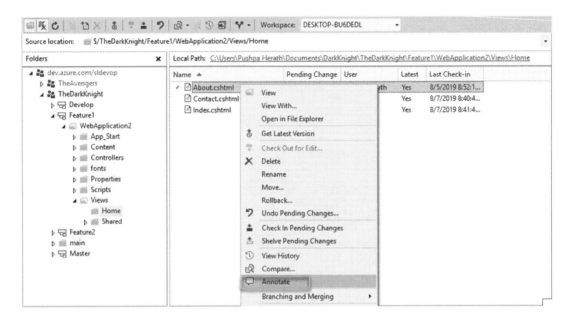

Figure 6-13. *Selecting Annotate*

After selecting Annotate from the pane, you will navigate to the page where you can see the changes made by each user. See Figure 6-14.

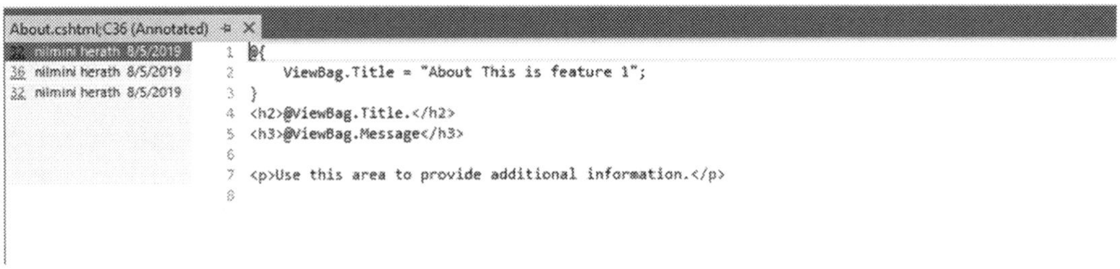

Figure 6-14. *Annotating a file with usernames*

This lesson explained how we can track the changes made by each user in the source files. This is a helpful feature while working in a team.

Summary

In this chapter, we discussed the available security control options of a TFVC repository in the Azure DevOps. Also, we discussed the ability to have different permissions for each file and folder in the source code. Finally, we discussed the ability to track the changes in the source code and identify who made each change in the source code by using annotations.

In the next chapter, we will get started with Azure Git Repos, which is the distributed version control system supported by Azure DevOps.

CHAPTER 7

Getting Started with Azure Git Repos

Git is a popular version control system with many developers. The ability of Git to be used on any platform and with almost any development tool makes it a great version control system. Azure DevOps Services comes with Azure Git Repos, which you can use with a development tool of your preference. Azure Git Repos also provides you with tight integration to Azure Boards and Azure Pipelines. You can leverage Azure Boards capabilities and track requirements alongside its implementation as well as automate builds and deployment easily with your code in Azure Git Repos.

In this chapter, let's explore how to get started with Azure Git Repos and use it to develop your code with Visual Studio and Visual Studio Code. It is expected that you are already familiar with general Git concepts, because this chapter introduces how to work with Azure Git Repos.

Lesson 7-1: Creating an Azure Git Repo

As discussed in the *Hands-on Azure Boards* book of this series, you can create a team project with Azure Git Repos or with Team Foundation Version Control (TFVC). Regardless of the way the team project is created, you can add one more Azure Git repositories to your team project in Azure DevOps. In this lesson, let's focus on creating a team project with Azure Git Repos and adding Azure Git repositories to a team project that is created with TFVC.

Creating a Team Project with Azure Git Repos

In Azure DevOps Services, you can create a team project and select the default version control type you want to set up for the team project. Creating a team project is explained in detail in the *Hands-on Azure Boards* book of this series. Select Git as the version control system and create a team project named LearnGit. See Figure 7-1.

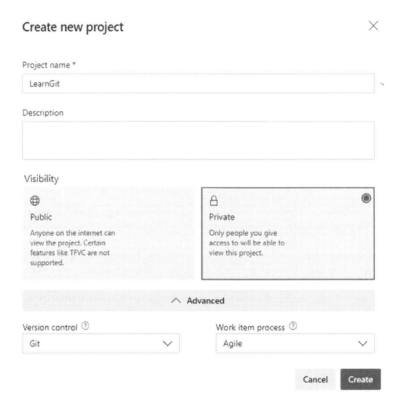

Figure 7-1. *Creating a team project with Git*

After the project is created, go to Repos in the left menu. An empty Git repo is created. See Figure 7-2.

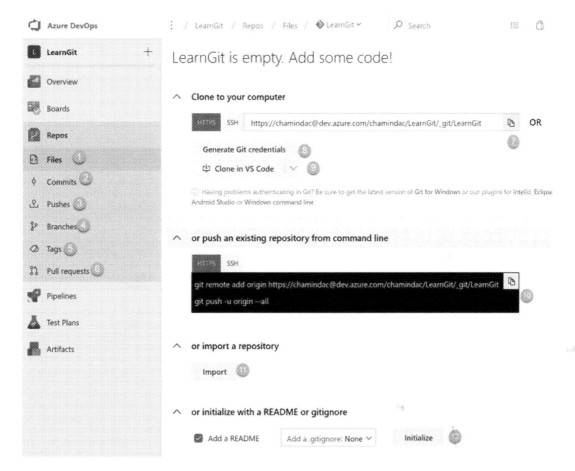

Figure 7-2. *Empty Git repo*

Let's get an overview of the functionality shown in Figure 7-2. We will be discussing some of these options in detail throughout the next few chapters.

1. You can click the Files submenu item to view the files of the repo.

2. Commits of the repo are listed on this page.

3. This page lets you view the code pushes.

4. Branches can be managed on this page.

5. You can manage pull requests from this page.

6. You can copy the clone URL to clone the repo using a development tool or the Git command line.

7.   "Generate Git credentials" lets you define credentials to access the
     Git repo. Or you can click the link to create a personal access token
     (PAT) scoped to the code. See Figure 7-3. PAT creation is explained
     in detail in the *Hands-on Azure Boards* book of this series.

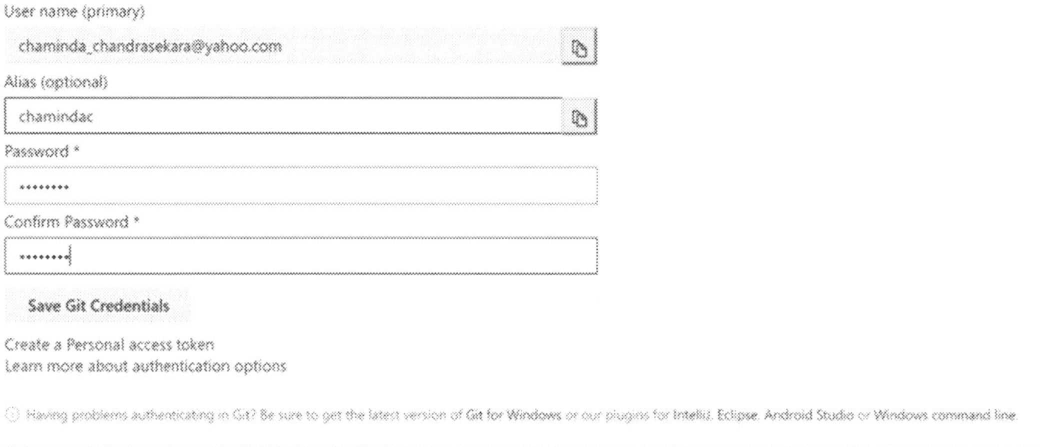

Figure 7-3. *Git credentials*

8.   This button and drop-down lets you select your preferred
     development tool and clone the repository in that tool.

9.   You can use these commands to push a local repository using the
     command line.

10.   You can import a remote Git repository or a TFVC repository in
     the current Azure DevOps organization using this option.

11.   You can initialize your repository with a .gitignore file.

Creating Additional Git Repos in a Team Project

You can create multiple Git repos in one team project unlike one TFVC repo per project.
To create additional Git repos, you can use the small drop-down option near the name of
the Git or TFVC repo in the breadcrumb. Then click "New repository." See Figure 7-4.

Figure 7-4. *New repository*

Then you can provide a name for the new Git repo, select Git as type of the repo, and create the new repo by clicking the Create button. You are allowed to create a `.gitignore` file while creating the repo to initialize it. See Figure 7-5.

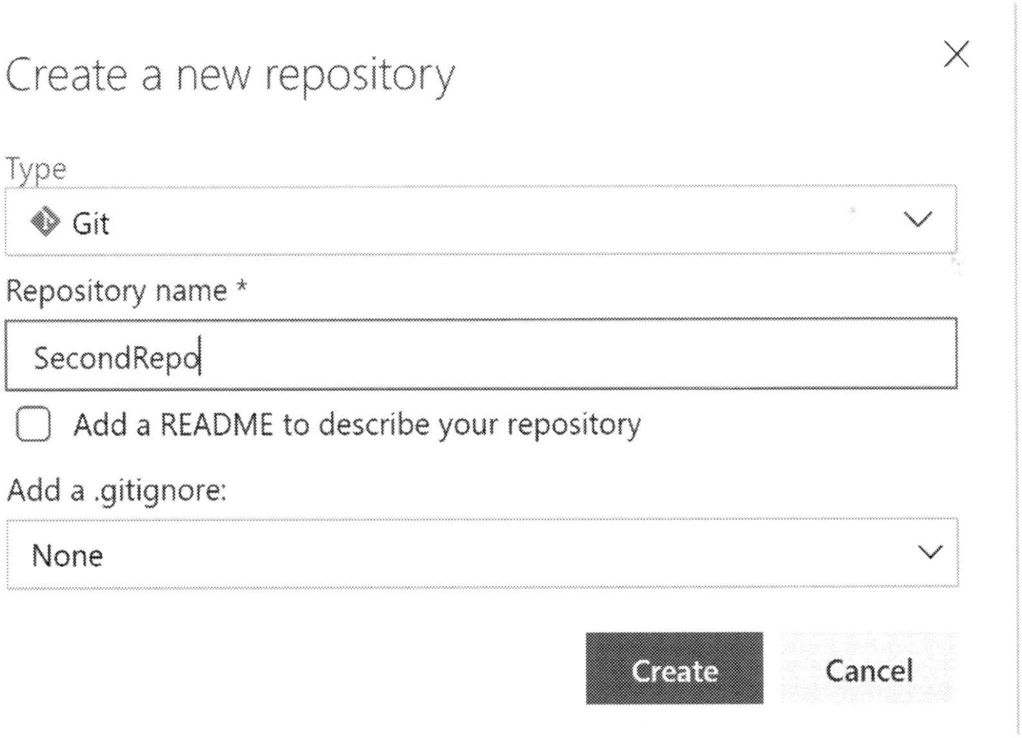

Create a new repository

Type

◈ Git

Repository name *

SecondRepo

☐ Add a README to describe your repository

Add a .gitignore:

None

Create   Cancel

Figure 7-5. *Creating a Git repo*

In this lesson, you learned how to create an Azure Git repo and how to create a new team project with a Git repo. Additionally, we looked at the options available on the empty repo page of a new Git repo.

Lesson 7-2: Cloning an Azure Git Repo

We are going to use Azure Git Repos with Visual Studio and Visual Studio Code in this book using a Windows environment. However, you can use Azure Git Repos with other development tools and on Linux and macOS environments.

Prerequisites: To use Git, you need to install Git for your operating system; you can download it from `https://git-scm.com/downloads`. You have created an Azure Git repo following the steps in the previous lesson.

VS Code

To clone the Azure Git repo, copy the clone URL from the empty Azure Git repo page, which was explained in the previous lesson. Open Visual Studio Code (you can download and install Visual Studio Code from `https://code.visualstudio.com/`). In the menu of VS Code, click View ➤ Command Palette or press Ctrl+Shift+P. In the command palette, type **Git:Clone**. See Figure 7-6.

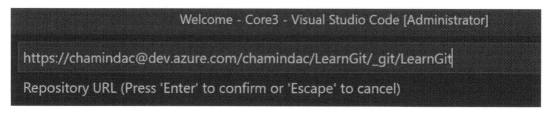

Welcome - Core3 - Visual Studio Code [Administrator]

>Git:Clone

Git: Clone   recently used

Figure 7-6. *Running the Git:Clone command*

Then paste the cloned URL into the command palette and press Enter. See Figure 7-7.

Welcome - Core3 - Visual Studio Code [Administrator]

https://chamindac@dev.azure.com/chamindac/LearnGit/_git/LearnGit

Repository URL (Press 'Enter' to confirm or 'Escape' to cancel)

Figure 7-7. *Pasting the Git repo clone URL in VS Code*

A pop-up dialog will appear asking for the clone's local folder path. Navigate to and select a folder to clone the repo and click the Select Repository Location button in the pop-up window. After cloning the repo, VS code will prompt you to open the repository. See Figure 7-8.

Figure 7-8. *Opening the repository*

If you do not open the repository with the previous option, you can go to the menu of VS Code, select File ➤ Open Folder, and select and open the repository folder from the pop-up window that appears.

Visual Studio

In Visual Studio, to clone and use an Azure Git repo, you have to connect to the team project. In the Team Explorer window of Visual Studio, click the Manage Connections toolbar icon and then click Manage Connections and Connect to a Project. See Figure 7-9.

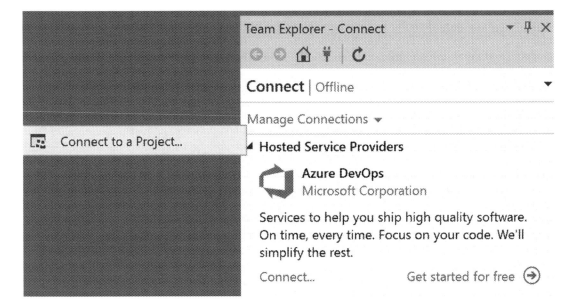

Figure 7-9. *Connecting to a team project*

A dialog window will appear, and you can select or add a Microsoft account or organization account that has access to the Azure DevOps organization. Then you can expand the Azure DevOps organization and see the team projects. Expand the LearnGit team project and select the Git repo. Provide a local path to clone the repository and click the Clone button. See Figure 7-10.

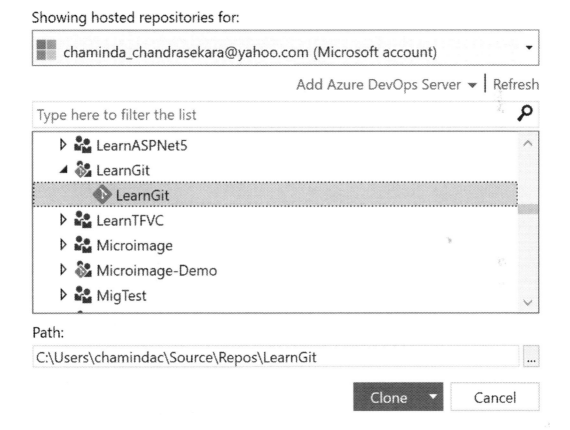

Figure 7-10. *Cloning the repository*

After you click the Clone button, you will see that the repository is successfully cloned in Visual Studio Team Explorer. See Figure 7-11.

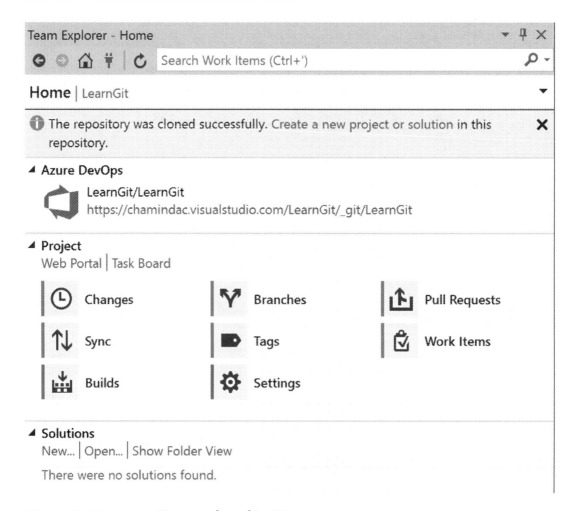

Figure 7-11. *Azure Git repo cloned in VS*

In this lesson, we discussed how to clone an Azure Git repository using Visual Studio Code or Visual Studio.

Lesson 7-3: Creating and Pushing Code to Azure Git Repos

Now that you have opened a repository folder in VS Code per the instructions in the previous lesson, you can start adding code files to it. Then you can take a look at how to add code using Visual Studio to Azure Git Repos in this lesson.

Prerequisites: You followed the previous lesson and have cloned an Azure Git repo using VS Code and VS.

Add a sample code file in the opened repository folder in Visual Studio Code. Once you add code, you will see the pending changes appear in VS Code. See Figure 7-12.

Figure 7-12. *Sample code*

Then you can provide a comment and use the Source Control menu in VS Code to stage, commit, and push changes. A commit will commit the changes in the local Git repo, and the changes will be pushed to the remote Azure Git repository once pushed. See Figure 7-13.

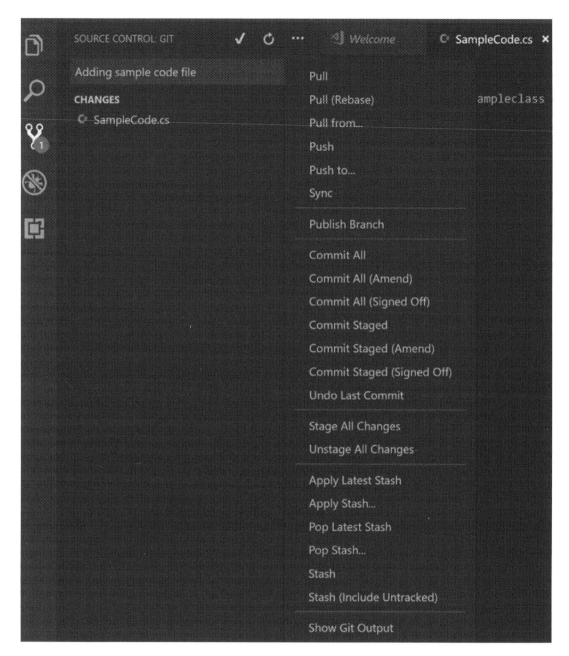

Figure 7-13. *Source Control menu options for Git*

If you view the repo in the Azure DevOps web portal, you will now see the sample code file in the master branch of the Azure Git repository. See Figure 7-14.

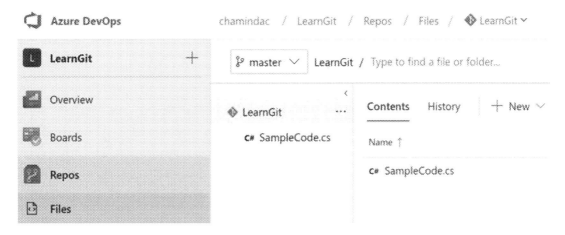

Figure 7-14. *Code in the master branch*

To get the changes in the master branch to Visual Studio in Team Explorer, click Branches. See Figure 7-15.

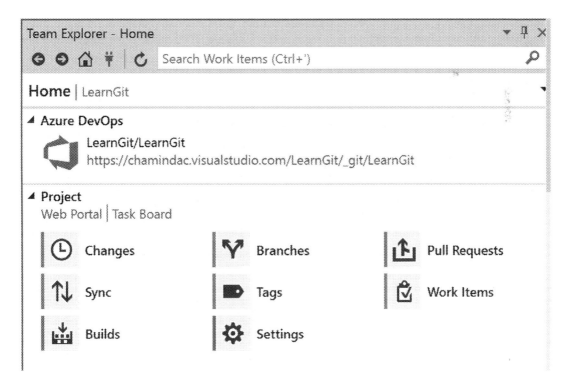

Figure 7-15. *Sync menu item*

Then expand the remote branches, right-click the master branch, and click Checkout in the context menu. See Figure 7-16.

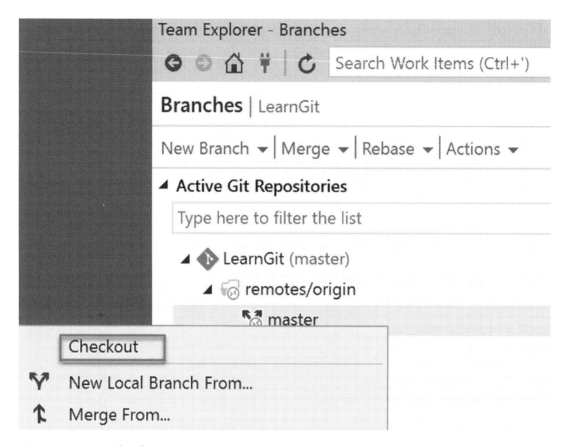

Figure 7-16. *Checkout menu item*

If you open the Solution Explorer in the folder view, you will able to see that the file that was pushed from VS Code is available in your local repo and checked out to the master branch. See Figure 7-17.

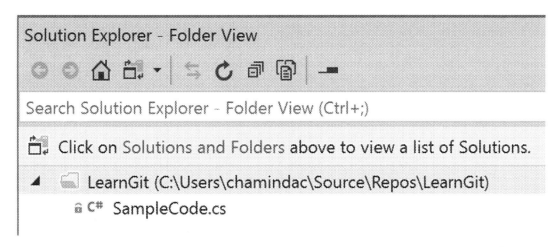

Figure 7-17. *Changes appearing in VS*

Now let's try to add project from VS to the repo. You can click New in the Team Explorer under Solutions to add a new solution. See Figure 7-18.

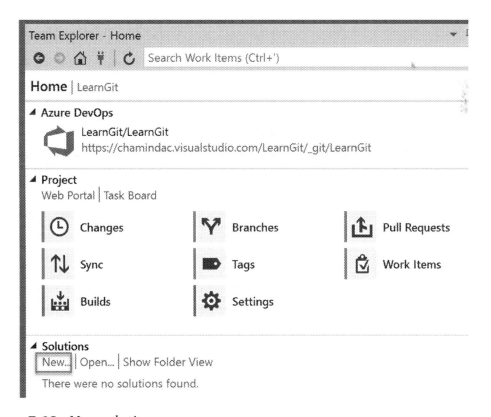

Figure 7-18. *New solution*

Then add an ASP.NET Core project. (Make sure you have the required .NET Core SDK available on your machine. Download the .NET Core SDKs from `https://dotnet.microsoft.com/download`.) The new solution path will be automatically set to the repo folder when you use the New solution button, as shown in Figure 7-18, to start creating the new solution. Once the solution is added, build the solution. Then in Team Explorer, click Changes. On the Changes page of Team Explorer, you can right-click the local items that should not be committed and ignore them, which will add a `.gitignore` file. Click + on the Changes page to stage the changes. See Figure 7-19.

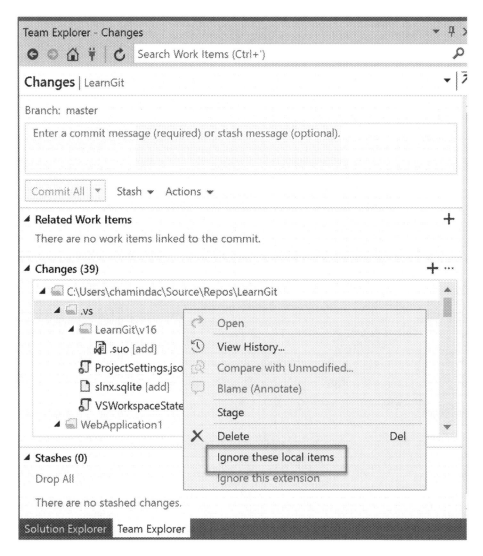

Figure 7-19. *Ignoring the local items*

You can provide a comment and then commit the staged changes. You can associate work items as we have done with TFVC when doing a commit in Azure Git Repos. There is an option to stash them, which can be used for the same purpose that we used a shelveset in TFVC, which we will discuss later in this chapter. See Figure 7-20.

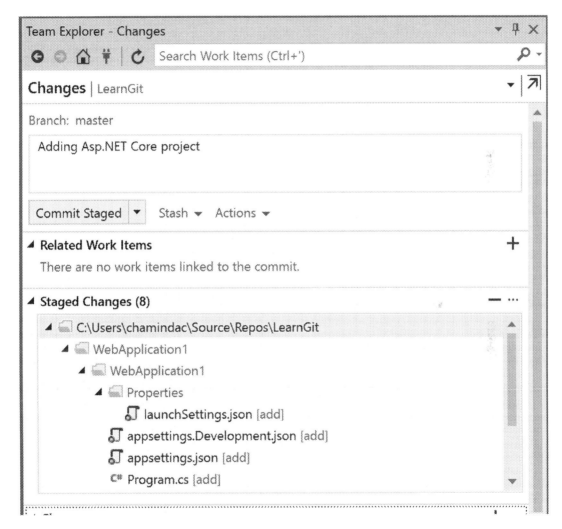

Figure 7-20. *Commit staged*

Then you can sync to share the changes, which will pull and push the changes. Click Sync in Team Explorer and on the Synchronization page of the Team Explorer sync. This will pull the master branch and then push your commit so that it is available in the remote repo. See Figure 7-21.

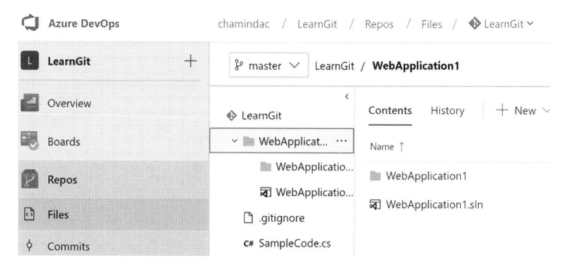

Figure 7-21. *Changes available in the Azure Git repo*

In this lesson, we discussed how to create code and push the changes to Azure Git Repos using Visual Studio and Visual Studio Code.

Lesson 7-4: Getting Changes from Others and Sharing Code

Now that we have an ASP.NET Core project in the Azure Git repository, we can try working with it using Visual Studio and Visual Studio Code. Let's look at how to get code changes and understand the difference between fetch and pull. Then we'll explore how to commit changes and share them by syncing.

Prerequisites: You followed the previous lesson.

Open VS Code and open the previously cloned repository folder in VS Code. In VS Code you can pull the changes using the Source Control menu options. See Figure 7-22.

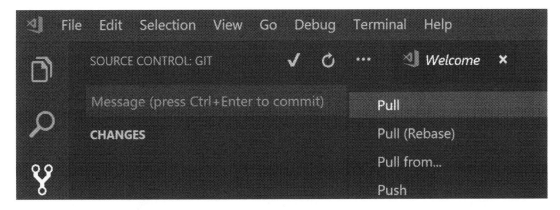

Figure 7-22. *Pulling in changes in VS Code*

You can see that the changes you made in Visual Studio and pushed to the Azure Git repository are now pulled to the VS Code local repository. See Figure 7-23.

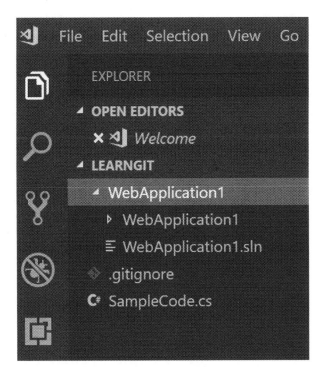

Figure 7-23. *Code pulled to VS Code*

Now make a small change in the code; for example, you can change the message at startup. See Figure 7-24.

```
Startup.cs ●
22          public void Configure(IApplicationBuilder app, IWebHostEnvironment env)
23          {
24              if (env.IsDevelopment())
25              {
26                  app.UseDeveloperExceptionPage();
27              }
28
29              app.UseRouting(routes =>
30              {
31                  routes.MapGet("/", async context =>
32                  {
33                      await context.Response.WriteAsync("Hello World! Today is great!!!");
34                  });
35              });
36          }
37      }
38  }
```

Figure 7-24. *Changing the code*

Then commit and push this change from VS Code to Azure Git Repos. Open Visual Studio, and in Team Explorer click Sync. On the synchronization page, click Fetch. You will see that the incoming changes are listed once fetched. The changes have not yet been merged to your local repo. Fetch in VS allows you to inspect the changes before getting them pulled to your local repo from the Azure Git repository. See Figure 7-25.

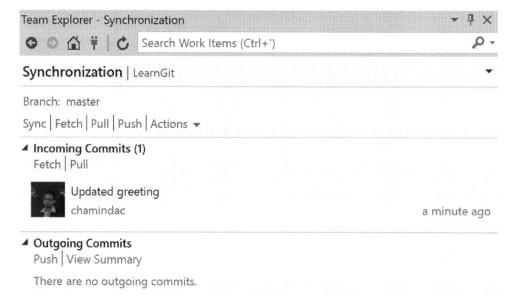

Figure 7-25. *Fetched changes in VS*

Double-click the incoming changes to view the details. You can see the commit details, and you will view the history, compare changes, and annotate changes. You can also create a Git tag for the commit or revert the changes. See Figure 7-26.

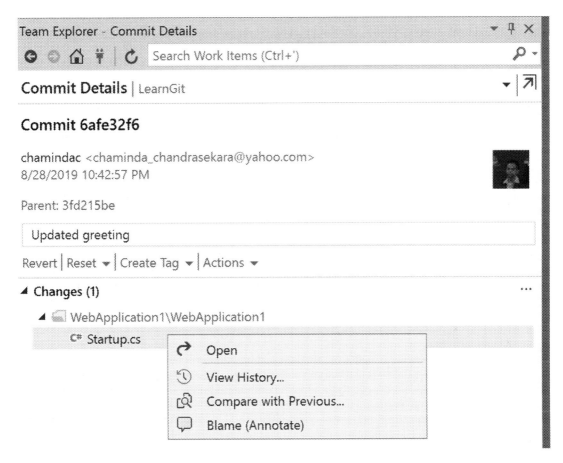

Figure 7-26. *Inspecting the incoming changes*

To get the changes to your local repo, do a pull on the Visual Studio Team Explorer synchronization page. Make another change in Visual Studio and commit the change. Click Sync in Team Explorer, and you will see the outgoing changes on the Synchronization page of Team Explorer. See Figure 7-27.

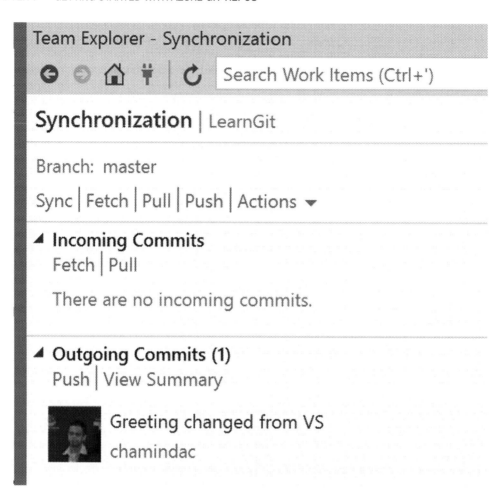

Figure 7-27. *Outgoing changes*

You can click Sync to pull and push changes or click Push to push the changes to Azure Git Repos.

In Visual Studio Code, by default automatic fetching happens before a pull. However, if you want to do a fetch in VS Code, you can open the command palette and type **Git:Fetch**. Make sure not to pull changes to VS Code.

In this lesson, we discussed fetching, pulling, and syncing changes with Visual Studio and Visual Studio Code in Azure Git Repos.

Lesson 7-5: Resolving Conflicts

When multiple team members work on a project, they may push changes to the same branch (we will discuss branch and merge conflicts in Chapter 8 of this book) and the same code file. Let's look at the conflict resolve options when using Azure Git Repos with VS Code and in Visual Studio.

Prerequisites: You followed the previous lesson.

Open VS Code, and in the web app make a code change in the same line that you made the change with Visual Studio in the previous lesson. For example, change the greeting message again, without doing a pull for the remote changes so that the change you made with VS in the previous lessen is not available in your local repo. Commit your change in VS Code, but do not push it. Instead, open the command palette after the commit and type **Git:Pull**, or click Pull in the Source Control menu in VS Code. You will see a message showing there are conflicts and can resolve them before committing. See Figure 7-28.

Figure 7-28. *Conflicts message*

You will see the incoming and current change conflicts in the file. See Figure 7-29.

```
◇ Startup.cs   ✕

22              public void Configure(IApplicationBuilder app, IWebHostEnvironment env)
23              {
24                  if (env.IsDevelopment())
25                  {
26                      app.UseDeveloperExceptionPage();
27                  }
28
29                  app.UseRouting(routes =>
30                  {
31                      routes.MapGet("/", async context =>
32                      {
Accept Current Change | Accept Incoming Change | Accept Both Changes | Compare Changes
33      <<<<<<< HEAD (Current Change)
34                          await context.Response.WriteAsync("Hello World! Today is great in vs code!!!");
35      =======
36                          await context.Response.WriteAsync("Hello World! Today is great isn't it!!!");
37      >>>>>>> de3ccb2c20329bb033520e07cb2542c90354f9cf (Incoming Change)
38                      });
39                  });
40              }
41          }
42      }
43
```

Figure 7-29. *Code conflicts*

You have the option to compare changes, which will open a side-by-side compare view. Accepting the incoming or current change or accepting both is possible for a conflict. Or you can manually resolve the conflict. Resolve the conflict to keep the change done in VS Code and commit the change and sync with the remote Azure Git repository.

Open Visual Studio, and without doing a pull, make a change to the same code line. Then commit the change in Visual Studio to the local repo. Now when you do a fetch in Visual Studio, you can see that the incoming and outgoing changes are there. See Figure 7-30.

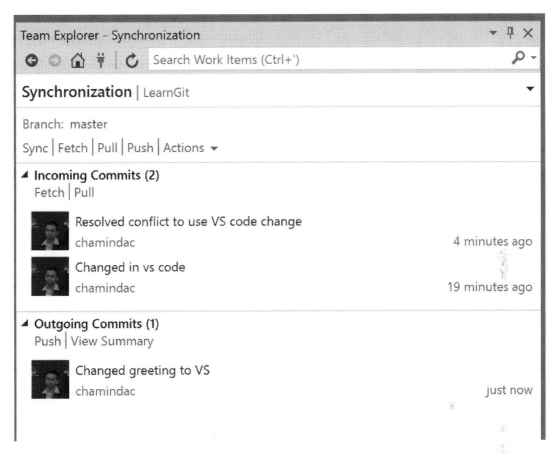

Figure 7-30. *Incoming and outgoing changes*

Now click Pull, and you will see that there is a conflict as you have changes in the same line of code. Click Conflicts to see the conflict details. See Figure 7-31.

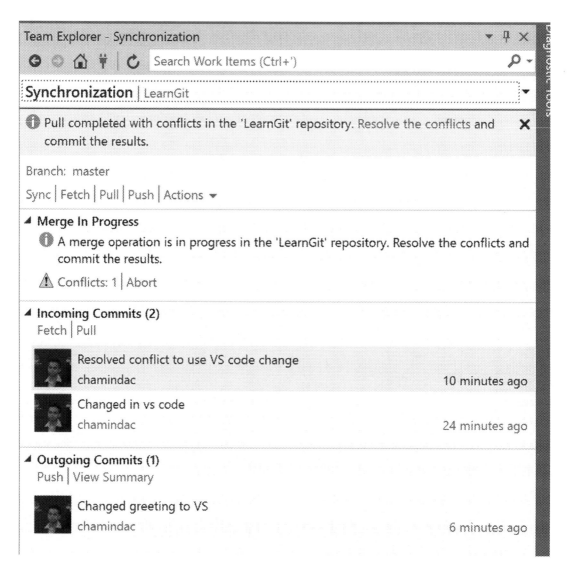

Figure 7-31. *Conflict shown in VS*

When you click Conflict, you will see the conflict files. When you click a conflicted file, you will compare the changes. You can keep the local changes or take the remote version. Click Merge to view in Compare mode and then merge. See Figure 7-32.

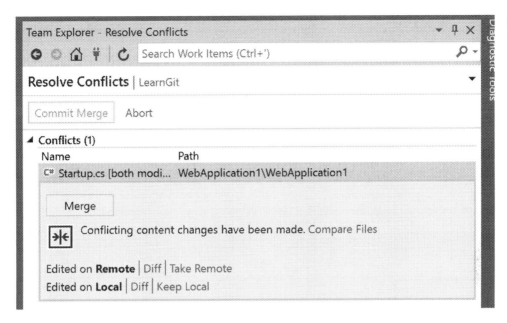

Figure 7-32. *Conflict file*

In the merge compare view, you can opt to select the remote or local change or both or manually edit and then accept the merge. See Figure 7-33.

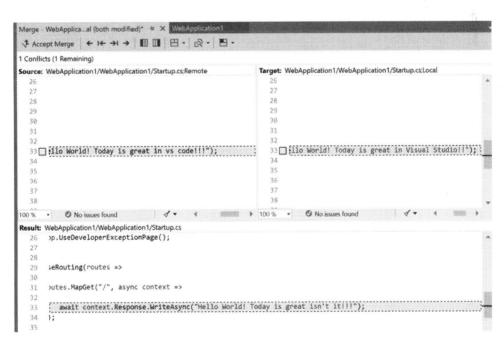

Figure 7-33. *Resolving a conflict*

Click Accept Merge after resolving conflicts with the preferred change and commit the merge when all the conflicts are resolved. See Figure 7-34.

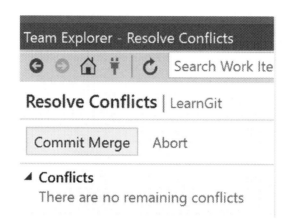

Figure 7-34. *Committing the merge*

You have to provide a comment to the merge commit and commit the changes to the local repository. Now you can sync to push the changes to the remote repo. If someone else added more changes, you may have to go through the resolve conflict procedure again.

In this lesson, we discussed how to resolve conflicts with Azure Git Repos using Visual Studio and Visual Studio Code.

Lesson 7-6: Stashing the Changes

Stashing helps you to save uncompleted work so that you can reapply it to your local repo when needed. Stash works the same way a shelveset in TFVC works. Let's look at how to use a stash in this lesson.

Prerequisites: You have completed all the lessons in this chapter and have the code available in the Azure Git repository and opened a local repo in VS Code and in Visual Studio.

In Visual Studio, open the solution from the local repo and make a code change. Then click the changes in Team Explorer; you will see the stash options on the commit changes page. See Figure 7-35.

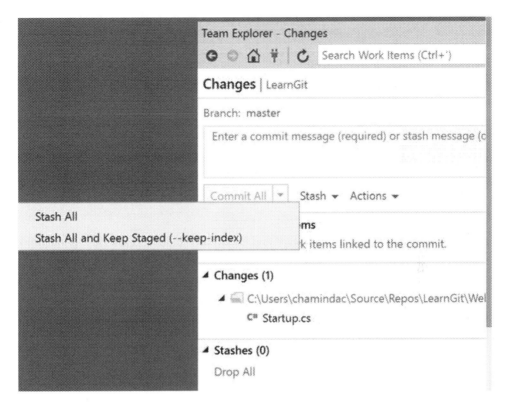

Figure 7-35. *Stash options*

Click Stash all if you want to do is create the stash and remove all the changes from the current branch. If you want to create the stash and still keep the changes, you can click Stash All and keep them staged. Once a stash is created, you can apply it to the branch again or pop it and apply. Pop will remove the stash, but Apply will keep the stash intact. See Figure 7-36.

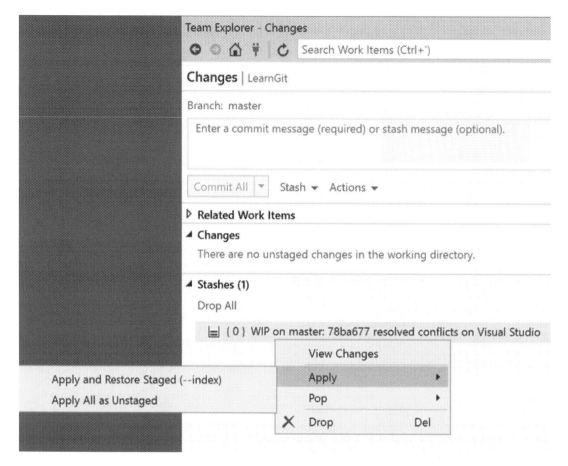

Figure 7-36. *Pop and Apply options for a stash*

In VS Code, as well, you can create a stash. When you make a change to the code, you can create a stash by typing **Git:Stash** in command palette or by using the Source Control menu stash. You will be prompted to provide a message for the stash and press Enter to create the stash. See Figure 7-37.

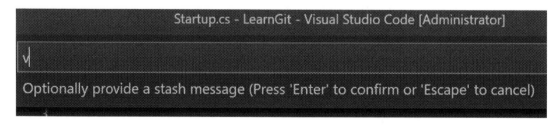

Figure 7-37. *Stash in VS Code*

You can apply or pop a stash in VS Code by clicking the relevant menu item in the Source Control menu or typing **Git: Apply Stash** or **Git: Pop Stash**. See Figure 7-38.

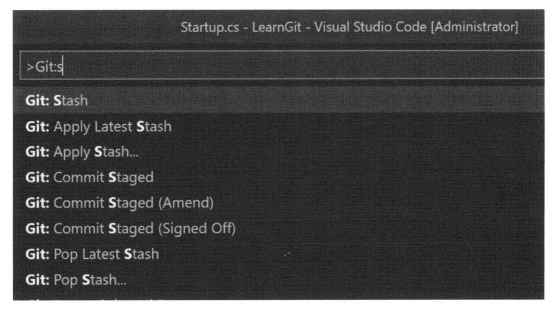

Figure 7-38. Git stash commands

The available stash will be listed, and you can pick one to pop or apply. See Figure 7-39.

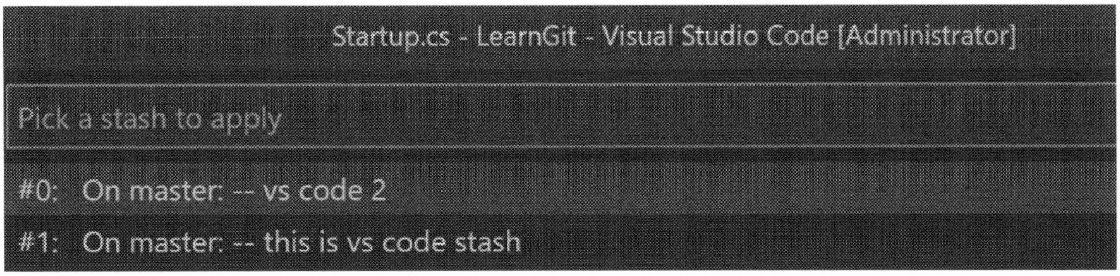

Figure 7-39. Available stash

We have explored stashes in this lesson, which are useful for keeping incomplete work saved in a Git repo using VS and VS Code.

Summary

In this chapter, we discussed how to get started with Azure Git Repos by creating a team project with an Azure Git repository in Azure DevOps. We used Visual Studio and Visual Studio Code to perform a few simple operations with Azure Git Repos in this chapter. The following is a list of common Git commands and their meaning for your reference.

- `git config`: Sets the username and e-mail for Git commits
- `git init`: Initializes a folder as a Git repo
- `git clone`: Clones a remote Git repo
- `git add`: Adds files to the staging area
- `git commit`: Commits changes to the repo
- `git diff`: Views differences not yet staged
- `git reset`: Unstages the files
- `git status`: Lists all files to be committed
- `git rm`: Deletes a file and stages it
- `git log`: Lists the version history of the current branch
- `git show`: Shows metadata and content changes of a commit
- `git tag`: Creates a tag for specific commit
- `git branch`: Creates a branch
- `git checkout`: Checks out a branch
- `git merge`: Merges a branch with another
- `git remote`: Connects the local repo to the remote server
- `git push`: Pushes changes of the current branch to the remote branch
- `git pull`: Fetches and merges changes from the remote server to the local repo
- `git stash`: Temporarily stores all tracked files

In the next chapter, we will be exploring the branching capabilities of Azure Git Repos, including the code review and pull request and branch policies application to protect branches.

CHAPTER 8

Branching with Azure Git Repos

Azure Git Repos is a distributed version control system that offers a great deal of flexibility to developers in how they use version control and share and manage code. Teams can use the tool to come up with consistent strategies to collaborate. Azure Git Repos branches help to isolate, review, share, and publish code when working with team members. You can adopt a branching strategy that suits your team's needs so that your team can collaborate in a consistent manner, spending less time on version control management and more on code development.

In this chapter, let's identify the available features in Azure Git Repos for branching, pull request management, and so, that will enable your team to efficiently collaborate, share code, and develop with the needed code isolation.

Lesson 8-1: Creating Branches

When we develop applications, we need to select the proper branching structure for the project. Branches allow team members to develop project features in a manageable way in isolation. You will learn about the Git branching features in Azure DevOps in this lesson.

Prerequisites:

- Azure DevOps project with Git version control as the source control system

- Azure DevOps project repo cloned and created with a sample MVC project

- The ability to log in to Azure DevOps as the administrator

171

© Chaminda Chandrasekara and Pushpa Herath 2020
C. Chandrasekara and P. Herath, *Hands-on Azure Repos*, https://doi.org/10.1007/978-1-4842-5425-7_8

Go to your Azure DevOps repository. Click the down arrow in front of the master branch. Select "New branch" in the pane. See Figure 8-1.

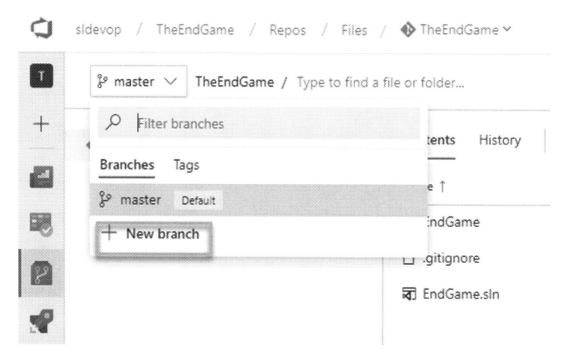

Figure 8-1. *Selecting a new branch*

The "Create a branch" window will pop up. You can give the branch a name such as feature41, select the based-on branch, and link up a work item. Finally, click "Create branch" to create the new branch. See Figure 8-2.

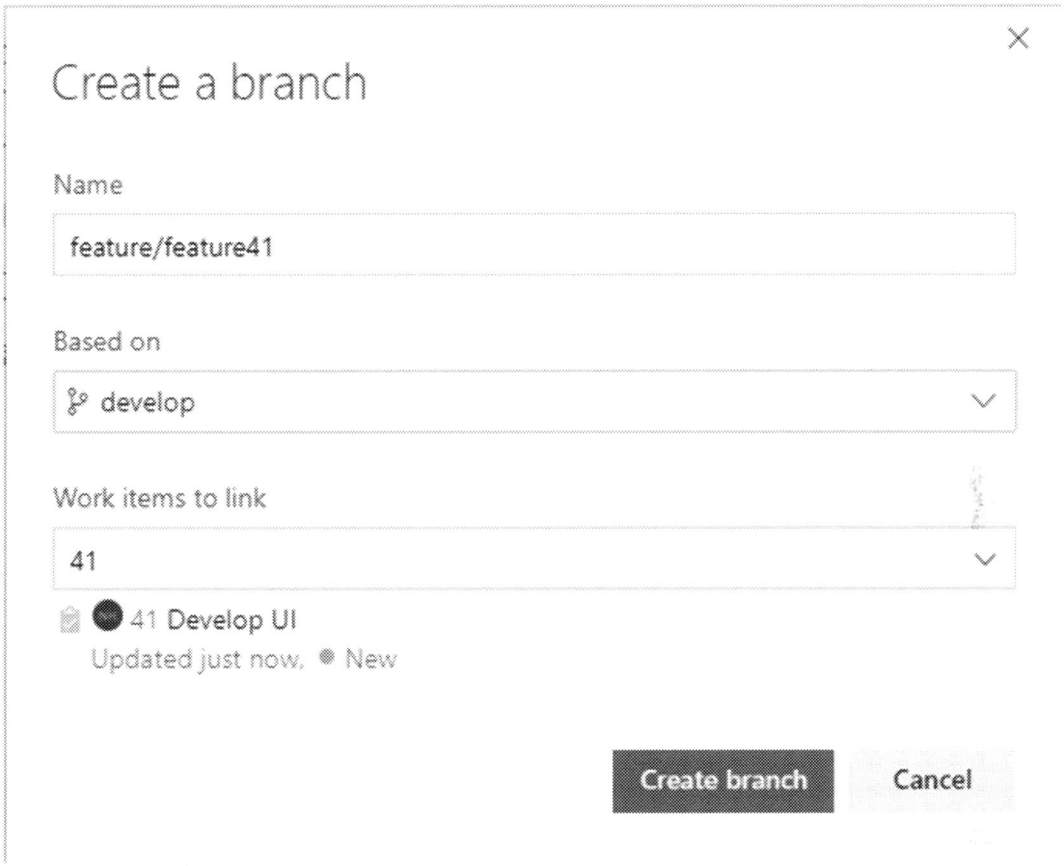

Create a branch   ✕

Name

feature/feature41

Based on

⌥ develop   ⌄

Work items to link

41   ⌄

📋 ⬤ 41 Develop UI
    Updated just now. ● New

[Create branch]   Cancel

Figure 8-2. *Creating a feature branch*

When we use a feature/branch name, we can create a feature branch inside a feature folder. Also, this feature branch is linked with the provided work item.

If you move to the Branches section under Repos, you will see the feature41 branch inside the feature folder. See Figure 8-3.

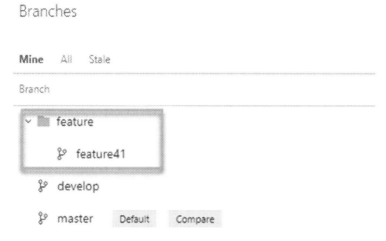

Figure 8-3. *The feature41 branch inside the feature folder*

This lesson explained how to create a Git branch using the Azure DevOps server. Also, you were able to get an idea of how to link the features with the work items while creating a new branch.

Lesson 8-2: Working with Branches in Visual Studio and VS Code

We discussed how to create Git branches with the Azure DevOps server. This lesson will explain how to work with branches in Visual Studio and VS Code. You will learn about the branch creation and checkout processes.

Prerequisites:

- Azure DevOps project with Git version control as the source control system

- Azure DevOps project repo cloned and created with a sample MVC project

- Cloned local workspace in the solution using Visual Studio

- Cloned local workspace in the solution using VS Code

In the first half of this lesson, we will discuss how to work with Azure Git Repos using the Visual Studio IDE.

Visual Studio

Go to Visual Studio. Move to the Team Explorer home. You will see the Branches link. Click the Branches link to move to the Branches section. See Figure 8-4.

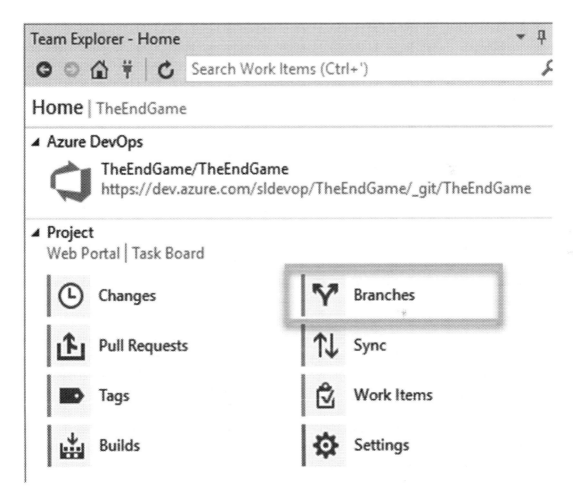

Figure 8-4. *Team Explorer branches*

The Branches page will display the active Git repositories available. See Figure 8-5.

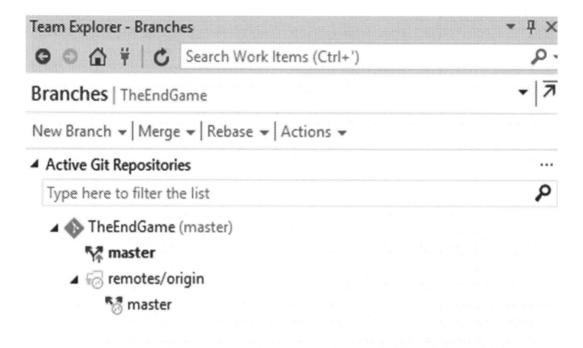

Figure 8-5. *Team Explorer's Branches page*

Let's identify the features available on the Branches page of Team Explorer.

Creating and Merging Branches

We can create new branches from here. To do that, click the New Branch link.

Give the new branch a name, and select the parent branch a name. Click the "Create a new branch" button to create a branch. See Figure 8-6.

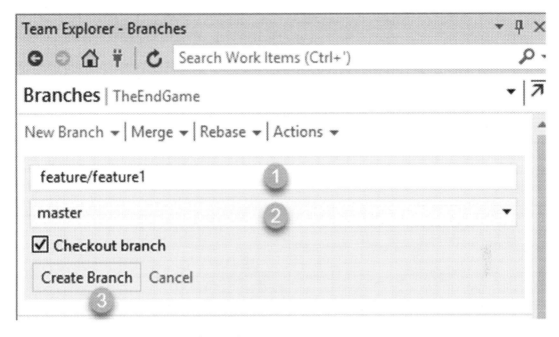

Figure 8-6. *Creating a new branch*

A new branch has been created in the local repo. We need to push the new branch to the remote repo. So, right-click the newly created branch to push the changes to the remote repository. See Figure 8-7.

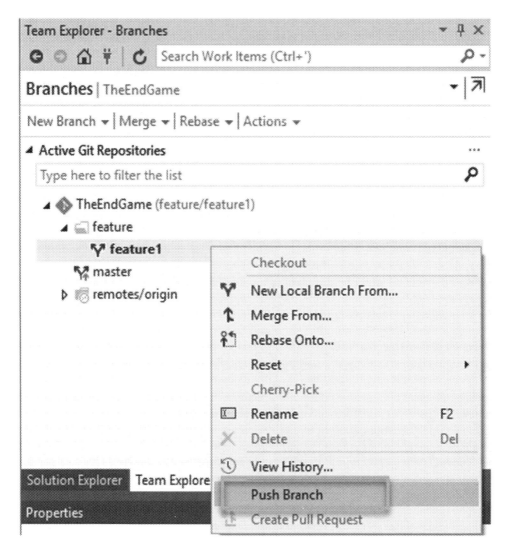

Figure 8-7. *Pushing a new branch*

If you go to Azure DevOps Repos, you will see the newly created branch is added to the remote repo.

Next we will discuss the merge options available. Click the Merge link on the Branches page. You will see the drop-down where you can set the "Merge from branch" option. By default, a merge is done to the current branch. See Figure 8-8.

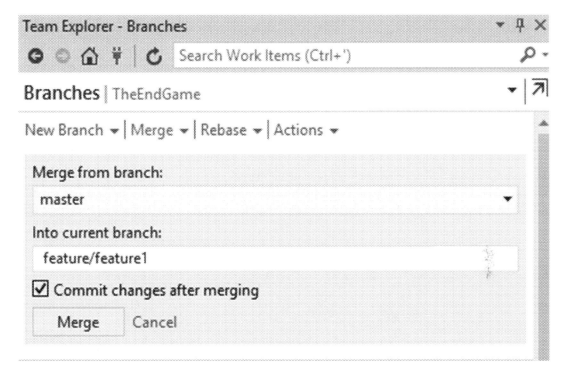

Figure 8-8. Merging branches

Rebase

We have discussed how to create a new branch and how to merge two branches. Now let's see another feature available in the Branches section of Team Explorer. That is Rebase.

Let's assume that while we are working with branches, we have created a feature1 branch from the master branch and done some development there. Let's say we have created another branch called feature2 and implemented another feature there. But after we merge the changes in the branches using a pull request, we can see the commits ordered by the commit date. Then we see that the commits done by each branch have overlapped. To keep this from happening, we can use the Rebase option. If we use Rebase, we can order the commits. We can add feature branch commits after the master branch commits. See Figure 8-9.

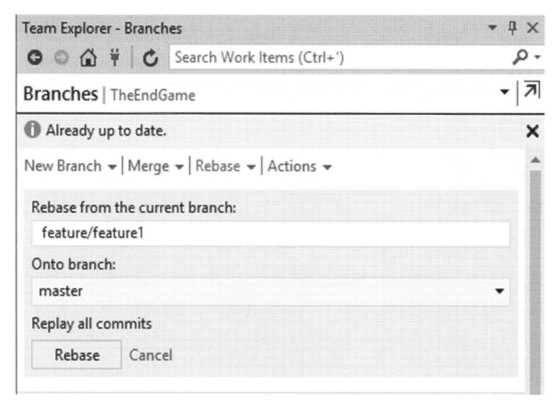

Figure 8-9. *Rebase option*

Using the Actions link in the Branches section, you can open File Explorer, open a command prompt, or view the history. See Figure 8-10.

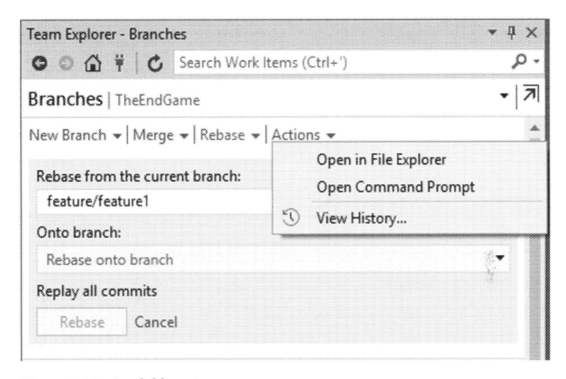

Figure 8-10. *Available actions*

So far, we have discussed the available features in Team Explorer's Branches section.

Checkout

Further, when we have multiple branches, we need to select the relevant branch from the list of the branches. To do that, you can right-click the local repo branch that you want to work on. A pane will open; click Checkout to move to the local branch. See Figure 8-11.

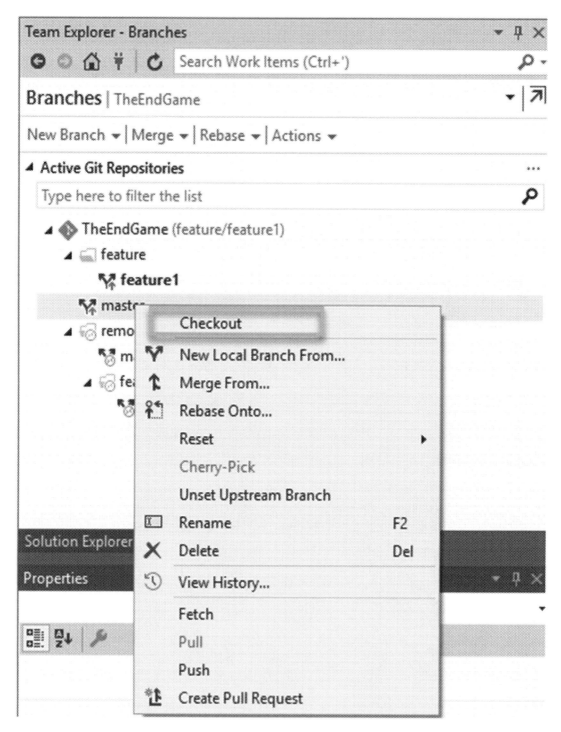

Figure 8-11. *Checking out the local repo*

VS Code

We have learned how to create new branches using Visual Studio. Let's see how to do this with VS Code.

Creating a New Branch

Open the command palette of VS Code. See Figure 8-12.

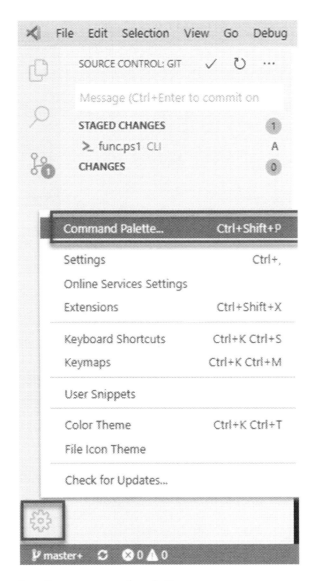

Figure 8-12. *Opening the command palette*

Type the command **Git: Create Branch From.** Then press Enter to move to the next step. See Figure 8-13.

Figure 8-13. *Selecting Git to create a branch from*

Give the new branch a name. Press Enter. See Figure 8-14.

Figure 8-14. *Branch name*

In the next step, it will allow you to select the parent branch. Go ahead and select the parent branch to create the new branch. See Figure 8-15.

Figure 8-15. *Selecting a parent branch*

So far, we have seen how we can create a new branch from an existing branch. Now let's see how we can check out the branches in VS Code.

Checkout

Open the command palette. Enter the command **Git: Checkout to**. See Figure 8-16.

Figure 8-16. *Running the Git: Checkout to command*

The branch list will open. Select the relevant branch from the list. See Figure 8-17.

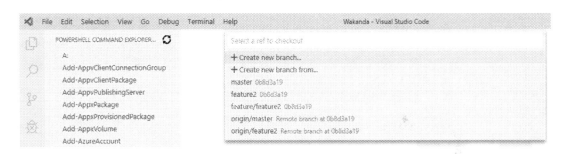

Figure 8-17. *Selecting the relevant branch*

In this lesson, we discussed how to create a new branch with Visual Studio and VS Code. Also, we discussed how to check out the branches using Visual Studio and VS Code.

Lesson 8-3: Merging Changes and Resolving Conflicts

We have discussed how to create branches with the Azure DevOps server, Visual Studio, and VS Code. This lesson will explain how to work with multiple branches using the Git source control system. We discussed TFVC in one of the previous chapters in this book. So, you will see the differences between Git and TFVC branches while reading this lesson. Now let's see how we can work with Git branches.

Prerequisites:

- Azure DevOps project with Git version control as the source control system

- Azure DevOps project repo cloned and created with a sample MVC project

- The ability to log in to Azure DevOps as the administrator

Open Visual Studio and check out the feature branch. Open the project file and modify the file. See Figure 8-18.

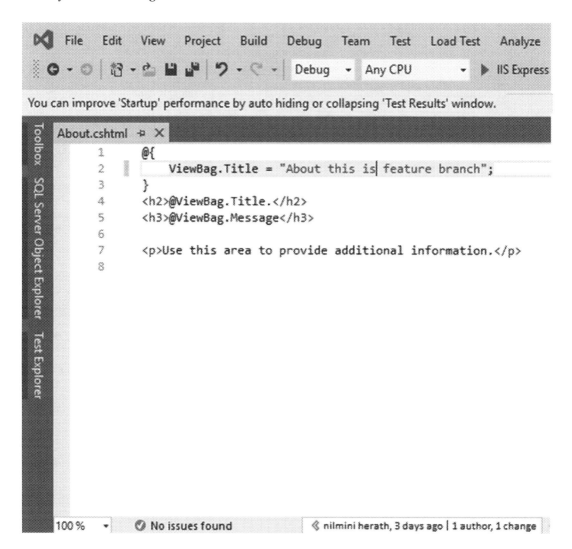

Figure 8-18. *Opening the About page and editing it*

After making modifications, we need to commit these changes to the local repository. To do that, open Team Explorer. Go to Changes. See Figure 8-19.

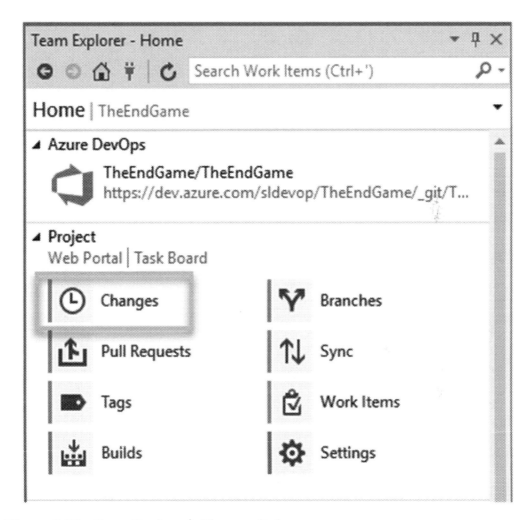

Figure 8-19. *Team Explorer's Changes link*

Clicking the Changes link will open the Changes page. On the Changes page, you will see the modified files. You can commit the changes to a local repo. See Figure 8-20.

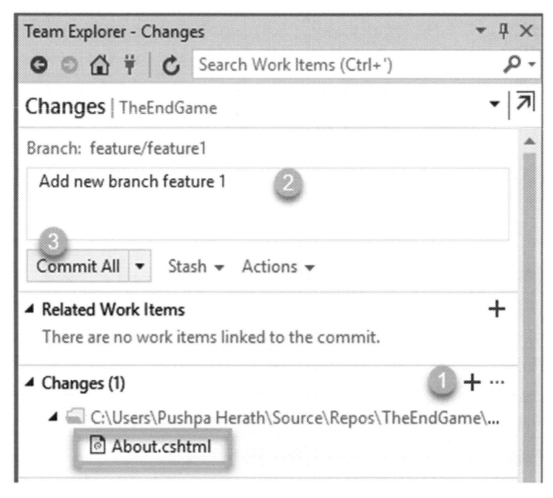

Figure 8-20. *Changes page*

1. You can stage the changes by clicking this plus icon.

2. Here you provide the commit comment.

3. Commit the changes to a local repo. After staging the changes, this button name will change to Commit Staged. If you click the arrow icon on the commit button, you will see other commit options available.

If you want to merge your changes to a remote repository, you can use the Commit and Sync option or Commit and Push option. If you only commit the changes, the changed files will display on the Sync page.

Now go to Team Explorer's Sync page. See Figure 8-21.

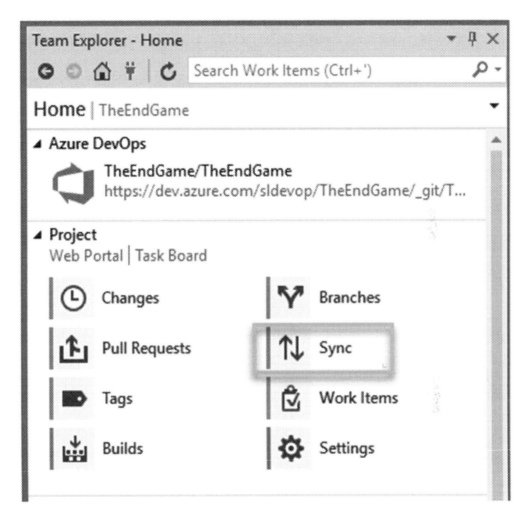

Figure 8-21. *Selecting Sync*

The Sync page will open. You will see the Outgoing commits section. Click Push to push changes to the remote branch. If you go to the Azure DevOps server, you will see the latest version of the code in the remote branch now. See Figure 8-22.

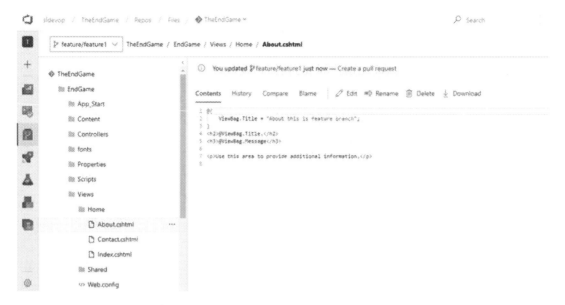

Figure 8-22. *Remote feature1 repo*

While working on the development project, team members often work on different features in parallel. So, a team will create a few feature branches for development. After completing the feature, each team will commit their changes to the remote development branch. So, when you commit the changes to the remote repo, it is required to get the latest version from the remote repo to the local repo before committing the changes. To do that, we can merge the changes from the remote repo. See Figure 8-23.

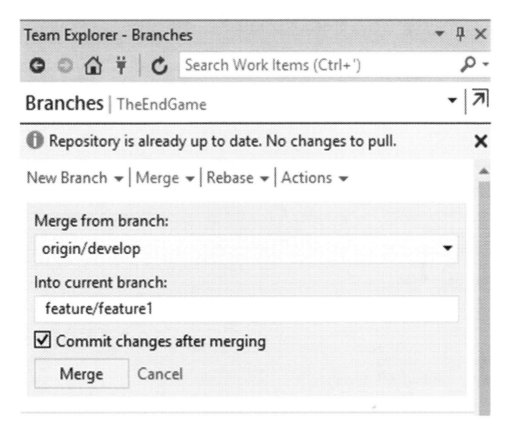

Figure 8-23. *Merging*

If there are any changes in the same file, it will mention the conflicts here. See Figure 8-24.

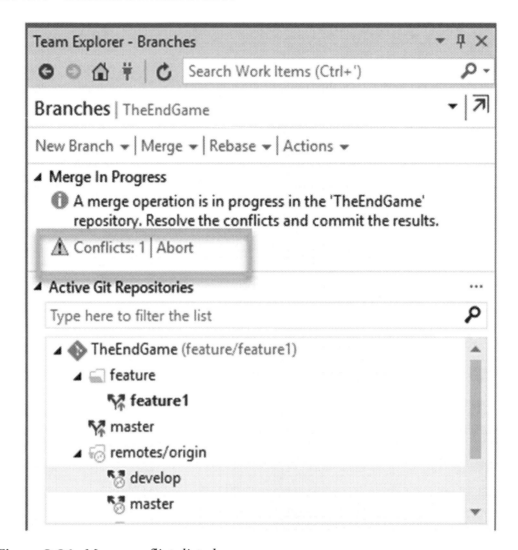

Figure 8-24. *Merge conflicts listed*

Click the Conflicts link to go to the Resolve Conflicts page. Click the file name on the Resolve Conflicts page. This will open the pane where you can find the link to compare the changes between the versions. See Figure 8-25.

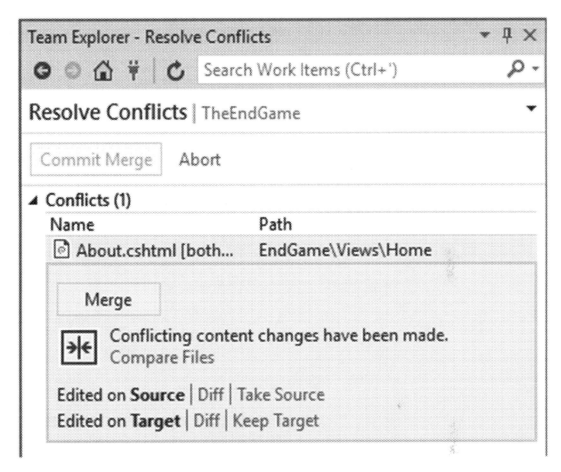

Figure 8-25. *Comparing the conflicts*

Click the Compare Files link to compare the files. See Figure 8-26.

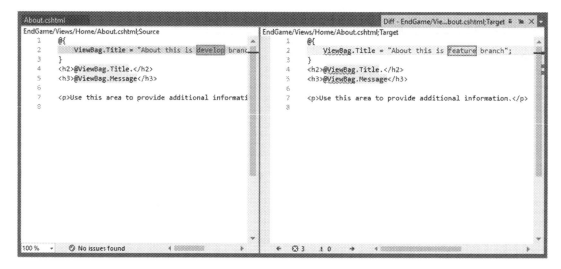

Figure 8-26. *Comparing the files*

You will see a Merge button on the Resolve Conflicts page. Click the Merge button to merge the files. You can decide on the version you need to keep in the branch. Click Accept Merge to merge the changes. See Figure 8-27.

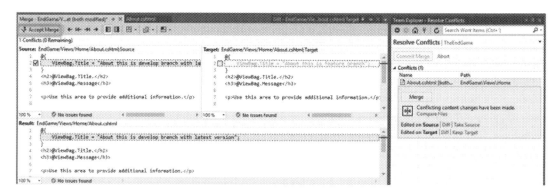

Figure 8-27. *Merging the changes*

While we work in multiple branches, we need to have a good idea of how to perform the merge correctly. Otherwise, the entire project is in trouble. If you haven't done the merge correctly, some versions and some code segments will disappear from the source. In this lesson, you learned the basics of Git branch merging and conflict resolving.

Lesson 8-4: Using Pull Requests and Code Reviews

As we all know, branch merging is an important action while working with any type of source control system. In the previous lesson, we discussed how to merge the changes between branches. But if every member of the team tried to do the merging, this process won't go smoothly. As a solution, we can control the merging permission for the team members as every member of the team shouldn't be able to merge to every branch. If the team members need to merge changes to the master or other important branches such as development, or merge a version branch from a feature branch, they can create a pull request to ask the responsible member to review and accept the modification. Let's discuss how we can do that with Azure DevOps Services in this lesson.

Prerequisites:

- Azure DevOps project with Git version control as the source control system

- Azure DevOps project repo cloned and created with a sample MVC project

- The ability to log in to Azure DevOps as the administrator

Go to the Azure DevOps Branches section. Click the three dots in front of the branch name. Select "New pull request" in the menu. See Figure 8-28.

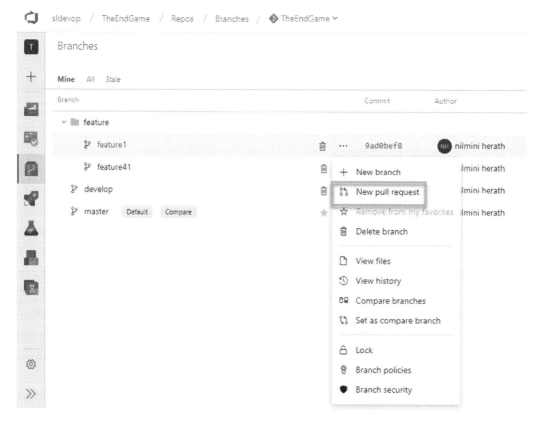

Figure 8-28. *"New pull request" menu item*

You will see the pull request creation page. You can select the branches to merge and set a reviewer on this page. See Figure 8-29.

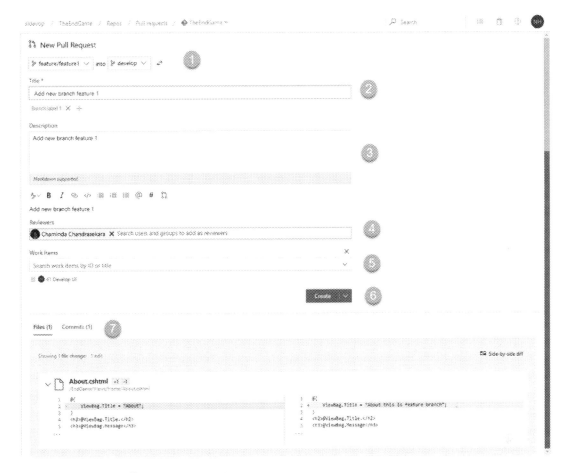

Figure 8-29. *Pull request creation*

1. Select branches to create the pull request.

2. Specify the title to request.

3. Enter a description for the request.

4. Select the reviewer.

5. Select a work item.

6. Click the Create button to create a request.

7. Do a code change comparison between the branches.

If you click the arrow in front of the Create button, you will see the "Create draft" option. See Figure 8-30.

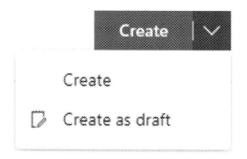

Figure 8-30. *"Create as draft" menu item*

This allows you to create a draft request to highlight to other collaborators that your code is ready to integrate with another branch. After clicking "Create as draft," you will see a page with a Publish button. Collaborators can give their comments on the changes going to be merged. See Figure 8-31.

Figure 8-31. *Draft pull request publish*

After creating a pull request, in some situations we get the conflict message shown in Figure 8-32.

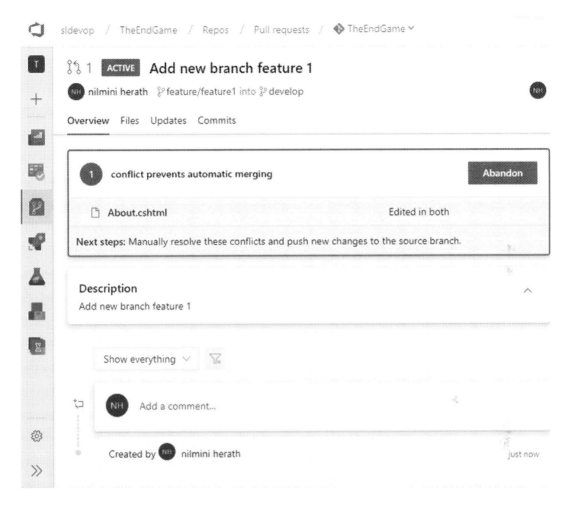

Figure 8-32. *Pull request conflict*

This happens when the development branch has some changes that the feature branch does not have. So, we need to resolve this before continuing.

To do that, go to Visual Studio. Go to the Branches section of Team Explorer.

Pull the development branch and feature branch. Merge the development branch changes with the feature branch. Now the feature branch has the latest changes from the developer branch (you might have to resolve any conflicts). Now, push the feature branch version to the remote repo.

Then go back to the Azure DevOps server. Navigate to the pull request section. You will see that the conflict in the pull request list disappears and the Approve button and the Complete button are enabled.

After creating a pull request, the approver gets a mail notification. See Figure 8-33.

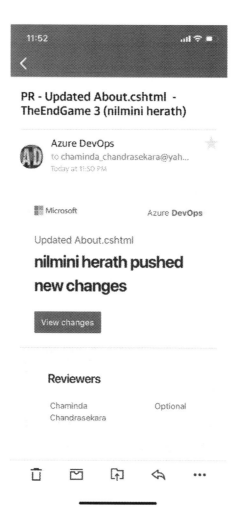

Figure 8-33. *Approver mail*

The approver can go to Azure DevOps and see the requested merge. They can decide whether this is ready to merge. If the changes are not ready, the approver can add comments by indicating the required updates. See Figure 8-34.

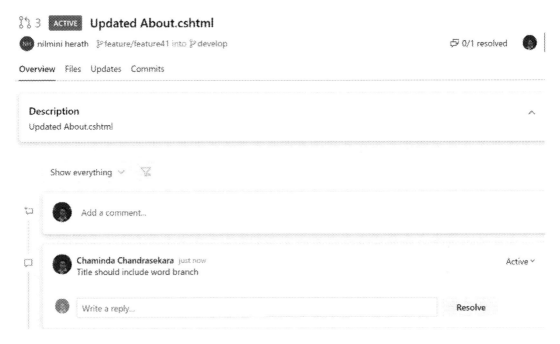

Figure 8-34. *Approver's comment*

Then the requester can read the comments and make any necessary changes. Finally, the approver will approve the request. See Figure 8-35.

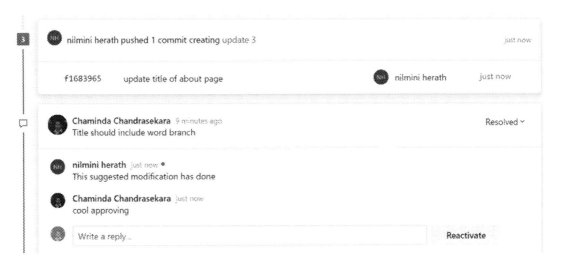

Figure 8-35. *Approving the request*

Click the arrow icon in front of the Approve button. You will see the other options available.

- **Approve**: Approve the pull request.

- **Approve with the suggestions**: Give some suggestions while approving.

- **Wait for author**: Do not approve the pull request and wait for the pull request author to address the comments. Once the comments are addressed, the author should inform the reviewer the pull request is ready for review again.

- **Reject**: Reject the request.

After approval, click the Complete button to finish the pull request. See Figure 8-36.

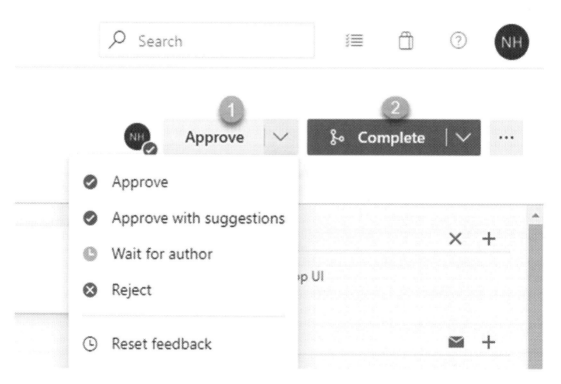

Figure 8-36. *Approving and completing the request*

After clicking the Complete button, you will see the "Complete pull request" pane. You can add a description and select the merge type from here. See Figure 8-37.

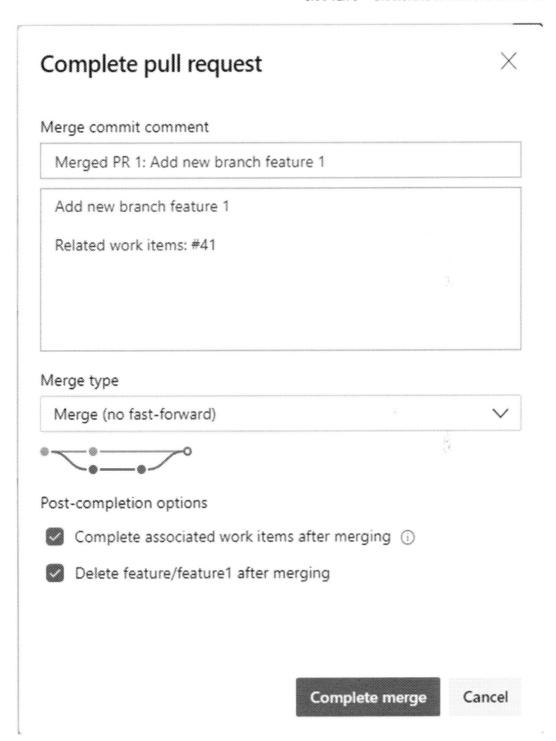

Figure 8-37. *Completing the pull request*

After completing the pull request, you will see the merge success message. See Figure 8-38.

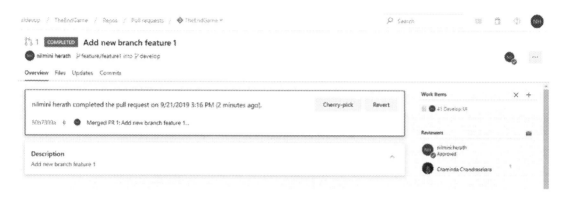

Figure 8-38. *Pull request completed*

Note that the requester can approve their own request. But in a real scenario, this process is not a best practice. So, you can control the approval by using branch policies. You will learn more about branch policies in Chapter 10.

This lesson explained how to create a pull request to request the merging between the branches. We discussed how to add reviewers to the request and how the reviewer responds to the request.

Lesson 8-5: Rebasing While Completing a Pull Request

We discussed Git branch creation, merge, and pull requests in this chapter. However, when you work with multiple branches, you might have modifications done parallelly in each branch. If you merge these changes, they will sort based on the date, and it is difficult to identify which change was done in which branch. To avoid this, there is a merge type called *rebase* that allows you to order the commits according to the branch. Let's learn how this rebase works.

Prerequisites:

- Azure DevOps project with Git version control as the source control system

- Azure DevOps project repo cloned and created with a sample MVC project

- The ability to log in to Azure DevOps as the administrator

- A pull request created, reviewed, and completed

While merging the changes between branches, there are several options available in Azure DevOps. We will discuss the rebase option in this lesson. As discussed in the previous lesson, when completing a pull request, the pull request completion pane opens. In that pane, you can select the merge type. See Figure 8-39.

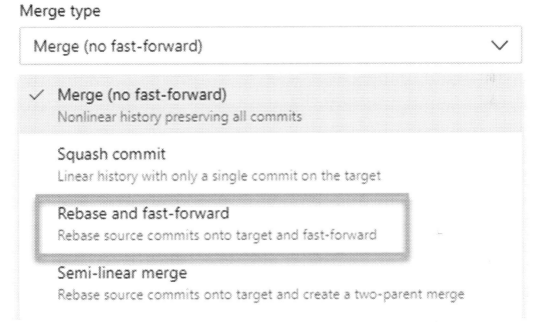

Figure 8-39. *Merge types*

Rebase is the merge type that adds all the feature branch changes/commits to the end of the developer branch changes/commits so the merge looks linear. See Figure 8-40.

Merge type

Rebase and fast-forward ⌄

Figure 8-40. *Rebase option*

In this lesson, we looked at the rebase option while completing a pull request.

Summary

This chapter explained how to work with Azure Git Repos branches using both Visual Studio and VS Code as well as the Azure DevOps Portal. We discussed how to create branches, merge changes, and resolve conflicts. Then we explored pull requests and the code review process as well as using the rebase option for a liner merge. The content of this chapter will help you to adopt a suitable branching strategy for your team since you have gained a good understanding of the available features in Azure Git Repos.

In the next chapter, we will discuss how to use the command-line options to work with Azure Git Repos.

CHAPTER 9

Using the Command Line with Azure Git Repos

Developers who use Git for source control mostly use the command line to perform actions, such as cloning repositories and pulling/pushing code. Many editors such as Visual Studio or Visual Studio Code support performing actions with Azure Git Repos using menu items. However, developers who are used to using Git as their version control system may prefer using the command line to work with Git Repos.

In this chapter, let's look at some examples of using the Azure Git Repos command line to clone repositories, push code, pull others' changes, etc. If you are beginner with Git Repos, this chapter will help you to get the basic understanding of how to use the command line with Azure Git Repos.

Lesson 9-1: Getting Started with the Command Line

As the first lesson, we need to get our development machines ready to use Azure Git Repos with the Git command line. Let's look at how to set up a machine to use a command line for Git.

Let's install Visual Studio Code as the preferred editor for the code editing in this chapter. Since the chapter uses Windows 10 as the OS, we can download VS Code for Windows from `https://code.visualstudio.com/#alt-downloads` and install it on the machine. You have the option to set up VS Code for the current user by installing the user setup, or you can download the system setup to install it for all users. Install the DotNet Core SDK on your machine. You can download it from `https://dotnet.microsoft.com/download`.

© Chaminda Chandrasekara and Pushpa Herath 2020
C. Chandrasekara and P. Herath, *Hands-on Azure Repos*, https://doi.org/10.1007/978-1-4842-5425-7_9

You have to install Git for your operating system to allow you to create local Git repositories and use Git commands. Go to `https://git-scm.com/downloads` and download Git for your operating system. In this chapter, you'll use Windows as the operating system. So, let's download Windows for Git and install it on the machine if it is not already installed. While installing, select VS Code as the default editor for Git. See Figure 9-1.

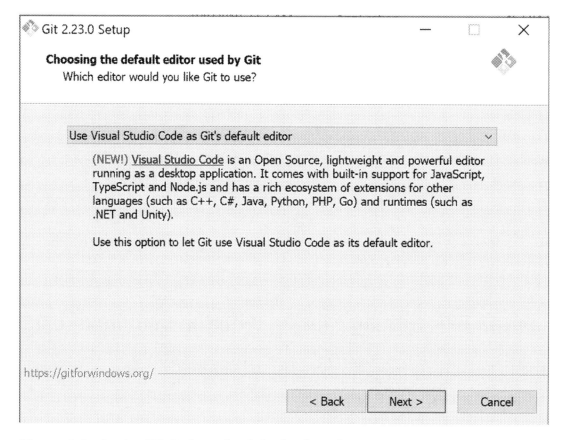

Figure 9-1. *Setting VS Code as the default editor for Git*

Let's get Azure CLI and add the Azure DevOps extension to Azure CLI so we can work with Azure Git Repos with a command line. You can set up Azure CLI following the instructions at `https://docs.microsoft.com/en-us/cli/azure/install-azure-cli?view=azure-cli-latest`. Once Azure CLI is installed, open a PowerShell window in administrator mode. The execute `az --version` to check the version installed. See Figure 9-2.

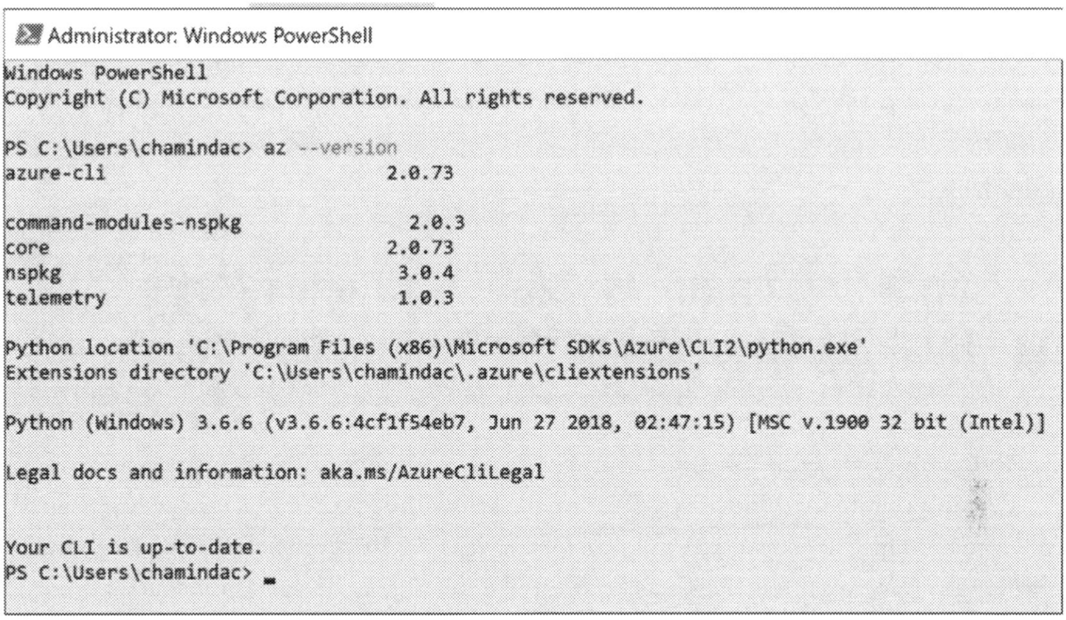

```
Administrator: Windows PowerShell
Windows PowerShell
Copyright (C) Microsoft Corporation. All rights reserved.

PS C:\Users\chamindac> az --version
azure-cli                          2.0.73

command-modules-nspkg                2.0.3
core                                2.0.73
nspkg                                3.0.4
telemetry                            1.0.3

Python location 'C:\Program Files (x86)\Microsoft SDKs\Azure\CLI2\python.exe'
Extensions directory 'C:\Users\chamindac\.azure\cliextensions'

Python (Windows) 3.6.6 (v3.6.6:4cf1f54eb7, Jun 27 2018, 02:47:15) [MSC v.1900 32 bit (Intel)]

Legal docs and information: aka.ms/AzureCliLegal


Your CLI is up-to-date.
PS C:\Users\chamindac>
```

Figure 9-2. *Azure CLI*

To add the Azure DevOps extension to Azure CLI, execute `az extension add --name azure-devops`. Then you can execute `az –version` to check that the Azure DevOps extension for Azure CLI is installed. See Figure 9-3.

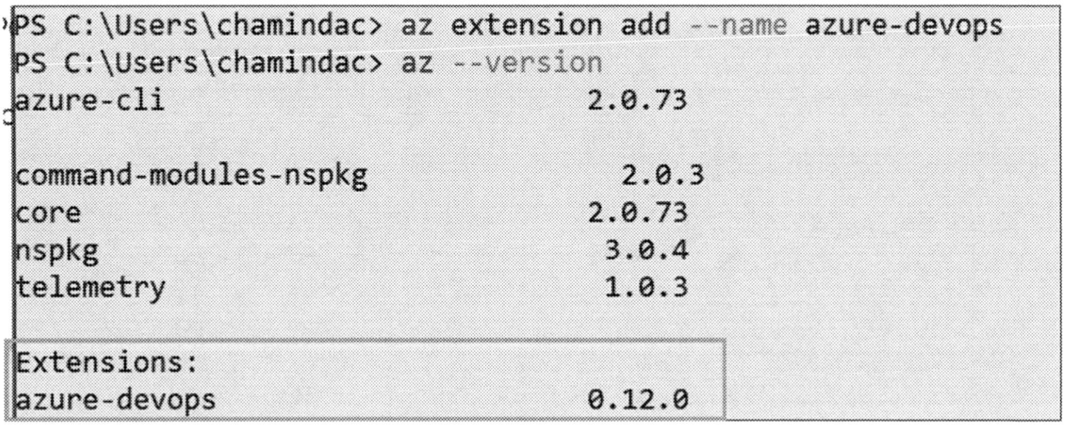

```
PS C:\Users\chamindac> az extension add --name azure-devops
PS C:\Users\chamindac> az --version
azure-cli                          2.0.73

command-modules-nspkg                2.0.3
core                                2.0.73
nspkg                                3.0.4
telemetry                            1.0.3

Extensions:
azure-devops                        0.12.0
```

Figure 9-3. *Azure DevOps extension*

In this lesson, we set up VS Code as the code editor and Git for Windows to support Git operations on a Windows 10 machine. Then we set up Azure CLI and the Azure DevOps extension to support the command line for Azure Git Repos. You can use the same tools in a Linux or macOS environment and perform the lessons in this chapter in a similar way.

Lesson 9-2: Cloning an Azure Git Repository and Pushing Code Using the Command Line

Let's discuss how to clone and push code to a newly created Azure Git repository using the command line in this lesson.

Create a new team project in Azure. We described how to set up a new team project in Azure DevOps in the *Hands-On Azure Boards* book of this series. To create the new Azure Git repository in the team project, you first need to log in to Azure DevOps. You can do this by executing az login if you are using an Azure Active Directory account or Microsoft account. If you want to use a personal access token (PAT) in Azure DevOps, you can execute az devops login. In a PowerShell window, type az login, and you will be prompted to log in to your account. See Figure 9-4.

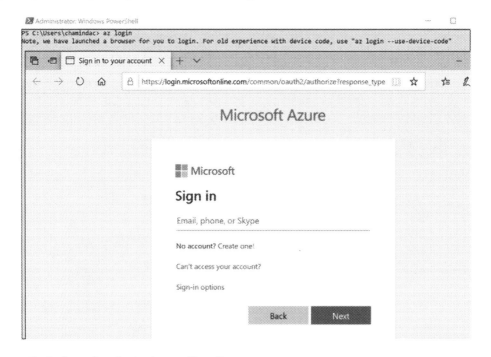

Figure 9-4. *Logging in to Azure DevOps*

Once you log in successfully, you can execute `az repos create --name GitCmd01 --organization` https://dev.azure.com/yourorg `--project yourteamproject` to create a new Azure Git repository in your team project. See Figure 9-5.

```
PS C:\Users\chamindac> az repos create --name GitCmd01 --organization https://dev.azure.com/chamindac --project LearnGit
{
  "defaultBranch": null,
  "id": "c74f95ce-83b9-4fce-9333-7856bd40786d",
  "isFork": null,
  "name": "GitCmd01",
  "parentRepository": null,
  "project": {
    "abbreviation": null,
    "defaultTeamImageUrl": null,
    "description": null,
    "id": "87187580-b408-43a8-8c39-70726c0e9b36",
    "lastUpdateTime": "2019-09-08T15:18:05.817Z",
    "name": "LearnGit",
    "revision": 459109619,
    "state": "wellFormed",
    "url": "https://chamindac.visualstudio.com/_apis/projects/87187580-b408-43a8-8c39-70726c0e9b36",
    "visibility": "private"
  },
  "remoteUrl": "https://chamindac.visualstudio.com/DefaultCollection/LearnGit/_git/GitCmd01",
  "size": 0,
  "sshUrl": "chamindac@vs-ssh.visualstudio.com:v3/chamindac/LearnGit/GitCmd01",
  "validRemoteUrls": null,
  "webUrl": "https://chamindac.visualstudio.com/DefaultCollection/LearnGit/_git/GitCmd01"
}
PS C:\Users\chamindac> _
```

Figure 9-5. *Creating a new Azure Git repository*

In the Azure DevOps web portal, you can see the new Azure Git repo created. Copy the clone URL of the new Azure Git repo. See Figure 9-6.

Figure 9-6. *Copying the clone URL*

Create a folder on your development machine named Repos. Open Git bash installed with Git as per the instructions in Lesson 9-1. Change the directory to the Repos folder in Git bash and then execute a Git clone with the URL of Azure DevOps Git repository. You will be prompted to log in to your Azure Git repository. Provide credentials and log in. See Figure 9-7.

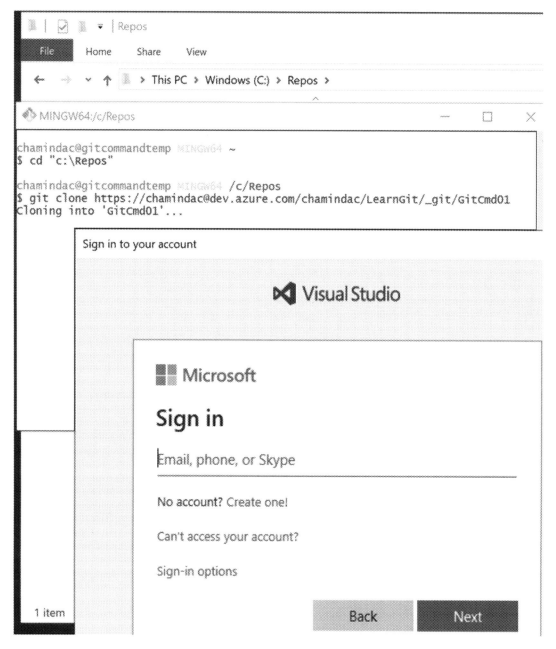

Figure 9-7. *Cloning the repo*

Launch Visual Studio Code and open the Repos/GitCmd01 folder in VS Code. Then press Ctrl+Shift+` or use the menu to open the terminal of VS Code. In the terminal, type dotnet new webapp to create a .NET Core web app in the folder. See Figure 9-8.

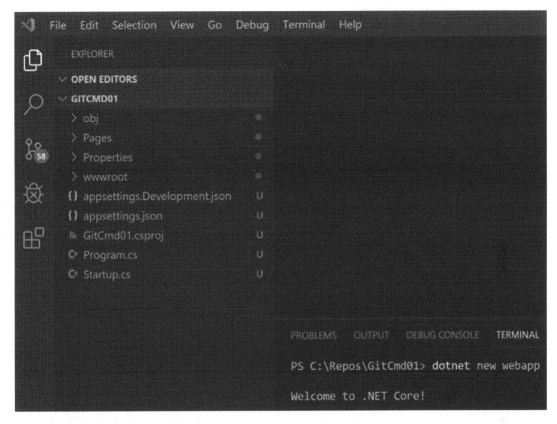

Figure 9-8. *Creating a new .NET Core web app*

You can add an extension to VS Code by pressing Ctrl+Shift+X. Search for *gitignore generator*. The install the .gitignore Generator, as shown in Figure 9-9.

Figure 9-9. *Installing the .gitignore Generator for VS Code*

Press Ctrl+Shift+P to launch a command palette in VS code. Type `generate .gitignore` in the command palette and press Enter. See Figure 9-10.

Figure 9-10. *Generating a .gitignore file*

In the next step, in the command palette, select visualstudiocode, windows, aspnetcore, and csharp, and click OK. See Figure 9-11 (the figure shows only two options selected, but you have to select all four).

Figure 9-11. *Selecting the app type for .gitignore*

A `.gitignore` file will be added to the code folder. Now we have to commit and push the code to Azure Git Repos. We can easily do this with VS Code. However, let's try to commit and push the code using a command line as in this lesson our purpose is to learn the command line with Azure Git Repos.

Open up the Git bash and change the directory to `Repos/GitCmd01`. You will see the branch name is master. See Figure 9-12.

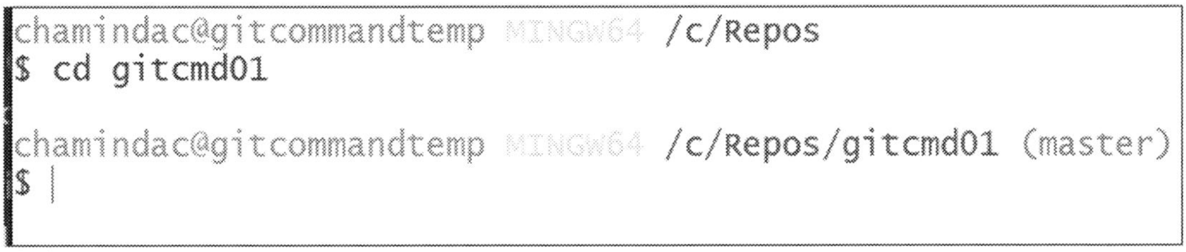

```
chamindac@gitcommandtemp MINGW64 /c/Repos
$ cd gitcmd01

chamindac@gitcommandtemp MINGW64 /c/Repos/gitcmd01 (master)
$ |
```

Figure 9-12. *Master branch*

Then execute a `git add .` to add the changes to Git as staged. You can commit the changes to an Azure Git repository locally by executing `git commit -m "the commit message"`. But since you have not provided the user information to Git, you might get an error message. See Figure 9-13.

```
chamindac@gitcommandtemp MINGW64 /c/Repos/gitcmd01 (master)
$ git add .

chamindac@gitcommandtemp MINGW64 /c/Repos/gitcmd01 (master)
$ git commit -m "adding sample code via command line"

*** Please tell me who you are.

Run

  git config --global user.email "you@example.com"
  git config --global user.name "Your Name"

to set your account's default identity.
Omit --global to set the identity only in this repository.

fatal: unable to auto-detect email address (got 'chamindac@gitcommandtemp.(none)
')

chamindac@gitcommandtemp MINGW64 /c/Repos/gitcmd01 (master)
$ |
```

Figure 9-13. *Attempting the git commit command*

As instructed in the message, you can execute a `git config –global user.email` command with your Azure DevOps account's login e-mail address to get the user information defined for Git. If you just want to set the identity to this repository, you can omit using `–global` in the command. Then you can attempt the commit again, which will succeed. See Figure 9-14.

Figure 9-14. *Setting the repository user and committing*

Now that we have the code committed to the local Azure Git repo, we can push it to the remote Azure Git repository by executing a `git push`. See Figure 9-15.

```
chamindac@gitcommandtemp MINGW64 /c/Repos/gitcmd01 (master)
$ git push
Enumerating objects: 72, done.
Counting objects: 100% (72/72), done.
Delta compression using up to 4 threads
Compressing objects: 100% (68/68), done.
Writing objects: 100% (72/72), 726.67 KiB | 3.38 MiB/s, done.
Total 72 (delta 11), reused 0 (delta 0)
remote: Analyzing objects... (72/72) (50 ms)
remote: Storing packfile... done (232 ms)
remote: Storing index... done (83 ms)
To https://dev.azure.com/chamindac/LearnGit/_git/GitCmd01
 * [new branch]      master -> master

chamindac@gitcommandtemp MINGW64 /c/Repos/gitcmd01 (master)
$
```

Figure 9-15. *Pushing to a remote Azure Git repository*

Go to Azure DevOps in a browser and check the GitCmd01 repository. You will be able to see that the new code pushed is available in the master branch. See Figure 9-16.

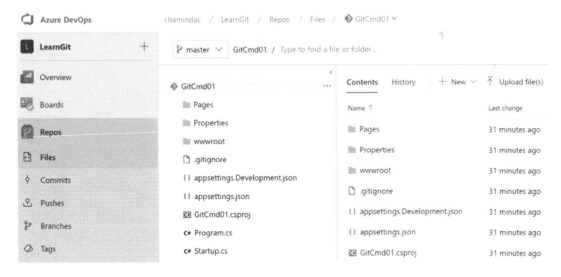

Figure 9-16. *Azure Git repository with code*

In this lesson, we discussed how to create an Azure Git repository, and then we cloned it using the command line to the local machine. Then we added some code and explored how to commit and push the code to Azure Git Repos with the command line.

Lesson 9-3: Creating a Git Repository Locally and Pushing It to Azure Git Repos

Let's see how we can create a local repository first and then push that to Azure Git Repos. This will help you to understand how you can use your existing local Git repositories and create Azure Git Repos repositories with them.

Create a directory in your machine named GItCmd02. Then change the directory to the newly created folder. See Figure 9-17.

```
chamindac@gitcommandtemp MINGW64 /c/repos
$ mkdir GitCmd02

chamindac@gitcommandtemp MINGW64 /c/repos
$ cd GitCmd02

chamindac@gitcommandtemp MINGW64 /c/repos/GitCmd02
$
```

Figure 9-17. *Creating a directory*

Execute git init to convert the folder into a Git repository. See Figure 9-18.

```
chamindac@gitcommandtemp MINGW64 /c/repos/GitCmd02
$ git init
Initialized empty Git repository in C:/Repos/GitCmd02/.git/

chamindac@gitcommandtemp MINGW64 /c/repos/GitCmd02 (master)
$
```

Figure 9-18. *Initializing a Git repository*

Open the GitCmd02 folder in VS Code, and in the VS Code terminal execute dotnet new webapp to create a .NET Core web application. See Figure 9-19.

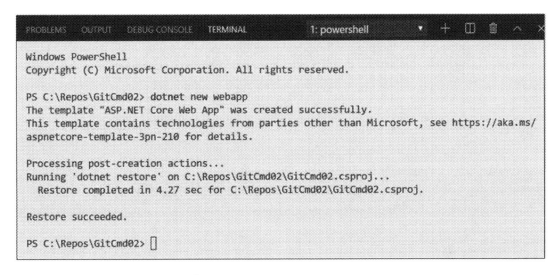

Figure 9-19. *Creating a web app*

Then do a git add . and add the user's e-mail to the repository. Execute git commit with a commit message to commit the code to the local Git Repos master branch in the GitCmd02 folder. See Figure 9-20.

```
chamindac@gitcommandtemp MINGW64 /c/repos/GitCmd02 (master)
$ git add .
warning: LF will be replaced by CRLF in .gitignore.
The file will have its original line endings in your working directory

chamindac@gitcommandtemp MINGW64 /c/repos/GitCmd02 (master)
$ git config user.email "chaminda_chandrasekara@yahoo.com"

chamindac@gitcommandtemp MINGW64 /c/repos/GitCmd02 (master)
$ git commit -m "Add code to local GitCmd02 repo master branch"
[master (root-commit) c8490b3] Add code to local GitCmd02 repo master branch
 54 files changed, 40194 insertions(+)
 create mode 100644 .gitignore
 create mode 100644 GitCmd02.csproj
 create mode 100644 Pages/Error.cshtml
 create mode 100644 Pages/Error.cshtml.cs
 create mode 100644 Pages/Index.cshtml
 create mode 100644 Pages/Index.cshtml.cs
 create mode 100644 Pages/Privacy.cshtml
 create mode 100644 Pages/Privacy.cshtml.cs
```

Figure 9-20. *Committing the code*

Now that we have the code committed to the local repository, we have to create a new repository in Azure DevOps to push the local repo to Azure DevOps. Open a PowerShell window and use `az login` or `az devops login` (if you are using a PAT) to log in to Azure DevOps. Then execute `az repos create --name GitCmd02 --organization https://dev.azure.com/your/orgname --project teamproject` to create an Azure Git repo named `GitCmd02`. See Figure 9-21.

```
PS C:\Users\chamindac> az repos create --name GitCmd02 --organization https://dev.azure.com/chamindac --project LearnGit
{
  "defaultBranch": null,
  "id": "5e6677a9-a929-493b-a2ba-30fa3cba2204",
  "isFork": null,
  "name": "GitCmd02",
  "parentRepository": null,
  "project": {
    "abbreviation": null,
    "defaultTeamImageUrl": null,
    "description": null,
    "id": "87187580-b408-43a8-8c39-70726c0e9b36",
    "lastUpdateTime": "2019-09-15T08:00:05.567Z",
    "name": "LearnGit",
    "revision": 459109620,
    "state": "wellFormed",
    "url": "https://chamindac.visualstudio.com/_apis/projects/87187580-b408-43a8-8c39-70726c0e9b36",
    "visibility": "private"
  },
  "remoteUrl": "https://chamindac.visualstudio.com/DefaultCollection/LearnGit/_git/GitCmd02",
  "size": 0,
  "sshUrl": "chamindac@vs-ssh.visualstudio.com:v3/chamindac/LearnGit/GitCmd02",
  "validRemoteUrls": null,
  "webUrl": "https://chamindac.visualstudio.com/DefaultCollection/LearnGit/_git/GitCmd02"
}
PS C:\Users\chamindac> _
```

Figure 9-21. *Creating an Azure Git repository*

Copy the remote URL in the output of the command `az repo create`. Then open the Git bash and navigate to the local repository folder called `GitCmd02`. Execute `git remote add origin "remote/clone url"`. See Figure 9-22.

```
chamindac@gitcommandtemp MINGW64 /c/repos/gitcmd02 (master)
$ git remote add origin "https://chamindac.visualstudio.com/DefaultCollection/Le
arnGit/_git/GitCmd02"

chamindac@gitcommandtemp MINGW64 /c/repos/gitcmd02 (master)
$ |
```

Figure 9-22. *Connecting the local repository to the Azure Git repository*

Run the command `git push origin master` to push the changes to the remote Azure Git repository. You will be prompted for credentials; log in with your Azure DevOps account. See Figure 9-23.

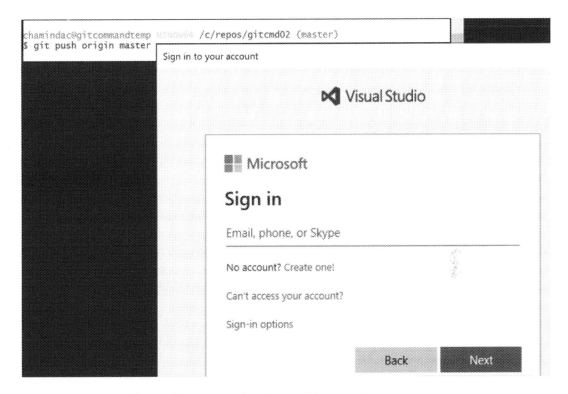

Figure 9-23. *Pushing changes to the Azure Git repository*

You can see that the code is available in the Azure Git repository after being pushed. See Figure 9-24.

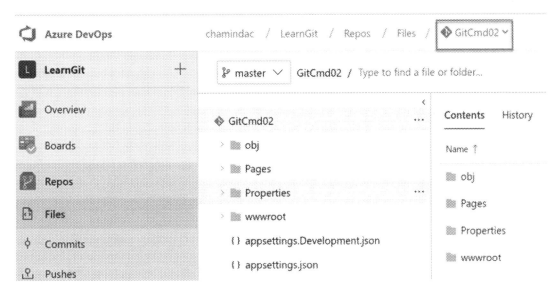

Figure 9-24. *Code pushed to the Azure Git repository*

In this lesson, you learned how to use a local available Git repository and push the code in that repository to an Azure Git repository.

Lesson 9-4: Creating Azure Git Repo Branches Using the Command Line

Now that we have the code in remote Azure Git repo, we can create branches using the Azure DevOps web interface, as discussed in Chapter 8. However, in this lesson, let's see how we can create a branch locally and push it to the remote Azure Git repository.

Prerequisites: You followed the previous lessons of this chapter.

Open Git and change directories to the cloned repository of Lesson 9-2. You should be in the master branch of the repository. If you execute the `git branch --list` command, you will be able to see that only the master branch is available. See Figure 9-25.

```
chamindac@gitcommandtemp MINGW64 /c/Repos/gitcmd01 (master)
$ git branch --list
* master

chamindac@gitcommandtemp MINGW64 /c/Repos/gitcmd01 (master)
$
```

Figure 9-25. *Listing branches*

Let's try to create a branch in the local Git repository and push it to the remote Azure Git repository. Execute `git branch develop` to create a branch called Develop from the master. Then you can switch to the Develop branch by executing `git switch develop` or `git checkout develop`. See Figure 9-26.

```
chamindac@gitcommandtemp MINGW64 /c/Repos/gitcmd01 (master)
$ git branch develop

chamindac@gitcommandtemp MINGW64 /c/Repos/gitcmd01 (master)
$ git switch develop
Switched to branch 'develop'

chamindac@gitcommandtemp MINGW64 /c/Repos/gitcmd01 (develop)
```

Figure 9-26. *Creating and switching to a new branch*

To push this new branch to the remote Azure Git repository, we cannot just use git push as there is no such remote branch available. We should execute git push --set-upstream origin develop to set the remote Develop branch and push the locally created Develop branch to the remote Azure Git repository. See Figure 9-27.

```
chamindac@gitcommandtemp MINGW64 /c/Repos/gitcmd01 (develop)
$ git push --set-upstream origin develop
Total 0 (delta 0), reused 0 (delta 0)
To https://dev.azure.com/chamindac/LearnGit/_git/GitCmd01
 * [new branch]      develop -> develop
Branch 'develop' set up to track remote branch 'develop' from 'origin'.

chamindac@gitcommandtemp MINGW64 /c/Repos/gitcmd01 (develop)
$
```

Figure 9-27. *Pushing the new branch Develop to the remote Azure Git repository*

You can see that the new branch is available now in the Azure Git repository by going to the web interface of Azure DevOps. See Figure 9-28.

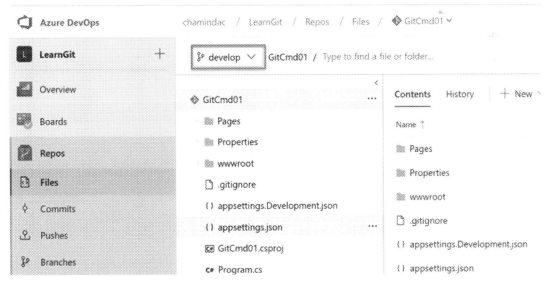

Figure 9-28. *Develop branch pushed*

You can check out a branch with `git checkout branchname` and then edit the code in the branch. Then you can commit the changes with `git add .` and `git commit`. To merge a branch to a given branch, you have to first check out the target branch and then execute `git merge sourcebranchname`. You can find a detailed command-line reference in the documentation at `https://docs.microsoft.com/en-us/azure/devops/repos/git/command-prompt?view=azure-devops`.

Summary

In this chapter, we explored managing Azure Git Repos repository with the command line. We looked at how to clone a repo and add code to it. Additionally, we discussed how to use a local Git repository to create an Azure Git repository. Then we explored the branching and discussed a few more commands. This chapter can be considered a good start to working with Azure Git Repos using the command line, and you can use the command-line reference available at `https://docs.microsoft.com/en-us/azure/devops/repos/git/command-prompt?view=azure-devops` to learn more.

In the next chapter, let's discuss the security and permissions related to Azure Git Repos.

CHAPTER 10

Azure Git Repos: Security

Security is an important aspect of any source control system. Permissions involve rights to create branches, commit code, check out branches, create pull requests, set permissions to merge changes into a given branch, etc.

In Azure Git Repos, you might want to protect your stable branches and apply additional security on given branches for specific teams. You might want to keep multiple repositories in a team project and apply permissions to individuals or teams in the team project.

In this chapter, you'll get a quick overview of all the permissions and permission levels available for Azure Git Repos and the options available for branch policies to protect Azure Git Repos branches.

Lesson 10-1: Setting Azure Git Repos Permissions

In Azure Git Repos, permissions can be applied for all repositories, individual repos, and their branches. Let's explore each of these permission levels.

Prerequisites: You have a team project with Azure Git Repos with branches and have code available in the repositories.

First navigate to a team project where you have multiple Git repositories with branches. Then click the "Project settings" tab and click Repositories in the Repos section. You will see a list of Azure Git repositories. See Figure 10-1.

© Chaminda Chandrasekara and Pushpa Herath 2020
C. Chandrasekara and P. Herath, *Hands-on Azure Repos*, https://doi.org/10.1007/978-1-4842-5425-7_10

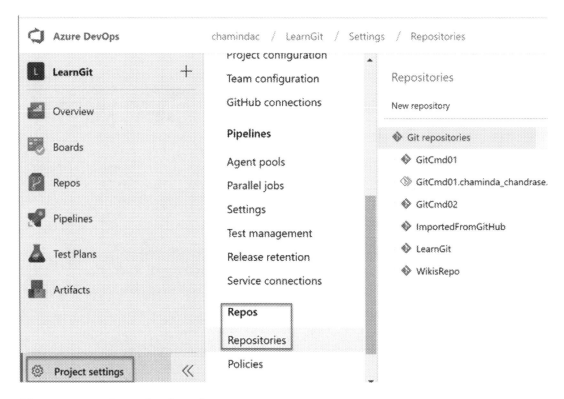

Figure 10-1. *Repositories tab*

In all the repositories, you can see there are several permissions available for each Azure DevOps security group. (We discussed these security groups in detail in the *Hands-on Azure Boards* book of this series.) See Figure 10-2.

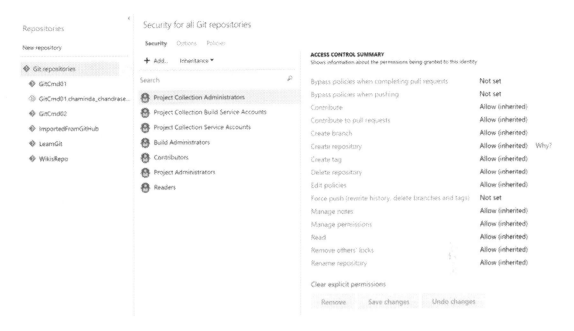

Figure 10-2. *All repositories permissions*

Some permissions are marked as Allow (inherited), which shows that the permission to a selected user or group is inherited from its membership in other groups or teams. You can click Why, which appears when you move your mouse over these permissions, to check how the permission is inherited. When a permission is denied, it gets priority always. If Denied is not set, the inheritance gets applied for the permission. Or you can explicitly allow a permission. Clicking a permission value changes the value from Not Set to Allow and from Deny to Not Set. All Git repositories permissions shown in Figure 10-2 are explained here:

- **Bypass policies when completing pull requests**: Branch policies can be ignored, and the user with this permission can complete and merge a pull request to any branch of any repository.

- **Bypass policies when pushing:** The user can push a change to any repo in any branch regardless of the branch policies.

- **Contribute**: The user can contribute (commit code) to any branch of any repo.

- **Contribute to pull requests**: The user can create pull requests targeting any branch in any repo.

- **Create branch**: The user can create a branch in any repo.

- **Create repository**: The user can create repositories in the team project.

- **Create tag**: The user can create tags in any branch of any repo.

- **Delete repository**: The user can delete an Azure Git repo from the team project.

- **Edit policies**: The user can edit branch policies in any branch of any repo.

- **Force push (rewrite history, delete branches and tags)**: The user can delete any branch of any repo and force push changes with history rewrite to any branch of any repo.

- **Manage notes**: The user can manage notes in any branch of any repo.

- **Manage permissions**: The user can manage the permissions of any repository and any branch.

- **Read**: The user can read code in any branch of any repo.

- **Remove others' locks**: The user can remove locks in any branch in any repo.

- **Rename repository**: The user can rename any repository.

You can use the Add button to add groups, teams, or users to grant them permissions explicitly. See Figure 10-3.

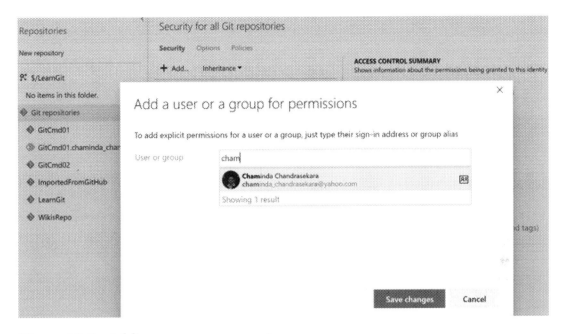

Figure 10-3. *Adding users, groups, or teams*

You can switch on/off inheritance for all repos in the Inheritance drop-down. See Figure 10-4.

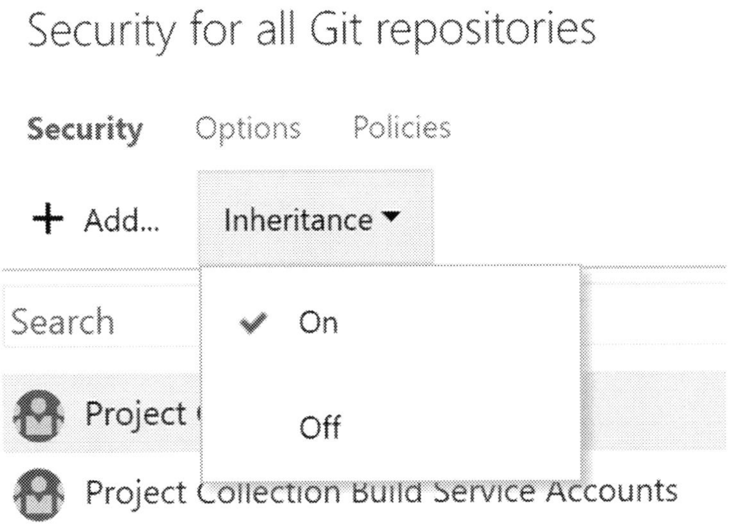

Security for all Git repositories

Security   Options   Policies

╋ Add...   Inheritance ▾

Search

✔ On

Off

Project

Project Collection Build Service Accounts

Figure 10-4. *Inheritance for permissions*

On the Options tab, you can allow Gravatars images from outside the enterprise. See Figure 10-5.

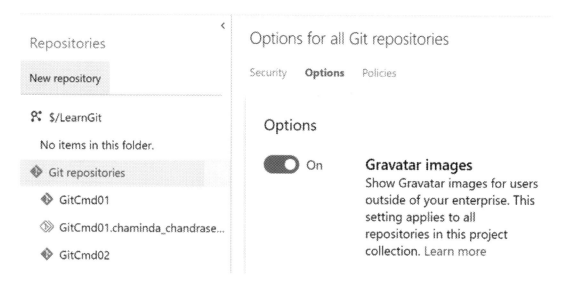

Figure 10-5. *Options*

You can set policies such as file size limits, path validations, etc., for all repositories using this tab. See Figure 10-6.

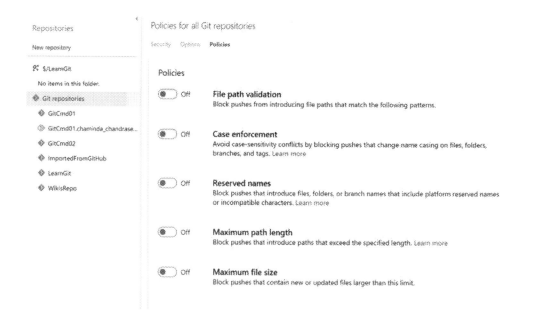

Figure 10-6. *Policies*

Click a repo to see the permissions of a given repo. Se Figure 10-7.

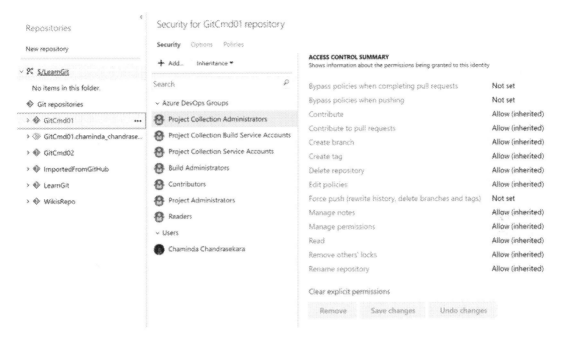

Figure 10-7.   *Repo permissions*

Similar to the permissions applied for all repositories, users, teams, and groups can be assigned with individual repo-scoped permissions.

In the options for an individual repo, you can set options allowing users to create forks, commit mention links, etc. See Figure 10-8.

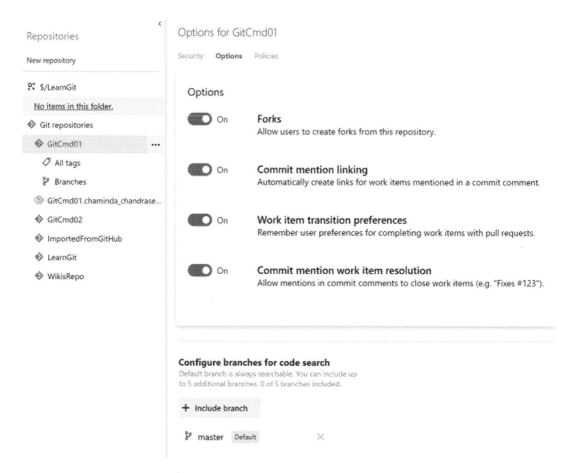

Figure 10-8. *Options of a repository*

The Policies tab allows you to set the same policies as in all the repositories in the scope of a selected repo. Forked repositories also have the same permissions, options, and policies.

In a repo for "All tags," you can set "Force push" permissions. See Figure 10-9.

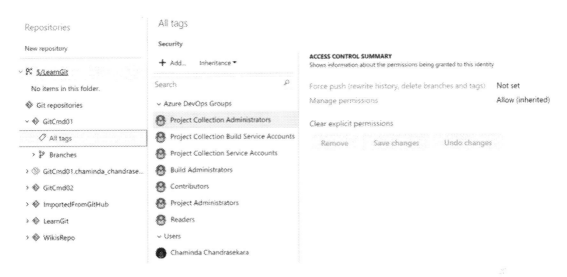

Figure 10-9. *"All tags" permissions*

You can set permissions for all branches in a selected repositories. The permission set for all branches is a subset of the repositories permissions scoped into a selected repo of all branches. See Figure 10-10.

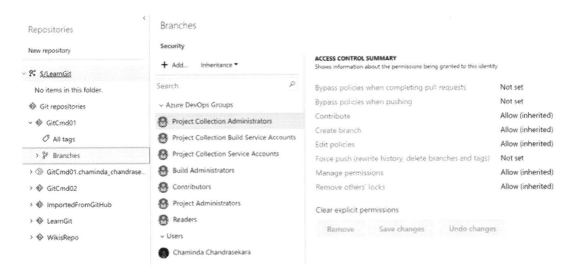

Figure 10-10. *All branch permissions*

For an individual branch, you can apply permissions. These are a subset of permissions from the all branch permissions, which are scoped to a selected branch. See Figure 10-11.

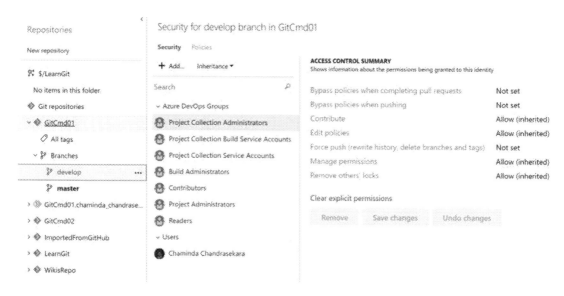

Figure 10-11. *Branch permissions*

When you click the Policies tab of a given branch, you will be taken to the branch's policy setup page, which we will discuss in the next lesson.

In this lesson, we explored the security permissions, options, and policies available in Azure Git Repos, which will help you to secure your code as per your team requirements.

Lesson 10-2: Setting Up Azure Git Repos Branch Policies

In addition to the Azure Git Repos permissions, each branch in a repo can be protected with policies. Let's look at the branch policies that are available in Azure Git Repos.

Prerequisites: You have a team project in Azure Git Repos with branches and have code available in the repositories.

As explained in the previous lesson, you can select a branch and click Policies on the Repositories page of the Repos section to access the branch policies page (see Figure 10-11). Or from Repos, you can go to Branches, and on the Branches page, you can use the Branch context menu to access the branch policies. See Figure 10-12.

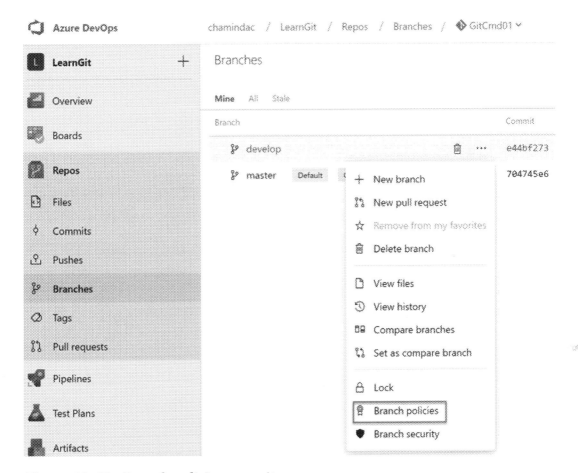

Figure 10-12. *Branch policies menu item*

On the policies page, you can protect a branch with several policy settings. See Figure 10-13.

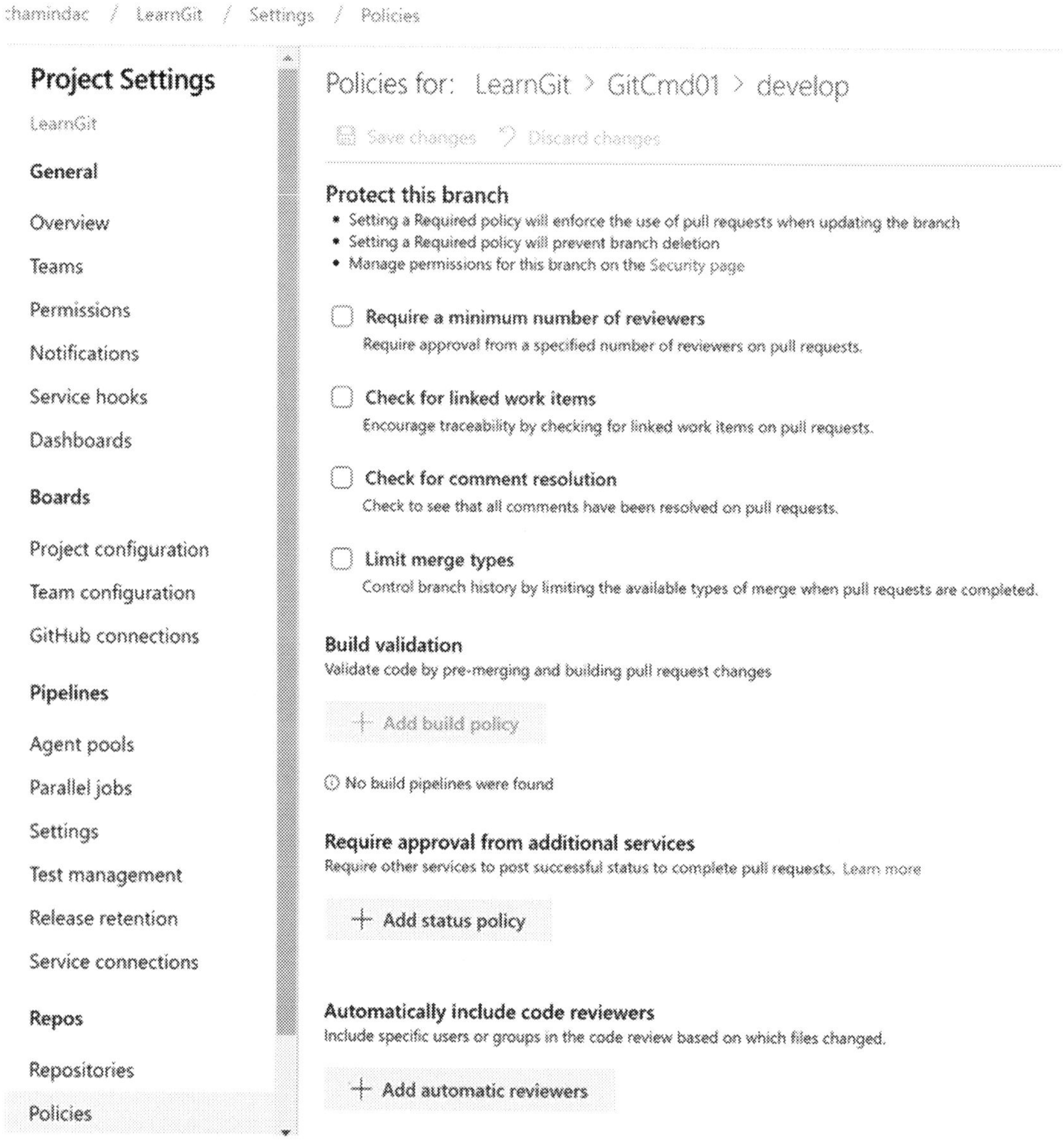

Figure 10-13. *Branch policies*

You can set the required number of reviews for incoming pull requests so that reviewers have to approve a pull request before merging to the branch. A few additional options for the number of reviewers can be set up, as shown in Figure 10-14.

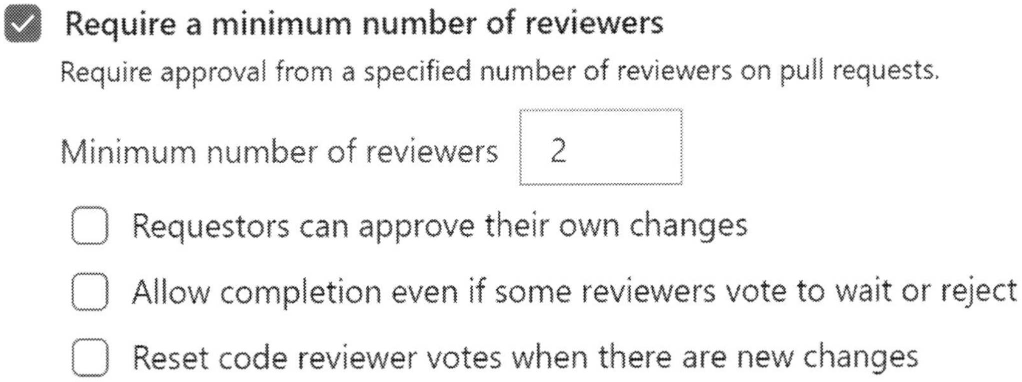

☑ **Require a minimum number of reviewers**

Require approval from a specified number of reviewers on pull requests.

Minimum number of reviewers   [2]

◻ Requestors can approve their own changes

◻ Allow completion even if some reviewers vote to wait or reject

◻ Reset code reviewer votes when there are new changes

Figure 10-14. *Requires reviewers policy*

The work item link policy enforces the requirement of a work item to be associated to the pull request. You can make this required or optional check with a warning. See Figure 10-15.

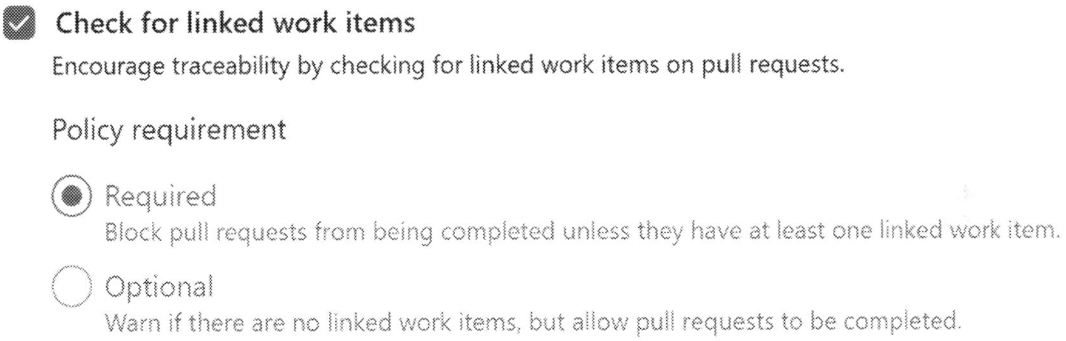

☑ **Check for linked work items**

Encourage traceability by checking for linked work items on pull requests.

Policy requirement

⦿ Required
Block pull requests from being completed unless they have at least one linked work item.

◯ Optional
Warn if there are no linked work items, but allow pull requests to be completed.

Figure 10-15. *Work item link policy*

Comments are made on a pull request by reviewers, and a policy can be set so that all the comments must be resolved before merging them to the branch. This policy again can be optional with a warning. See Figure 10-16.

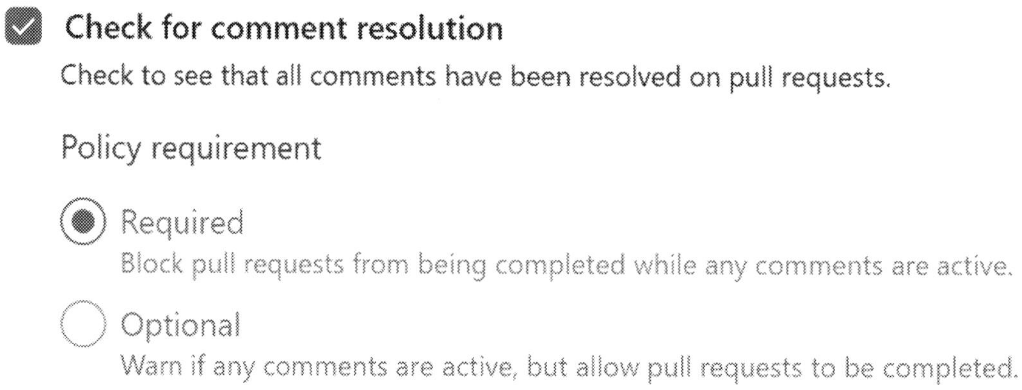

☑ **Check for comment resolution**
Check to see that all comments have been resolved on pull requests.

Policy requirement

◉ Required
Block pull requests from being completed while any comments are active.

◯ Optional
Warn if any comments are active, but allow pull requests to be completed.

Figure 10-16. *Comment resolution policy*

Merge types can be set as a branch policy so that only allowed merge types of pull requests are possible to the branch. See Figure 10-17.

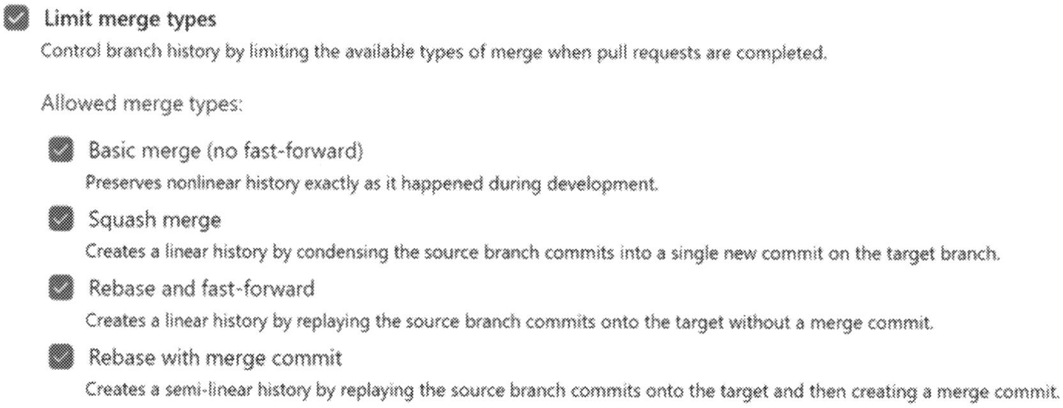

☑ Limit merge types
Control branch history by limiting the available types of merge when pull requests are completed.

Allowed merge types:

☑ Basic merge (no fast-forward)
Preserves nonlinear history exactly as it happened during development.

☑ Squash merge
Creates a linear history by condensing the source branch commits into a single new commit on the target branch.

☑ Rebase and fast-forward
Creates a linear history by replaying the source branch commits onto the target without a merge commit.

☑ Rebase with merge commit
Creates a semi-linear history by replaying the source branch commits onto the target and then creating a merge commit.

Figure 10-17. *Merge types policy*

One you click add "Build policy," you can select an available Azure pipeline build and set a policy so that it requires the build to be successful to merge the pull request. See Figure 10-18. You can add more than one build as the build policy. We discuss builds in more detail in the *Hands-on Azure Pipelines* book of this series.

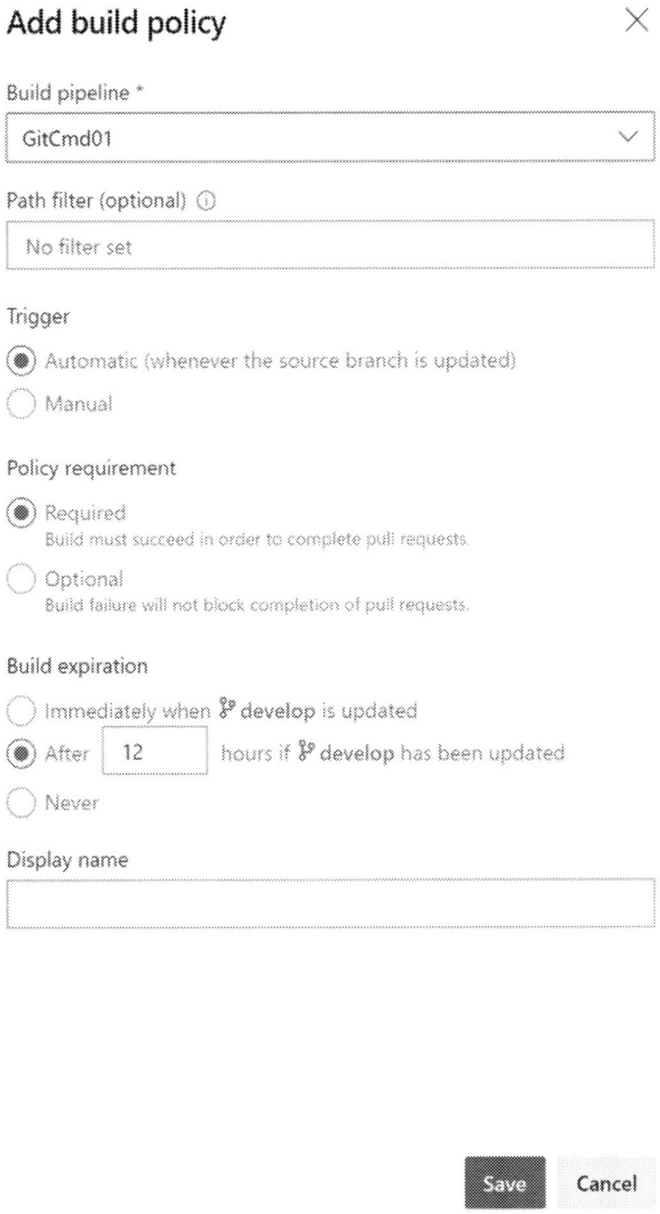

Add build policy   ✕

Build pipeline *

GitCmd01	⌄

Path filter (optional) ⓘ

No filter set

Trigger

◉ Automatic (whenever the source branch is updated)

◯ Manual

Policy requirement

◉ Required
　Build must succeed in order to complete pull requests.

◯ Optional
　Build failure will not block completion of pull requests.

Build expiration

◯ Immediately when ⑂ **develop** is updated

◉ After `12`　hours if ⑂ **develop** has been updated

◯ Never

Display name

[Save] Cancel

Figure 10-18. *Build policy*

The status policy lets you check the status applied to a pull request by an external service using the REST (Representational State Transfer) API. How to use REST APIs is explained in Chapter 12. The automatic reviews policy lets you add reviewers automatically to the PR when created. See Figure 10-19.

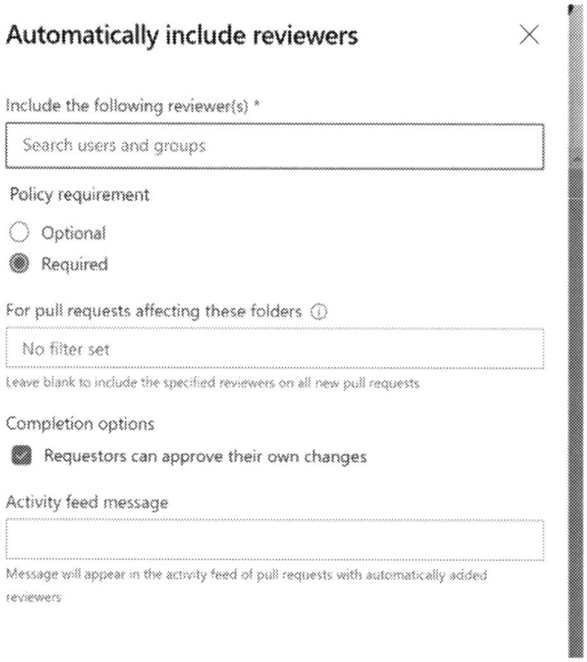

Figure 10-19. *Automatic reviewers*

In this lesson, we explored the policies that can be used to protect a branch, in addition to the permissions available in Azure Git Repos.

Summary

We discussed the permissions, options, and policies in Azure Git Repos. In addition, we discussed how to protect branches with branch policies.

In the next chapter, we will discuss features such as creating forks, tagging importing external repos, and creating wikis with Git Repos markdown files.

CHAPTER 11

Azure Git Repos Extras

We have discussed many Azure Git Repos operations that you can perform. There are a couple of additional common Git operations such as creating Git tags and forking that we will be exploring in this chapter. Further, we will talk about importing other repositories to Azure Git Repos and creating wikis in Azure DevOps via markdown files stored in Azure Git.

Lesson 11-1: Using Git Tags

A tag is helpful to mark a specific point in the commit history of a Git repo. Azure Git Repos supports two types of tags, lightweight tags and annotated tags. A *lightweight* tag is a tag for the commit, while an *annotated* tag marks a commit and includes a tagger, which is a message for the tag with the date.

Prerequisites: You followed Chapters 6, 7, and 8 and have created an Azure Git repository with a few commits in it.

Creating Tags with the Azure DevOps Web Portal

The tags you create using the Azure DevOps Portal will be always annotated tags. You can open an Azure Git repository in the Azure DevOps Portal and on the History tab use the context menu of a given commit to create a tag. See Figure 11-1.

© Chaminda Chandrasekara and Pushpa Herath 2020
C. Chandrasekara and P. Herath, *Hands-on Azure Repos*, https://doi.org/10.1007/978-1-4842-5425-7_11

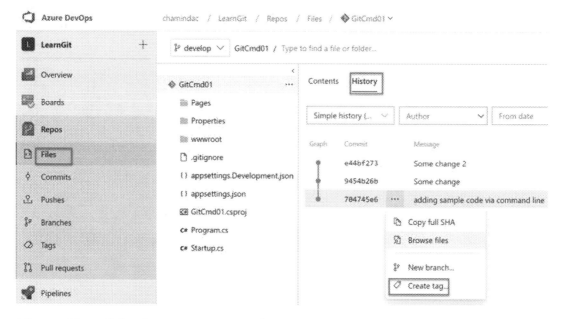

Figure 11-1. *Selecting to create a tag for a commit*

In the pop-up window, provide a tag name and a description and create the tag for the commit. See Figure 11-2.

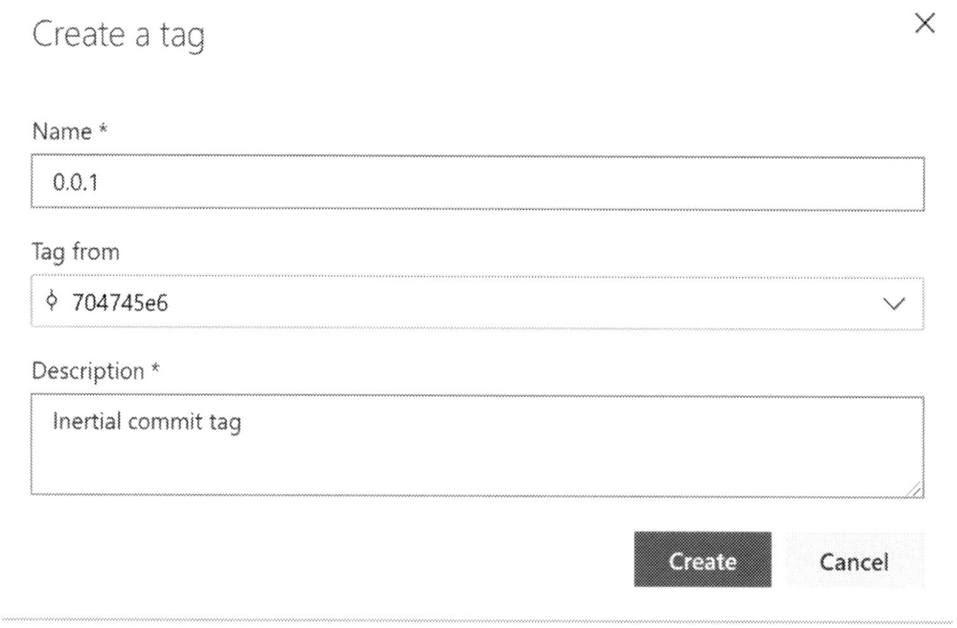

Create a tag ✕

Name *

    0.0.1

Tag from

    ⬦ 704745e6   ⌄

Description *

    Inertial commit tag

                                        [Create]   Cancel

Figure 11-2. *Creating the first tag*

The tag will be visible in the commit. See Figure 11-3.

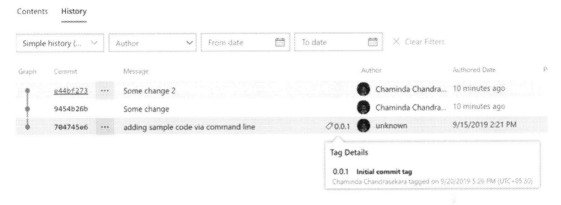

Figure 11-3. *The tag visible in the commit*

You can create and view tags on the Tags page of the Azure DevOps Portal. See Figure 11-4.

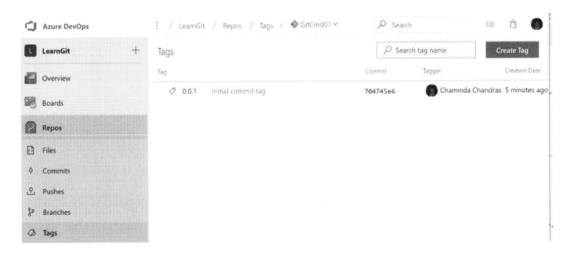

Figure 11-4. *Tags page*

When you click Create Tag, the "Create a tag" pop-up window will open. In the drop-down of the tag creation pop-up, you can select a branch for which to create a tag. See Figure 11-5.

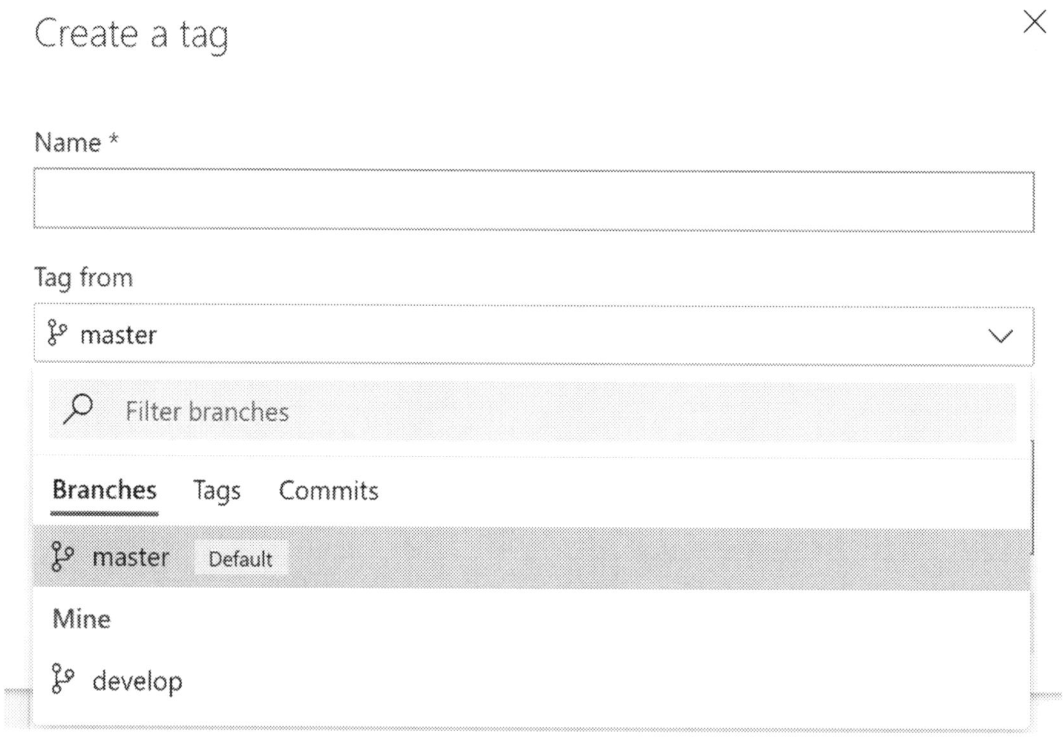

Create a tag   ✕

Name *

[   ]

Tag from

⎇ master   ⌄

🔍 Filter branches

Branches   Tags   Commits

⎇ **master**   Default

Mine

⎇ develop

Figure 11-5. *Branch for a tag*

You can select a specific commit by searching for it using the first four characters of the commit ID. See Figure 11-6.

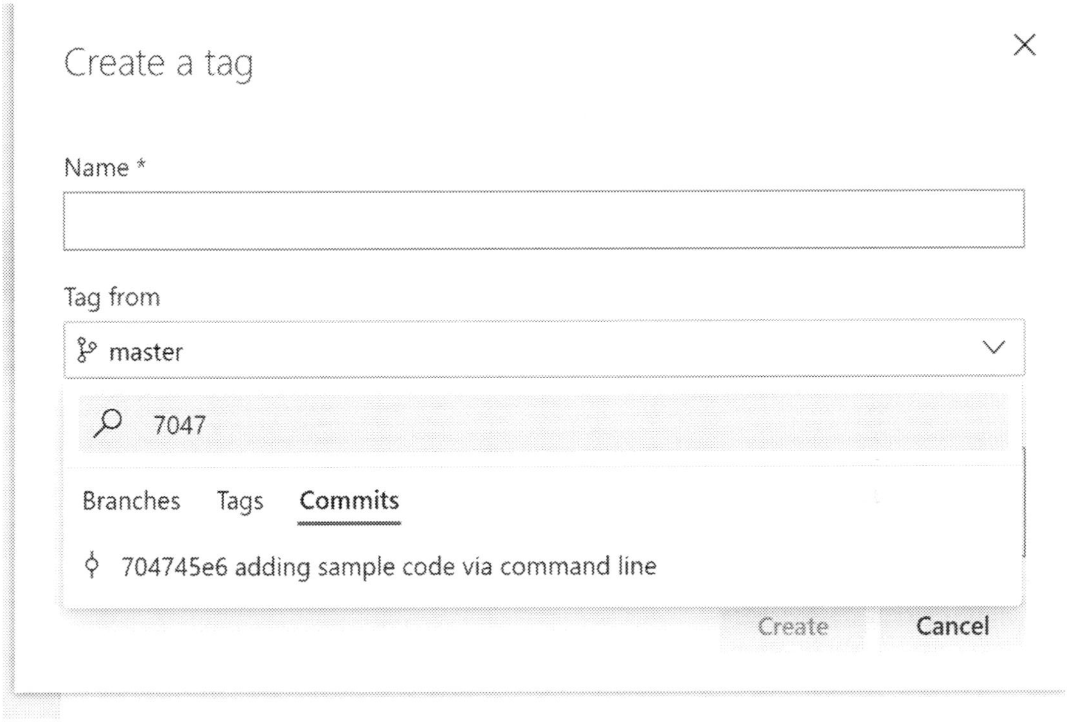

Create a tag

Name *

Tag from

🔗 master

🔍 7047

Branches   Tags   **Commits**

♦ 704745e6 adding sample code via command line

Create   Cancel

Figure 11-6. *Selecting a commit for the tag*

You can create multiple tags for a single commit if required. See Figure 11-7.

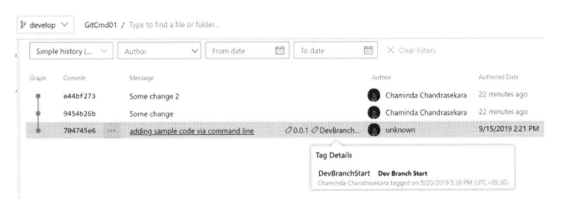

Figure 11-7. *Multiple tags for a commit*

The tag context menu allows you to create a branch, download the tagged commit version's source code as a zip file, view files in a tagged commit version, view history from the tagged commit, and delete the tag. See Figure 11-8. In addition, you can set the tag as a compare tag to compare the files of two commits for changes.

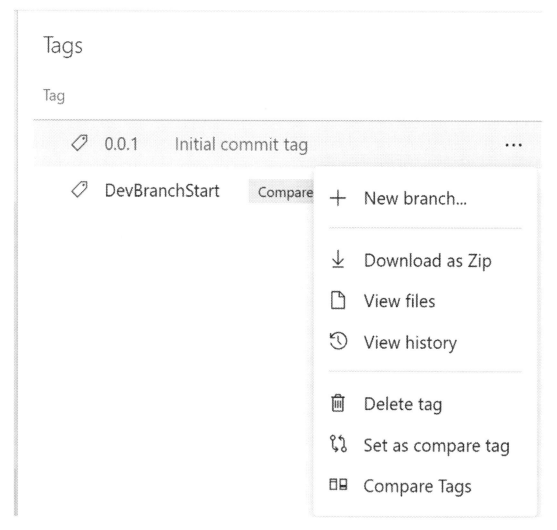

Figure 11-8. Tag context menu

Creating Tags with Visual Studio

You can clone an Azure Git repository using Visual Studio, as we discussed in Chapter 7. In Visual Studio Team Explorer, you can click Tags. See Figure 11-9.

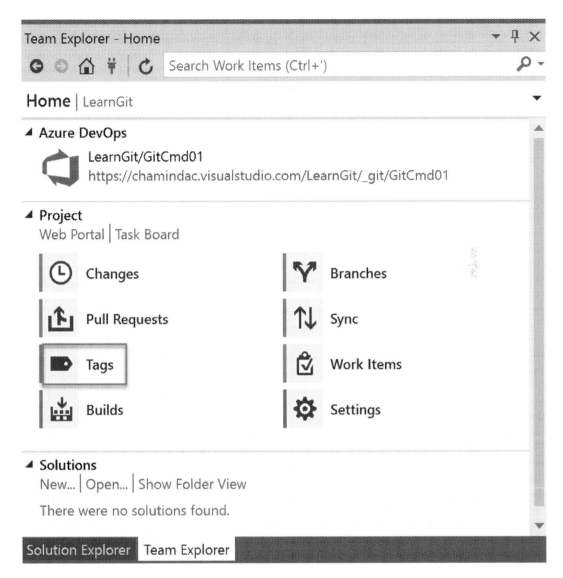

Figure 11-9. *Tags in VS Team Explorer*

The tag context menu in Visual Studio lets you perform several actions. You can check out a branch of the tag, view the history, view the details of the tagged commit, delete the tag locally in the repository, and push a local tag to a remote repository. The links on the Team Explorer tags page allow you to create new tags, push all tags to a remote repository, or create a local branch from a given tag. See Figure 11-10.

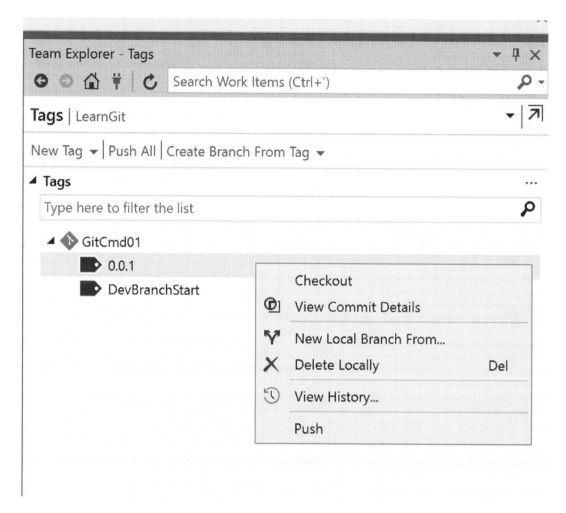

Figure 11-10. *Tag context menu in VS*

From Visual Studio, you can view a branch's history, as explained in Chapter 8. In the commit history, you can get the context menu for a commit by right-clicking a commit and using Create Tag to create a new tag for the commit. See Figure 11-11.

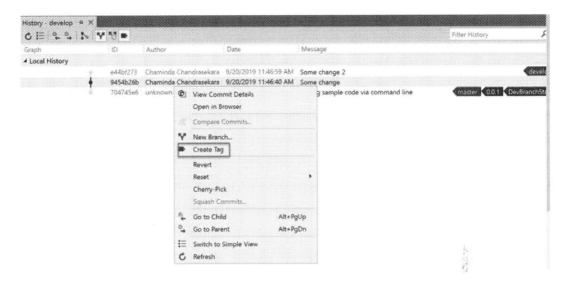

Figure 11-11.   *Creating a tag from the commit history in VS*

In the Commit Details page opened in Team Explorer, you can specify the tag and a message and then create the tag. See Figure 11-12.

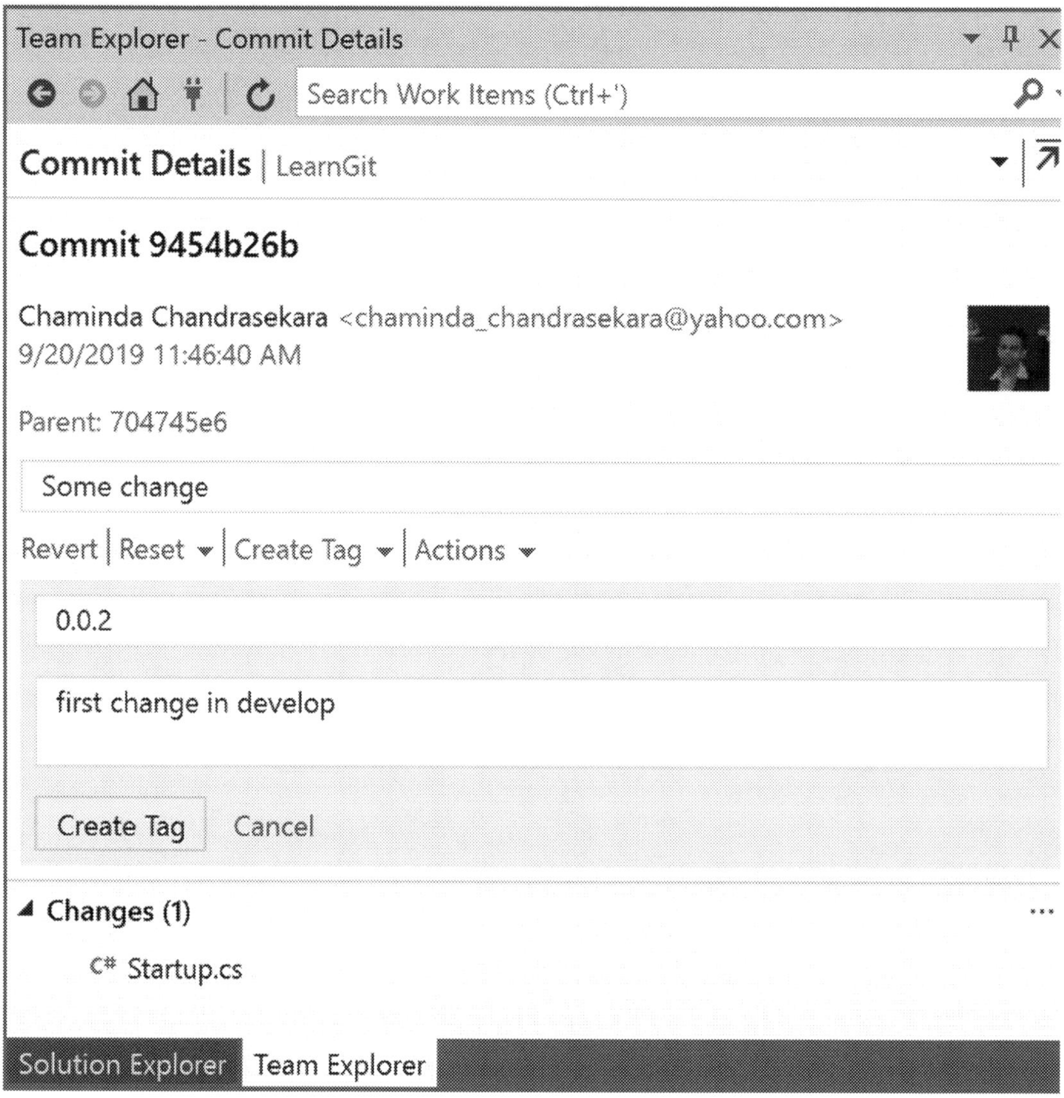

Figure 11-12. *Creating a tag in VS*

One the tag is pushed, it is available in the remote Azure Git repo. See Figure 11-13.

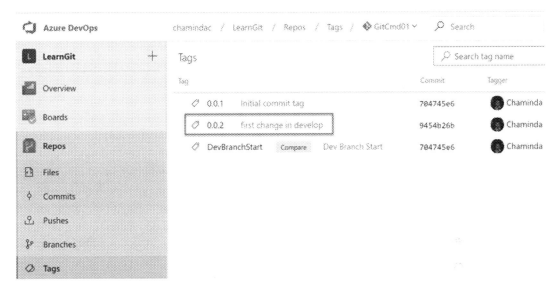

Figure 11-13. *Tag in Azure Git repo after push*

Creating Tags with the Command Line

You can list the tags available in a branch by executing git tag or git tag -l or git tag --list from the branch at the command line in Git bash. See Figure 11-14.

Figure 11-14. *Listing tags*

You can filter the tags by using wildcards. For example, git tag -l "0.0*" will list the tags starting with 0.0. It is a must to use -l or --list when you are using a filter. See Figure 11-15.

```
chamindac@vs2019dev MINGW64 ~/source/repos/GitCmd01 (develop)
$ git tag -l "0.0*"
0.0.1
0.0.2

chamindac@vs2019dev MINGW64 ~/source/repos/GitCmd01 (develop)
$
```

Figure 11-15. *Listing tags with a filter*

To create a tag, you can use git tag tagyouwanttocreate. A tag will be created for the latest commit. See Figure 11-16.

```
chamindac@vs2019dev MINGW64 ~/source/repos/GitCmd01 (develop)
$ git tag "0.0.3"

chamindac@vs2019dev MINGW64 ~/source/repos/GitCmd01 (develop)
$ git tag -l "0.0*"
0.0.1
0.0.2
0.0.3
```

Figure 11-16. *Creating a tag*

To create an annotated tag, use -a with the command. Using -m, you can provide a descriptive message for the annotated tag. See Figure 11-17.

```
chamindac@vs2019dev MINGW64 ~/source/repos/GitCmd01 (develop)
$ git tag -a "anotatedtag01" -m "tag message 01"

chamindac@vs2019dev MINGW64 ~/source/repos/GitCmd01 (develop)
$
```

Figure 11-17. *Creating an annotated tag*

You can use git show tagname to view a tag. If the tag is not an annotated tag, tag and commit the details shown. See Figure 11-18.

```
chamindac@vs2019dev MINGW64 ~/source/repos/GitCmd01 (develop)
$ git show 0.0.3
commit e44bf2734bebd5d9b1a5f588f7570b19384d9673 (HEAD -> develop, tag: anotatedt
ag01, tag: 0.0.3, origin/develop)
Author: Chaminda Chandrasekara <chaminda_chandrasekara@yahoo.com>
Date:   Fri Sep 20 11:46:59 2019 +0000

    Some change 2

diff --git a/Startup.cs b/Startup.cs
index 60bb776..26a19a2 100644
--- a/Startup.cs
+++ b/Startup.cs
@@ -21,7 +21,7 @@ namespace GitCmd01

        public IConfiguration Configuration { get; }

        // This method gets called by the runtime. Use this method to add servi
ces to the container. Some change
+       // This method gets called by the runtime. Use this method to add servi
ces to the container. Some change2
        public void ConfigureServices(IServiceCollection services)
        {
            services.Configure<CookiePolicyOptions>(options =>

chamindac@vs2019dev MINGW64 ~/source/repos/GitCmd01 (develop)
```

Figure 11-18. *Viewing a tag that is not annotated*

For an annotated tag, the creator of the tag, the message for the tag, and the date of the tag creation is shown in addition to the commit details. See Figure 11-19.

```
chamindac@vs2019dev MINGW64 ~/source/repos/GitCmd01 (develop)
$ git show anotatedtag01
tag anotatedtag01
Tagger: Chaminda Chandrasekara <chaminda_chandrasekara@yahoo.com>
Date:    Fri Sep 20 14:20:31 2019 +0000

tag message 01

commit e44bf2734bebd5d9b1a5f588f7570b19384d9673 (HEAD -> develop, tag: anotatedt
ag01, tag: 0.0.3, origin/develop)
Author: Chaminda Chandrasekara <chaminda_chandrasekara@yahoo.com>
Date:    Fri Sep 20 11:46:59 2019 +0000

    Some change 2

diff --git a/Startup.cs b/Startup.cs
index 60bb776..26a19a2 100644
--- a/Startup.cs
+++ b/Startup.cs
@@ -21,7 +21,7 @@ namespace GitCmd01

        public IConfiguration Configuration { get; }

        // This method gets called by the runtime. Use this method to add servi
ces to the container. Some change
+       // This method gets called by the runtime. Use this method to add servi
ces to the container. Some change2
        public void ConfigureServices(IServiceCollection services)
        {
            services.Configure<CookiePolicyOptions>(options =>
```

Figure 11-19. *Showing an annotated tag*

To delete a tag, you should execute git tag -d tagname. You can push the tags by
using git push tagname. If you have multiple tags to push, you should execute git push
--tags. See Figure 11-20.

```
chamindac@vs2019dev MINGW64 ~/source/repos/GitCmd01 (develop)
$ git push --tags
Enumerating objects: 1, done.
Counting objects: 100% (1/1), done.
Writing objects: 100% (1/1), 177 bytes | 88.00 KiB/s, done.
Total 1 (delta 0), reused 0 (delta 0)
remote: Analyzing objects... (1/1) (66 ms)
remote: Storing packfile... done (200 ms)
remote: Storing index... done (84 ms)
To https://chamindac.visualstudio.com/DefaultCollection/LearnGit/_git/GitCmd01
 * [new tag]         0.0.3 -> 0.0.3
 * [new tag]         anotatedtag01 -> anotatedtag01

chamindac@vs2019dev MINGW64 ~/source/repos/GitCmd01 (develop)
$
```

Figure 11-20. *Pushing tags*

In this lesson, we looked at various ways to create Git tags to mark a specific commit.

Lesson 11-2: Forking a Repo

Forking a repo allows you to make an entire copy of an Azure Git repo. Then you can work on the fork without affecting the original repo. If required, you can make a pull request to merge the changes from a fork to the original Azure Git repository. Forking repos is useful when you want to create a fully isolated copy of a Git repository. Let's look at how to fork an Azure Git repository in this lesson.

Prerequisites: You followed Chapters 6, 7, and 8 and have created an Azure Git repository with a few commits in it.

Click the Fork button in the Azure Git repository to create a fork. See Figure 11-21.

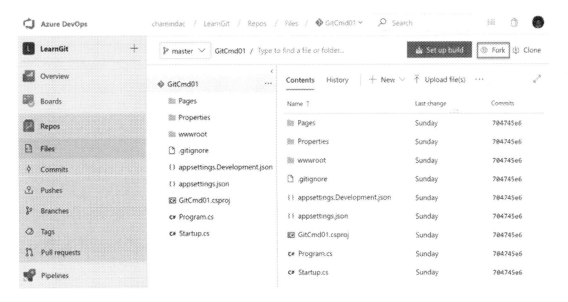

Figure 11-21. *Forking a repo*

In the pop-up, you are allowed to decide whether to create the fork with all branches or with the default branch only. Additionally, you can fork a repository into another team project of the Azure DevOps organization. This is useful when you want to start a new project with the same codebase. Let's fork all the branches to the same team project. See Figure 11-22.

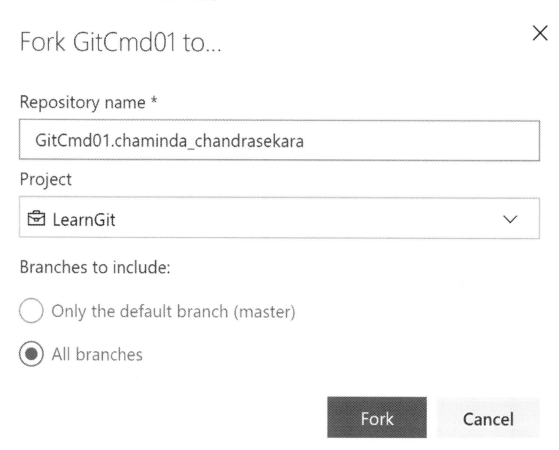

Figure 11-22. *Creating a fork*

Now go ahead and make a change in the newly forked repository in a branch. Then when you try to create a pull request, you are given an option to make the pull request to the original Azure Git repo's desired target branch. Of course, you can create a pull request within the forked repo. See Figure 11-23.

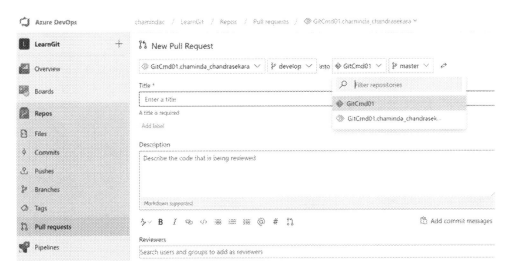

Figure 11-23. *Pull request from a fork*

We explored fork creation in the Azure Git repositories in this lesson.

Lesson 11-3: Importing from an External Repository

You can easily import external Git repos or TFVC repos into an Azure DevOps organization as Git repos. Let's look at the steps required to import a repo in Azure Git Repos.

Prerequisites: Create a repository in GitHub and add some code to it. Then copy the clone URL of the GitHub repository.

Click the drop-down near the Azure Git repository name to view the options to import a repository. See Figure 11-24.

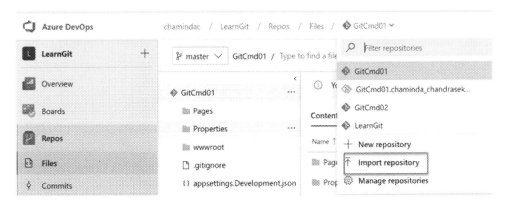

Figure 11-24. *Importing a repository*

In the drop-down you can select Git or TFVC. You can import TFCV repos in the current Azure DevOps organization as Git repositories. See Figure 11-25.

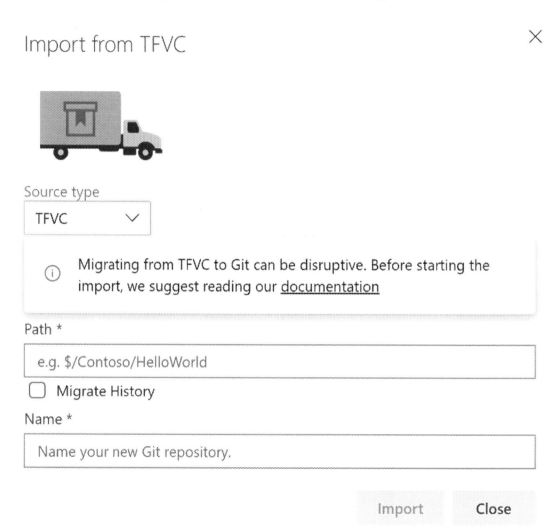

Figure 11-25. *Option to import a TFVC repo*

Copy a clone URL from the GitHub repo that was created, as mentioned in the prerequisites. Select Git as the import type and paste the clone URL. Provide a username and password for the GitHub account. See Figure 11-26.

Import a Git repository

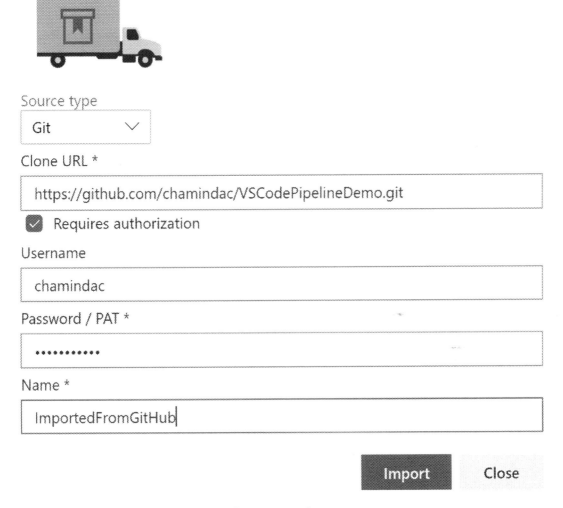

Source type

```
Git                    ∨
```

Clone URL *

```
https://github.com/chamindac/VSCodePipelineDemo.git
```

☑ Requires authorization

Username

```
chamindac
```

Password / PAT *

```
••••••••••
```

Name *

```
ImportedFromGitHub
```

Import   Close

Figure 11-26. *Importing a repo from GitHub*

Once the import operation completes, refresh, and you will be able to see that the GitHub repository is imported to the Azure Git repository with the history. See Figure 11-27.

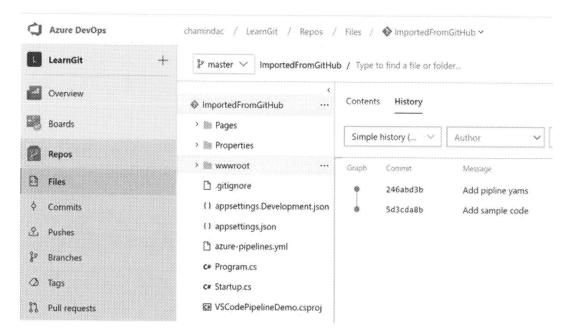

Figure 11-27. *Imported repository from GitHub*

In this lesson, we discussed how to import a repository to Azure Git Repos.

Lesson 11-4: Setting Up Azure Git Repos Markdown Files as a Wiki

Azure DevOps allows you to use Azure Git Repos markdown files to set up wikis. Wikis are useful to communicate valuable instructions and information to your teams. In this lesson, let's look at the steps to create a wiki using markdown files in an Azure Git repository.

Prerequisites: You are familiar with markdown files.

As the first step, create a new Azure Git repository named WikisRepo in a team project. Make sure to select the option to add a readme file to initialize the repo. See Figure 11-28.

Create a new repository   ×

Type

❖ Git   ⌄

Repository name *

WikisRepo

✅ Add a README to describe your repository

Add a .gitignore:

None   ⌄

Create   Cancel

Figure 11-28. *Creating WikisRepo*

In the repository, click the menu icon and create a new folder. See Figure 11-29.

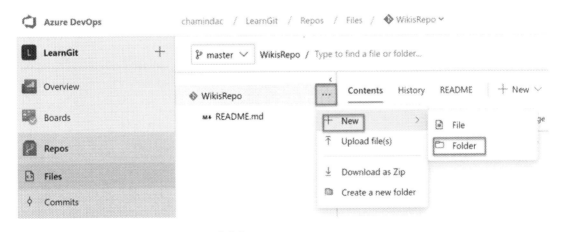

Figure 11-29. *Creating a new folder*

Then create a folder named DevWikis in the repo and add a markdown file. See Figure 11-30.

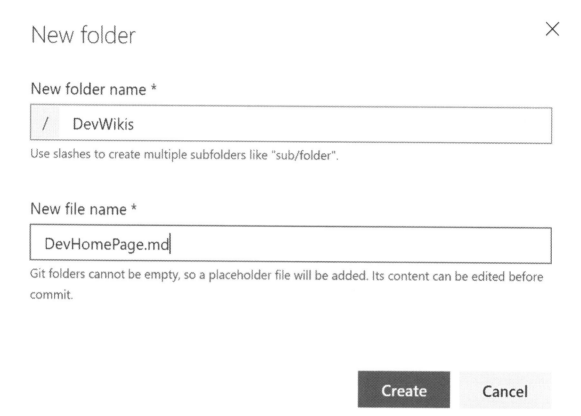

Figure 11-30. *Adding a folder and a markdown file*

Add some simple markdown content and commit the changes to the repo. See Figure 11-31.

Figure 11-31. *Adding markdown content*

Then go to Overview ➤ Wikis and click "Publish code as wiki." See Figure 11-32.

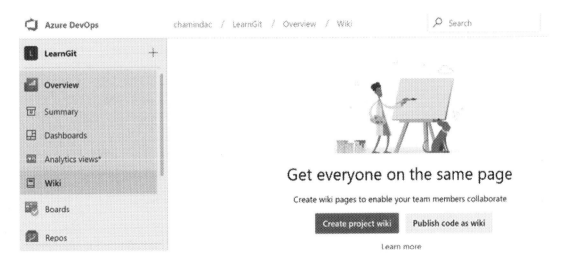

Figure 11-32. *Publishing the code as a wiki*

In the side pane that opens, select the WikisRepo branch and folder that contains the markdown files. Then provide a name for the wiki and click Publish. See Figure 11-33.

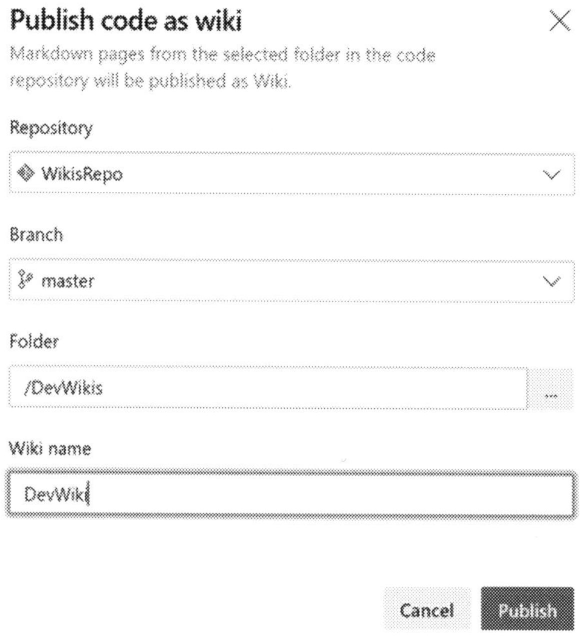

Publish code as wiki   ✕

Markdown pages from the selected folder in the code
repository will be published as Wiki.

Repository

◈ WikisRepo   ∨

Branch

ᛘ master   ∨

Folder

/DevWikis   ...

Wiki name

DevWiki

Cancel   **Publish**

Figure 11-33. *Publishing the wiki*

The wiki will be published, and you can keep adding markdown files to the
repository to add more wiki pages. See Figure 11-34.

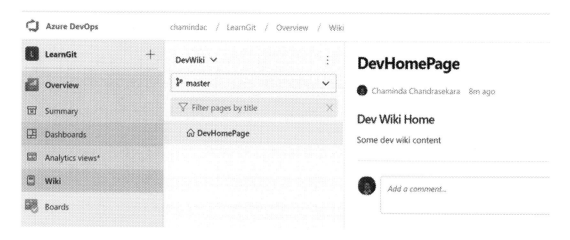

Figure 11-34. *Wiki published*

In this lesson, we explored the options to create a wiki in Azure DevOps using
markdown files available in an Azure Git repository.

Summary

In this chapter, we discussed a few operations that we can perform with Azure Git Repos such as creating tags, forking repos, importing external repos to Azure Git Repos, and setting up wikis using markdown files in an Azure Git repository. These lessons have provided you with starting guidelines and steps so that you can leverage the capabilities to build great solutions with your teams using Azure Git Repos.

In the next lesson, let's discuss the REST API of Azure DevOps in relation to TFVC and Azure Git Repos, which will allow you to build additional reporting capabilities as well as operational automation capabilities with scripting languages such as PowerShell.

CHAPTER 12

REST APIs for Azure Git and TFVC Repos

The Representational State Transfer (REST) APIs in Azure DevOps are service endpoints supporting HTTP operations. They allow you to retrieve, create, and update resources in Azure DevOps, including Azure Git and TFVC repositories. The REST APIs facilitate the development of extensions to Azure DevOps and help to integrate Azure DevOps with third-party tools. There are many extensions for Azure DevOps developed based on the REST APIs in the Visual Studio marketplace (`https://marketplace.visualstudio.com/`), and they can be used to add features and enhancements to Azure DevOps.

In this chapter, let's look at how we can use REST APIs with Azure Git Repos and TFVC, which will allow you to build useful reports based on version control data and perform actions on the version control to automate any desired actions.

Lesson 12-1: Using Repo REST APIs from a Browser to Retrieve Data

Using a browser is the simplest way to access a REST API to retrieve data in Azure DevOps. Let's look at a few simple REST API calls against Azure Git Repos and TFVC repos using a browser.

Prerequisites: You have team projects in Azure DevOps and have Git and TFVC repos with code.

A REST API GET URL generally has the following format for Git repositories. This GET request retrieves all the repositories in a team project. (We discussed the REST API URL components in detail in the *Hand-on Azure Boards* book of this series.)

```
https://dev.azure.com/{organization}/{project}/_apis/git/
repositories?api-version=5.1
```

© Chaminda Chandrasekara and Pushpa Herath 2020
C. Chandrasekara and P. Herath, *Hands-on Azure Repos*, https://doi.org/10.1007/978-1-4842-5425-7_12

First log in to your Azure DevOps organization using a browser. Then execute the previous URL with the correct organization and team project name. See Figure 12-1.

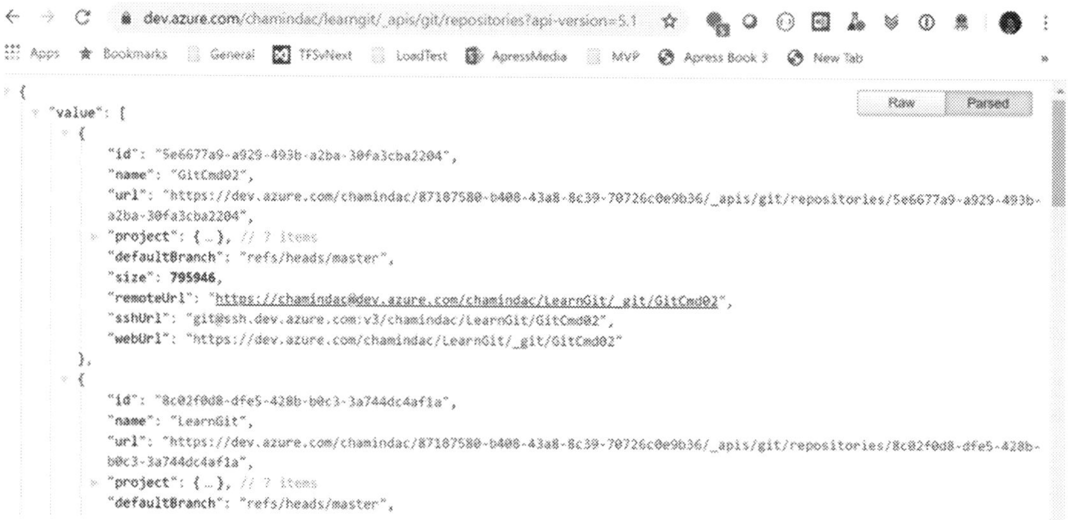

Figure 12-1. *Getting all the repositories using REST APIs*

You can pass additional URL parameters such as `includeLinks`. You can find documentation about Git repositories at `https://docs.microsoft.com/en-us/rest/api/azure/devops/git/?view=azure-devops-rest-5.1`.

Similar to retrieving Git repos in a team project, you can get all the changesets in a team project's TFVC repo using a REST API.

```
https://dev.azure.com/{organization}/{project}/_apis/tfvc/
changesets?api-version=5.1
```

You should use the Azure DevOps organization name and your team project name to retrieve the changeset information. See Figure 12-2.

```
"count": 2,
"value": [
    {
        "changesetId": 773,
        "url": "https://dev.azure.com/chamindac/Learntfvc/_apis/tfvc/changesets/773"
        "author": {
            "displayName": "Chaminda Chandrasekara",
            "url": "https://spsprodeus22.vssps.visualstudio.com/Abee6738c-dee5-443d-
            bbff-69f0dc00aa02",
            "id": "84f2a6cb-7327-4dca-bbff-69f0dc00aa02",
            "uniqueName": "chaminda_chandrasekara@yahoo.com",
            "imageUrl": "https://dev.azure.com/chamindac/_api/_common/identityImage?
        },
        "checkedInBy": {
            "displayName": "Chaminda Chandrasekara",
            "url": "https://spsprodeus22.vssps.visualstudio.com/Abee6738c-dee5-443d-
            bbff-69f0dc00aa02",
            "id": "84f2a6cb-7327-4dca-bbff-69f0dc00aa02",
            "uniqueName": "chaminda_chandrasekara@yahoo.com",
            "imageUrl": "https://dev.azure.com/chamindac/_api/_common/identityImage?
        },
        "createdDate": "2019-08-20T17:15:51.43Z",
        "comment": "Adding new console app"
    },
    {
```

Figure 12-2. *Getting TFVC changesets using a REST API*

You can refer to the TFVC REST API reference at `https://docs.microsoft.com/en-us/rest/api/azure/devops/tfvc/?view=azure-devops-rest-5.1` to learn more about REST API methods available for TFVC.

In this lesson, we explored the simplest way to call the Azure DevOps REST API to retrieve information for Azure Git Repos and TFVC.

Lesson 12-2: Creating a PAT to Use with REST APIs for Repos

Personal access tokens (PATs) in Azure DevOps allow you to authenticate and authorize third-party applications, scripts, or tools to access Azure DevOps REST APIs. We discussed how to create a PAT in detail in the *Hands-on Azure Boards* book of this series. Let's create a PAT to allow access to Azure Git Repos and TFVC in this lesson.

Click your user profile in Azure DevOps and click Security in the context menu. See Figure 12-3.

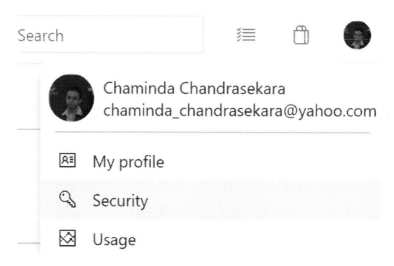

Figure 12-3. *Security for a user*

On the Personal Access Tokens page, click New Token. A side pane will open; select Full and Status for the scope to create a new PAT. See Figure 12-4.

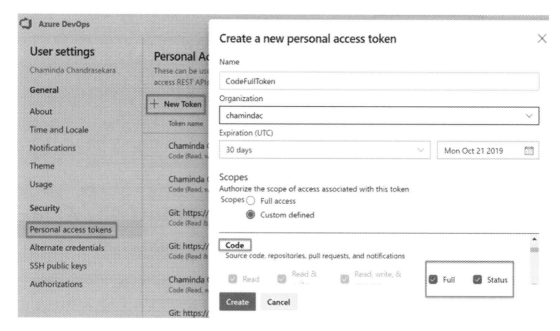

Figure 12-4. *Creating a PAT for code repositories*

Once you click the Create button, a PAT will be generated. Make sure to copy and save it in a secure location as you will not be able to see the token value again once you close the side pane. See Figure 12-5.

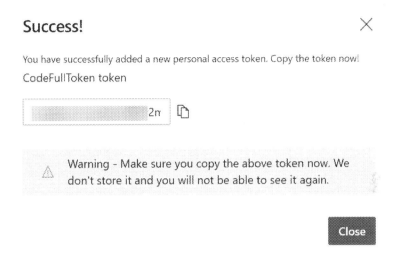

Figure 12-5. *Generated PAT*

In this lesson, we created and saved a PAT to use with the REST API for Azure Git Repos and TFVC.

Lesson 12-3: Using the Repo REST APIs from Postman

Postman is a popular tool used by developers to test REST APIs and more. There is a free version you can download from `https://www.getpostman.com/downloads/`. Let's look at how to use Postman to work with Azure Git Repos and TFVC REST APIs.

Prerequisites: Download and install Postman.

Open Postman. You may have to sign in or sign up. Once Postman is opened, go to the Authorization tab. Select Basic Auth. Then for the password, provide the token we generated in Lesson 12-2. For the username, type any text. Provide the TFVC changeset and get REST API URL, `https://dev.azure.com/{organization}/{project}/_apis/tfvc/changesets?api-version=5.1`. Then click Send. See Figure 12-6.

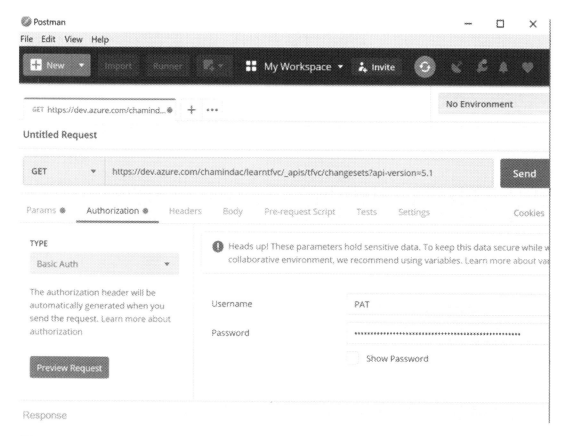

Figure 12-6. *Postman to execute REST API GET*

The REST API returned value is displayed in the Postman app. See Figure 12-7.

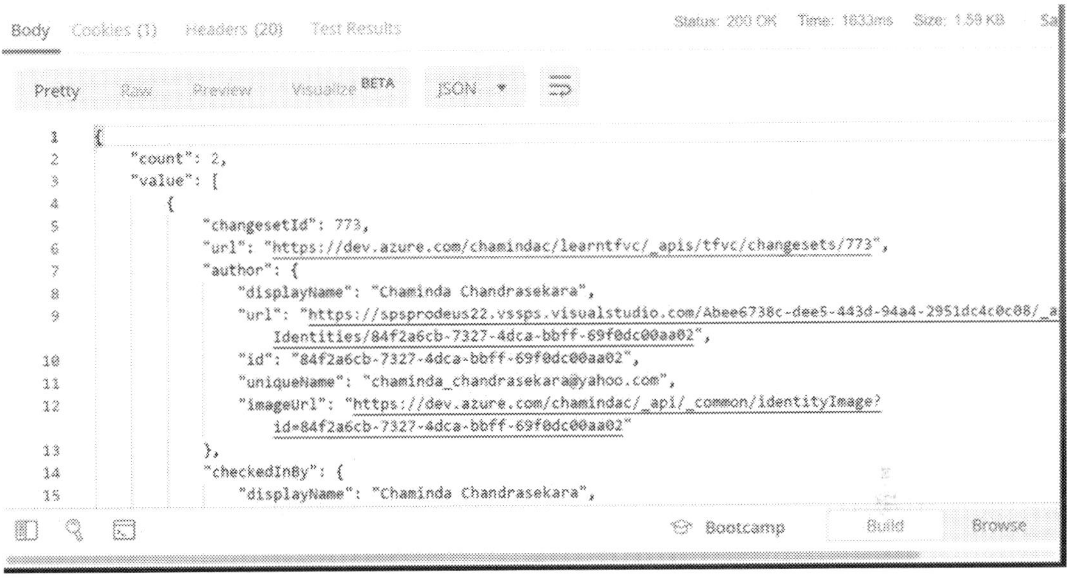

Figure 12-7. REST API returning changesets

In this lesson, we explored how to set up Postman to use a REST API for Azure TFVC repos. In the same way, you can call the Azure Git Repos REST APIs in Postman.

Lesson 12-4: Using the Repo REST APIs from PowerShell

PowerShell is now supported on all platforms in addition to just the Windows platform. PowerShell can be used to call REST APIs for Azure Git Repos and TFVC. Let's discuss the steps to call Azure Git Repos REST APIs so that you can retrieve data from Azure Git Repos and use the same steps to get data from TFVC repos via REST APIs.

Prerequisites: You have team projects with Azure Git Repos and TFVC repositories.

You need to create an authorization header as the first step to call a REST API in Azure DevOps. The following code can be used in PowerShell to create an authorization header:

```
param(
    [Parameter(Mandatory=$true)]
    [string] $token,
    [Parameter(Mandatory=$true)]
```

```
    [string] $collectionUri,
    [Parameter(Mandatory=$true)]
    [string] $teamProjectName,
    [string] $restAPIversion = '5.1'
)

$User=""

# Base64-encodes the Personal Access Token (PAT) appropriately
$base64AuthInfo = [Convert]::ToBase64String([Text.Encoding]::ASCII.
GetBytes(("{0}:{1}" -f $User,$token)));
$header = @{Authorization=("Basic {0}" -f $base64AuthInfo)};
```

Additional parameters other than the $token in the code can be discussed later in the chapter. The token is used with the username (which can be an empty string) to generate the Base64-encoded Authorization token. Then it is added to a variable named $header in order to pass it as the header of the REST API call.

As the next step, we can add code to call the REST API to retrieve all Azure Git Repos repositories in a team project.

```
$Uri = $collectionUri + '/' + $teamProjectName + '/_apis/git/
repositories?api-version=' + $restAPIversion

$repositories = Invoke-RestMethod -Method Get -ContentType application/json
-Uri $Uri -Headers $header
```

Then we can loop though the repositories to print each repo's name.

```
foreach($repo in $repositories.value)
{
    Write-Host ("Repository name: {0}" -f $repo.name)
}
```

The complete PowerShell code is as follows:

```
param(
    [Parameter(Mandatory=$true)]
    [string] $token,
    [Parameter(Mandatory=$true)]
```

```
    [string] $collectionUri,
    [Parameter(Mandatory=$true)]
    [string] $teamProjectName,
    [string] $restAPIversion = '5.1'
)

$User=""

# Base64-encodes the Personal Access Token (PAT) appropriately
$base64AuthInfo = [Convert]::ToBase64String([Text.Encoding]::ASCII.
GetBytes(("{0}:{1}" -f $User,$token)));
$header = @{Authorization=("Basic {0}" -f $base64AuthInfo)};

$Uri = $collectionUri + '/' + $teamProjectName + '/_apis/git/
repositories?api-version=' + $restAPIversion

$repositories = Invoke-RestMethod -Method Get -ContentType application/json
-Uri $Uri -Headers $header

foreach($repo in $repositories.value)
{
    Write-Host ("Repository name: {0}" -f $repo.name)
}
```

You can call this script with the following syntax and print the repo names. See Figure 12-8.

```
.\GetAzureGitRepos.ps1 -token patvalue' -collectionUri 'https://dev.azure.
com/orgname' -teamProjectName 'teamprojectname'
```

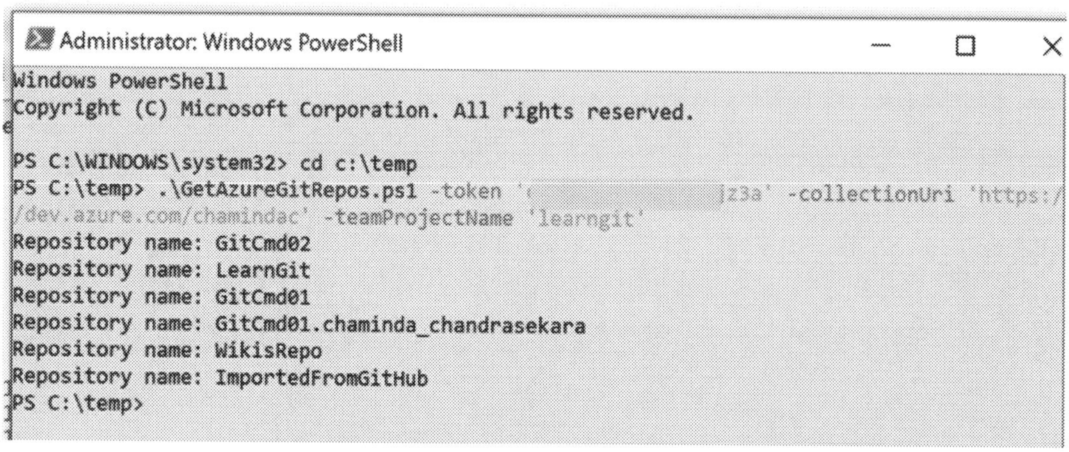

Figure 12-8. *Retrieving repository data with PowerShell from the REST API*

In this lesson, we discussed how to use PowerShell to connect to the Azure Git Repos REST API to retrieve data. In the same way, you can call TFVC REST APIs to retrieve data.

Summary

In this chapter, we discussed how to use Azure DevOps REST APIs to retrieve data from Azure Git Repos and TFVC repos. You can use this knowledge to create useful reports or work with REST APIs to perform actions on repositories.

In this book, we discussed how to use repositories to support your version control needs in Azure DevOps. We looked at setting up TFVC and Azure Git Repos in team projects and the options to create branches, do pull requests, and review code. Further we explored security, REST APIs, command-line options, and many other features available in Azure DevOps repositories to give you a comprehensive overview.

In the next book of the series, *Hands-on Azure Pipelines*, we will be discussing the CI/CD capabilities of Azure DevOps in detail.

Index

A

Azure DevOps organization, 2
Azure Git Repos
    branching structure, 171–174
    branch permissions, 225–234
    command line (*see* Command
        line)
    import external Git repos, 257–260
    pull request, 195–205
    push local repo, 218–222
    rebase option, 204
    resolve conflict, 185–194
    setting up wikis, 260
        add markdown
          content, 263
        add markdown file, 262
        creation, 261
        Publish code, 263, 264
        wiki pages, 264
    tags
        branch, 244
        commit ID, 245
        context menu, 246
        creation, 242
        multiple tags, 245
        name and description, 242
        page, 243
        visible commit, 243

B

Branching strategy
    development isolation, 106
    feature isolation, 107
    main only, 106
    release isolation, 107
    service and release
        isolation, 108
Branch policy, 234
    automatic reviewers, 240
    build policy, 239
    comment resolution
        policy, 238
    menu item, 235
    merge policy, 238
    reviewers policy, 237

C, D

Command line
    az devops login, 210
    Azure CLI, 209
    Azure DevOps extension, 209
    branch creation, 222–224
    command palette, 214
    copying clone URL, 211
    git commit command, 215
    .gitignore Generator, 213, 214

Command line (*cont.*)
    git push, 217, 218
    master branch, 215
    NET Core web app, 213
    repository user setting, 216
    VS code setting, 208

E

End-user license agreement (EULA), 112

F, G, H, I, J, K, L, M, N, O

Forking repo, 255–257

P, Q

Personal access token (PAT), 142

R

REST API
    PAT creation, 269–271
    Postman app, 271–273
    PowerShell code, 273–276
    retrieve data, 267–269

S

Shelvesets, 55
    Azure DevOps Services/
        Server, 59
    context menu, 60
    My Work window, 64
    resume work, 68
    sample code, 56
    Shelve button, 58

    Suspend button, 65
    Team Explorer window, 57
    unshelve changes, 62
    unshelving, 60
Source Control Explorer, TFVC
    add/edit workspace, 34
    change file, 39
    changeset details window, 48
    changesets comparison, 50
    compare window, 40
    conflicts window, 46
    local mode, 33
    local workspace mode, 36
    menu items, 37
    merge tool, 46
    pending changes window, 44
    server mode, 33
    server workspace mode, 36
    source control pane option, 41
    undeleting file, 53
    Visual Studio menu, 51
    workspace option, 33
Source Control Merge wizard, 94

T, U

Team Foundation Version
    Control (TFVC)
    auditing changes
        compare option, 135
        select Annotate, 136
    Azure Git Repos (*see* Azure Git Repos)
        button creation, 143
        conflict file, 161–167
        create team project, 140
        empty Git repo, 141

new Git repo, 142

pull changes, 156–160

pushing code, 148–156

stash commands, 166–169

Visual Studio, 145–148

VS code, 144

branch creation, 85–88

branch/folder file level, 129

access control, 129

branch permission, 131

security control, 133, 134

security option, 130

branching (*see* Branching strategy)

branch structure, 92

Check-In Policy tab, 79

cherry-picking option, 103–105

code review, 68–76

command-line client, 111

comment policy, 80

Compare icon, 98

convert branch option, 89–91

developer command prompt, 109

enable/disable web editing, 128

Feature1 branch, 97

Lock file dialog, 77

Locking/unlocking file, 76

merge branch comparison, 98

merge conflicts, 99

merging and resolving conflicts, 91

Repos menu, 3

security controls, 125, 126

source branch version, 95

Source Control Explorer (*see* Source Control Explorer, TFVC)

team project (*see* Team project, creation)

Track Changeset icon, 100–103

Visual studio (*see* Visual Studio Team Explorer)

VS code

access token method, 25

Azure Repos extension, 24

connect repo, 26

enter code, 26

extensions tab, 23

team sign-in, 25

work item query policy, 81

workspace command, 113–117

Team project, creation, 118

add command, 120

checkin command, 121

checkout command, 121

get command, 119

rename command, 122

undo command, 122

V, W, X, Y, Z

Visual Studio, 175

branch creation, 177

checkout option, 182

merge branch, 179

rebase option, 179, 180

Visual Studio team explorer, 5

add account, 6

check-in note, 21

check-in policy, 20

check-out settings, 20

connect URL, 7

file types, 16

local workspace, 19

Map & Get button, 8

pending changes, 22

server workspace, 18

Visual Studio team explorer (*cont.*)
    solution explorer window, 8–16
    source control settings, 19
VS code
    branch creation, 183, 184
    checkout command, 185

VS tags
    command line, 251–255
    commit history, 249
    context menu, 248
    creation, 250
    team explorer, 247